LABOUR RELATIONS IN CENTRAL EUROPE

Contemporary Employment Relations

Series Editor: Gregor Gall

Professor of Industrial Relations and Director of the Centre for Research in Employment Studies, University of Hertfordshire, Hatfield, UK

The aim of this series is to publish monographs and edited volumes on all aspects of contemporary employment relations including human resource management, employee branding, shared services, employment regulation, the political economy of employment, and industrial relations. Topics such as mergers, corporate governance and the EU – in the context of their affect upon employment relations – also fall within the scope of the series. Aimed primarily at an academic readership this series provides a global forum for the study of employment relations.

Other Titles in the Series

Child Labour in South Asia
Edited by Gamini Herath and Kishor Sharma
ISBN 978-0-7546-7004-9

Trade Unions and Workplace Democracy in Africa
Gérard Kester
ISBN 978-0-7546-4997-7

Human Resource Management in Russia
Edited by Michel E. Domsch and Tatjana Lidokhover
ISBN 978-0-7546-4876-5

Changing Working Life and the Appeal of the Extreme Right
Edited by Jörg Flecker
ISBN 978-0-7546-4915-1

Employment Contracts and Well-Being Among European Workers
Edited by Nele De Cuyper, Kerstin Isaksson and Hans De Witte
ISBN 978-0-7546-4575-7

Labour Relations
in Central Europe
The Impact of Multinationals' Money

JOCHEN THOLEN
University of Bremen, Germany

with

LUDOVIT CZÍRIA
EIKE HEMMER
WIESLAWA KOZEK
ZDENKA MANSFELDOVÁ

LONDON AND NEW YORK

First published 2007 by Ashgate Publishing

Reissued 2018 by Routledge
2 Park Square, Milton Park, Abingdon, Oxon OX14 4RN
605 Third Avenue, New York, NY 10017

First issued in paperback 2021

Routledge is an imprint of the Taylor & Francis Group, an informa business

A Library of Congress record exists under LC control number: 2006103146

Notice:
Product or corporate names may be trademarks or registered trademarks, and are used only
for identification and explanation without intent to infringe.

Publisher's Note
The publisher has gone to great lengths to ensure the quality of this reprint but
points out that some imperfections in the original copies may be apparent.

Disclaimer
The publisher has made every effort to trace copyright holders and
welcomes correspondence from those they have been unable to contact.

ISBN 13: 978-0-8153-9010-7 (hbk)
ISBN 13: 978-1-3511-5444-4 (ebk)
ISBN 13: 978-1-138-35828-7 (pbk)

DOI: 10.4324/9781351154444

Contents

List of Figures and Tables

Figure

Tables

List of Authors

Dr Jochen Tholen, Senior Researcher, Departmental Head of the Institute Labour and Economy at the University of Bremen.

Dr. Ludovit Czíria, Senior Researcher, Deputy Director of the 'Centre for Work and Family Studies' (formerly 'Research Institute of Labour, Social Affairs and Family') at the Labour Ministry of the Slovakian Republic.

Eike Hemmer, Researcher, Institute Labour and Economy at the University of Bremen.

Prof. Wieslawa Kozek, Institute for Sociology, University of Warsaw.

Dr. Zdenka Mansfeldová, Senior Researcher, Deputy Director in the Institute for Sociology at the Czech Academic of Sciences in Prague.

Acknowledgements

Thank you to all those who have contributed to the success of this study:

- The Hans Boeckler Foundation and the Otto Brenner Foundation for the financial support of the project
- The Friedrich Ebert Foundation (Warsaw) for the financial and organizational support of the project conclusion conference
- The cooperation partners in the German trade unions IG Metall, IG BCE and NGG as well as the respective trade unions in Poland, Czech Republic and Slovakia for their contextual collaboration and organizational support
- The European trade union federations EMF, EMCEF and EFFAT
- The conversational willingness of the German, Czech, Polish and Slovakian employers'/business enterprise associations of the metal, chemical and food industries as well as the Union of Industrial and Employers' Confederations of Europe (UNICE)
- The employment ministries in Poland, Czech Republic and Slovakia as well as the European Commission / GD Employment and Social Affairs
- Altogether, the representatives of business enterprises and companies, trade unions and employers' associations in the concerned countries (Germany, France, Switzerland, Poland, Czech Republic, Slovakia and on the EU level) who were available for expert interviews and/or declared their willingness for the implementation of the case studies
- The project advisory council for the consistent critical-positive accompaniment, and in particular Gerlinde Doerr, Wilhelm Eberwein, Bela Galgóczi and Hermann Ribhegge for the checking of the manuscript and many valuable information
- The Friedrich Ebert Foundation (Warsaw office), the Hans-Boeckler-Foundation, the Otto Brenner Foundation and the University of Bremen for supporting financially the translation from German into English
- The helpful comments of the Publisher's anonymous reviewers.
- Florian Smets for laying out the book.

List of Abbreviations

ÁPB	Branch Council (Hungary)
AZZZ SR	Federation of Employers Association of the Slovak Republic
BASTUN	Baltic Sea Trade Union Network
BDA	Federation of the German Employers' Associations
BVE	Federation of the German Food and Drink Industry
CAEF	Committee of Associations of European Foundries
CAPE	Chambers Accession Programme for Eastern Europe
CEE	Central and Eastern Europe
CEEC	Central and Eastern European Countries
CIAA	Confederation of the Food and Drink Industries of the EU
CIC	Chamber of Industry and Commerce
CMKOS	Confederation of Bohemian-Moravian Trade Unions
CSR	Republic of Czechoslovakia
CWC	Corporate Works Council
DGB	German Trade Union Confederation
DIHK	Top organization of the 82 German Chambers of Industry and Commerce
DIHT	the German Chamber of Industry and Commerce
DIW	German Institute for Economic Research, Berlin
EBRD	European Bank for Reconstruction and Development
EEA	European Economic Area
EFFAT	European Federation of Food, Agriculture, Tourism Trade Unions
EIC	Euro Info Centre (Dresden)
EMCEF	European Mine, Chemical and Energy Workers Federation
EMF	European Federation of Metalworkers
ERT	European Roundtable of Industrialists
ÉTOSZ	Consultant Service for Interest Protection (Hungary)
ETUC	European Trade Union Confederation
ETUI	European Trade Union Institute
EU	European Union
EWC	European Works Council
FAST e.V.	Research Institute for Foreign Trade, Structure and Technology, Berlin
FDI	Foreign Direct Investment
FES	Friedrich Ebert Foundation, Germany
FZZ	Trade Union Forum Poland
GD	GD Employment and Social Affairs (EU Commission)
IFE	Industrial Forum on Enlargement
ILO	International Labour Organization

ITUC	Interregional Trade Union Councils
IUF	International Union of Food, Agricultural, Hotel, Restaurant, Catering, Tobacco and Allied Workers' Associations
JWC	Joint Works Council
KOVO	The Czech Trade Union of Metal Workers
KOZ SR	Confederation of Trade Unions of the Slovak Republic
KPP	Confederation of Polish Employers
MEDEF	Mouvement des Entreprises de France/French Employers' Association
MNC	Multinational Company
NGG	Trade Union for Food, Beverages, Hotel and Catering Workers/ Gernany (Gewerkschaft Nahrung, Genuss, Gaststätten)
NGO	Non Governmental Organisation
NSZZ	(Solidarnosc 80), Trade Union Solidarity 80 (Poland)
OECD	Organization for Economic Cooperation and Development
ÖGB	Confederation of Austrian Trade Unions
OPZZ	All-Polish Trade Union Confederation
OZP	Slovak Trade Union of Food Workers
PKPP	Polish Confederation of Private Employers
PHARE	Poland and Hungary Assistance for the Reconstruction of Economy (EU Financial Assistance for CEEC)
R&D	Research and Development
RTD	Research and Technology Development
RWI	Rhine-Westphalian Economic Research Institute, Essen
SE	(SocietasEuropaea) European Public Company
SME	Small and Medium-sized Enterprises
SMECA	Small and Medium-sized Enterprises, Community acquis
SOCR	Confederation of Industry and Transport in the Czech Republic
TAIEX	Office for the Exchange of Information and Technical Assistance/EU
UEAPME	European Association of Small and Medium-sized Craft Enterprises
UFTE	UNICE Task Force on Enlargement
UNCTAD	United Nations Commission for Trade and Development
UNICE	Union of Industrial and Employers' Confederations of Europe (Union des Confédérations de l'Industrie et des Employeurs d'Europe) – renamed in February 2007 as BusinessEurope
USD	US Dollar
VISEGRÁD	Visegrád Countries (Poland, Czech Republic, Slovakia, Hungary)
WCA	Works Constitution Act

Chapter 1

Study Concept, Hypotheses and Approach

Since 1990, Foreign Direct Investments (called FDI in the following) have brought about a modernization jump amongst the respective Central and Eastern Europe (CEE) national economies. This is only incompletely illustrated through the FDI portion of 10 per cent of the overall investment amounts in Central and Eastern Europe in the period 1993–2003.

New management concepts, corporate organizations and technology on a global scale have been implemented in many cases.

But how does the situation look like with regard to the so-called 'soft factors', and in this context, particularly in the realm of relations between corporate/site management and the workforce?

The vocational/technical qualifications of the workforce in Central and Eastern Europe were – at least in the technical/natural science professions – already available. The foreign investors were able to develop their investments quite well on this basis. However, industrial relations as an essential creative factor within a company were at the commencement of the investments either characterized by the conditions during the communist time or otherwise – in the case of Greenfield investments – were able to be/had to be entirely reconfigured.

Was there also a 'modernisation jump' in this realm? And if so, what did the West European – in particular German – investors bring with them? What did they take over? What did they redevelop?

Thus said, the essential starting points of a research project are very briefly outlined, and the results will be presented in the following. In general, what does 'modernisation jump' mean?

This question leads us directly to the theoretical frame within which this survey is embedded. Since the emergence of sociology in the nineteenth century, social theory and theories of modernity have formed an inseparable unity, albeit a contradictory and often paradigm-shifting unity.

Just to mention some contradictions and shifts: from the early works of Marx's historical materialism (1857/58); Max Weber's volumes on the role of bureaucracy (1915/18/21) and the Protestant ethic (1905); Polyani's arguments about the roots of capitalism (1944); Schumpeter's theory of the contradictory or dialectic processes of developing and self-destroying capitalism (1942); to modern authors such as Giddens with his works on the consequences of modernity (1990); Habermas' theory of communication as *the* process of today's modernity (1981); the criticism by Lyotard (1984) that modernity has become obsolete and society has entered a 'postmodern' condition, and last but not least counter-critics for example Baumann

(1997) – all these and many other social theories of modernity were/are focused only on the Western, the 'developed' part of the world. Furthermore, they were and are narrow-minded and are describing only partially the process of modernization – they do not consider sufficiently issues like gender, environmental problems, the IT revolution, and so on.

Coming from this, our understanding is that the truly *global* process of modernization has just started not only because of the economic and social developments in China and other (mainly Far East) countries, but because of the growing importance of issues beyond traditional theories of modernity, such as equal opportunities in general, environmental issues (global warming, and so on), the unpredictable development of IT and its impacts not only on the economy, but on politics and daily life. This widening of our perspective, started on a broader level in the last two decades of the twentieth century, and came together with the velvet revolutions in the former Eastern Bloc and the breakdown of the Soviet Union in the years 1989–1991. The famous transformation process then started – in this form as a historically singular process. Economies, politics and social life had to be transformed from a planned economy with in principle no private property with a one party dictatorship into a market orientated, capitalistic society under democratic conditions. Foreign Direct Investment (FDI) played, and is playing, a crucial role in modernizing the national economies and thus the societies. However, the economic and social transformation as a catching-up process, assisted by FDI inflows into the Central and Eastern European Countries (CEEC), is only a part of the *global*, more comprehensive process of modernization which started in the outgoing twentieth century.

And this process is propelled by a growing corporate power in a globalizing world (Carroll, 2004), which shifted our interest to the micro – that means the companies' – level.

And this is trendy insofar as within the academic and business community there is a growing interest in the relationship between corporate governance and employment relations (Heery and Wood, 2003).

The concept of the study, its leading research hypotheses and the empirical procedure will be explained in the first chapter.

The specific analytical reference points, embedded in the general theoretical frame of 'global modernity' are of great importance for the practical arrangement of the study and the interpretation of the empirical results (including the evaluation of documents and other studies) (Chapter 2).

Subsequently, in the third chapter there are several figures pertaining to the extent and significance of foreign direct investments in Central and Eastern Europe as well as a comparative presentation of the industrial relations in Poland, Czech Republic and Slovakia (as selected host countries of foreign direct investments). These figures are intended to substantiate the essential underlying conditions for the development of industrial relations in the Central and Eastern European Countries (CEEC).

The expert interviews on the supra-company level with representatives of trade unions, employers' associations and labour/economics ministries in Poland, Czech Republic, Slovakia and Germany as well as on the EU level (Chapter 4) were an initial empirical step towards preparation of the case studies.

Nine business enterprises (seven of them from Germany, one Swiss and one German/French enterprise) from the metal and electrical industry (including car industry), the food processing industry, and the chemical and energy industry in the differing configuration of the industrial relations with respect to their CEE subsidiary enterprises will be introduced in Chapter 5.

Ultimately, the model of the arrangement of the industrial relations will be summarily discussed in Chapter 6, from which action recommendations for actors can also possibly be derived. In conclusion, the very tempting – but perhaps not sufficient in the final analysis – question will be carefully posed: in what direction could the industrial relations on site/company level in the CEEC evolve?

We point out that on account of its specific subject matter this study can only depict a partial extract of the evolution of industrial relations in Central and Eastern Europe.

Concept

The object of the study is the industrial relations on the *site/corporate level*. In terms of content, this focusing is substantiated through the transformation process brought into play in the new EU member states themselves in 1990; the decentralization and fragmentation of the economic structures in these nations contributed to a substantial strengthening of the corporate/site level within the scope of the respective national industrial relations. This transformation process has been more or less completed through the EU membership of the eight CEEC on 1 May 2004.

The subject matter is the influence of direct investments by West European, mostly German companies on the industrial relations on the company/site level in selected CEEC (Poland, Czech Republic, Slovakia), which all – together with five other CEEC – joined the European Union on 1 May 2004. FDI play an important role in the redefinition of industrial relations in the national economies of these countries, and the investments from Germany are first and foremost here.

An essential orientation framework in this connection is the increasing Europeanization of industrial relations in the different countries, whether it now pertains to the EU-15 (as countries of origin for the investments) or the new EU members (as host countries) in their efforts regarding practical implementation of *acquis communautaire* (EC acquis).

At the same time, the main weight of this study has been placed on the industrial relations in the FDI *host countries*.

The general objective of this research project was the analysis of the effects of direct investments – mainly from German companies – on the development of industrial relations in the CEE subsidiary enterprises, whose external conditions are characterized by a considerable change dynamism.

The project time span (December 2002 to May 2005) comprised two essential phases of the enlargement process. The first phase, up to immediately before the accession date (May 2004), was above all characterized through the implementation of *acquis communautaire* in the respective national law of the three CEE states ('pre-accession period'). The second phase, immediately after accession, entailed initial *practical* experiences in the three CEEC concerned as new EU member states.

Research Hypotheses

Research hypothesis 1: Differing motives of the investing companies bring about differing models of industrial relations in the CEE subsidiary enterprise

Starting point
There are a vast number of strategies from companies for conclusion of FDI. In summary, two strategies (which absolutely can be mixed in practice) can be differentiated: the first motive pertains to reasons of cost (labour costs, taxes, charges and subsidies, exchange equalization, and so on), whereas the second motive concerns market reasons (opening up new markets, proximity to major customers, presence of competition, and so on). The size of the respective company, branch affiliation and ranking in the process chain quite frequently determine the investment strategy.[1]

Hypothesis
These investment strategies/reasons are an independent variable for the study. We act on the assumption of the working hypothesis, according to which there is a connection between a specific investment strategy and the characterization of industrial relations in the respective CEE subsidiaries:

1. Reasons of cost are quite frequently embedded in short-term profit maximization expectations. Here the corporate management entities indicate indifference vis-à-vis the CEE subsidiaries with respect to the configuration of industrial relations. Much is left to coincidence – or better, lopsided – on the part of the business management, which is by no means to be equated with conflict-free industrial relations.
2. Long-term expectations dominate with regard to market reasons as an overriding investment strategy. Stable and dependable industrial relations have a much greater significance here. Stronger inclusion of workforces (in any form whatsoever), solution-orientated cooperative willingness and conflict settlement mechanisms are elements of this strategy. All in all, the different investment strategies also bring about quite different characterization models of industrial relations in the CEE subsidiary enterprises.

Research hypothesis 2: The nature of investment (Brownfield or Greenfield) quite often determines the degree of involvement amongst trade unions and representatives on the site/company level

Starting point
Foreign direct investments met/meet with conditions which are frequently described as Brownfield or Greenfield investments.

---

1   See the detailed, separate *Forschungsbericht* [research report] J. Tholen, Hemmer (2005) concerning this.

Hypothesis

In relation to the industrial relations, Brownfield investments signify the existence of path-dependent (unilaterally characterized in the host country of the investments) patterns of labour relations in the workplace (mostly trade union representatives), whereas Greenfield investments signify 'union-free' zones.

In the future, such a differentiation could lose significance through the following two tendencies:

1. In the course of development many original Brownfield investments have been/will be expanded on account of subsequent technical, organizational, structural and other changes expanded around Greenfield investments. These expansions could have different causes: success of the original investment and thus increased demand, alteration of the corporate group's investment objective (from short-term to long-term strategies), and so on. As a result, different models of industrial relations can be developed. This ranges from the path dependency of the existing model in the host country of the investments to lopsided path dependencies in the country of origin of the investments up to third-nation influences such as the EU – including all mixed forms.

2. As a result of the statutory introduction of representatives in the Czech Republic, Slovakia and partially also in Poland (that is perhaps even including a 'model' of dualism), the nature and conditions of industrial relations in these countries could change on a long-term basis. A crucial question as to what extent the trade unions in the CEEC integrate these new forms of representatives on the site/company level in their strategy or whether these new forms of workforce representatives might emerge as a bad competition for the traditional trade union representatives.

Research hypothesis 3: Europeanisation of industrial relations on the corporate/company/site level – the increasing role of European Works Councils with regard to mediation between industrial relations in the host countries and those in the FDI countries of origin

Starting point

A complementary level emerges through the Europeanization of industrial relations, in which the national systems continue to exist and are additionally supplemented through elements of European industrial relations.

The European Works Councils (hereinafter referred to as EWC) are the strongest expression for this.

Hypothesis

The EWC is increasingly using a 'bridge function' between the industrial relations of the countries of origin and host countries with respect to the investments.

As a result of its existence and mode of operation, the EWC has not only been able to contribute European standards of *industrial relations* on the corporate/site level, but at the same time could also be able to introduce European standards of *management concepts*. Together with the respective trade unions, the EWC could also be an institution to make rational discussion accessible and to keep it within limits pertaining to the continuously discussed danger of wage dumping and the lowering of standards – for example in occupational health and safety protection, exactly through this transparent feedback effect.

However, it will be pointed out that even there, where representatives from the sites in the CEEC are in existence in the EWC, not all CEEC sites are represented in the EWC, since these subsidiaries are too small in accordance with the EWC directive.

Empirical Approach

The empirical approach essentially encompasses three steps:

In the first step, a *secondary empirical collection and evaluation of relevant studies* of the industrial relations in Poland, Czech Republic and Slovakia follows, and is focused on the changes through the eastward enlargement of the EU and through foreign direct investments.[2]

In a second step: in 2003/beginning of 2004 (a total of 64) *expert interviews on the supra-company level* were held with representatives of trade unions and employers' associations of selected industries. Also included were representatives from labour ministries on national levels (in Germany, Poland, Czech Republic and Slovakia) and on the EU level for development of industrial relations on the site/ corporate level in general, and in particular regarding the influence of foreign direct investments on the industrial relations in the transformation countries.

As a result of these expert interviews, information was collected and evaluated, which goes far beyond the concerned enterprises – indeed, even beyond the selected branches (but within the manufacturing industry), and thus enhances the *general* reporting character of the project (Chapter 4).

At the same time this step serves as preparation of nine smaller case studies: *Expert interviews were held on the corporate/site level* in a third empirical step. In this case we concentrated on the CEE subsidiaries as well as their parent enterprises. Altogether we selected nine companies (three from the metal/electrical industry, two from the food processing industry, three from the chemicals industry and one company from the energy industry). Five parent enterprises have subsidiaries in all three CEEC, two have subsidiaries in two CEEC (but with different country combinations), and three parent enterprises each also have only one subsidiary enterprise in the two host countries of investment selected on our part (a total of 21 CEE subsidiary enterprises/investments).

In addition to an in-depth document analysis in the nine parent enterprises as well as in their 21 CEE subsidiary enterprises (in the second half of 2004/beginning of 2005) expert interviews were held with the management (managing director and/or personnel manager) as well as the trade union representatives or respective

---

2   In this regard, see the publication: Tholen, Czíria, Hemmer, Mansfeldová, Sharman: EU-Enlargement und Labour Relations. New Trends in Poland, Czech and Slovak Republic, IAW Working Paper 3/2,003, University of Bremen.

works councils (if available). This resulted in an average of three interviews per site/subsidiary/parent company (Chapter 5).

The objective of this step was to identify common interests and differences in the single subsidiary enterprises, also in the direction of a standardization (see the conclusions in Chapter 6 concerning this).

Chapter 2

Analytical Reference Points

The analytical reference points are of great importance for the arrangement of the study and the interpretation of the empirical results (including the evaluation of documents and other studies). The theory of industrial relations, the change of the (Germanic) production model through globalization and utilization of new techniques, the process of Europeanization and the path (in)dependence of national (industrial relations) models are essential references in this study.

Regarding the Theory of Industrial Relations

At this point it is not necessary to enlarge on an extensive theory of industrial relations. In accordance with Mueller-Jentsch (despite all criticism through Weitbrecht in 2001), an analysis framework – which refers to several theory strands – is offered for the project at hand:

> As a theoretical guide for the presentation and the analysis of the circumstances relevant to industrial relations, I propose an expanded, actor-related institutional approach, an integration of historical and control-theoretic institutionalism with action-theoretic (mainly negotiation-theoretic) concepts. This approach consists of three theoretical 'building blocks':
>
> 1. the historic-genetic analysis,
> 2. the arena concept, and
> 3. the bargaining concept (Mueller-Jentsch, 1996, p. 57).

This approach offers the advantage of recording different determining moments in their change dynamism. In this context, the specific form of the linkage and weighting of the various elements remains an unsolved theoretical problem. Nevertheless, this differentiation appears as the adequate form for recording the different qualities and functions of industrial relations on the various levels of multilevel regulation within the scope of the EU.

The historic-genetic analysis refers to the evolutionary character of industrial relations, which have been created in the various countries under specific power relationships in the different national systems. Country-specific developmental paths ensue, which are particularly manifested in deep-rooted institutional structures and well-established behavioural patterns of the involved actors.

> However, a typical sequence and a generalised result are to be ascertained for all industrial-capitalistic countries of the West (Mueller-Jentsch, 1996, p. 57).

These common interests ultimately result from the functional requirements which are placed on industrial relations, starting from the economical necessities of capitalist economic systems.

The arena concept refers to the functional differentiation of industrial relations and thus results in the subdivision of different subsystems, for instance through the six levels of the industrial relations diagram in Poland, Czech Republic and Slovakia in the following Chapter 3.2. Despite all links, these six subsystems have a relative degree of independence as discussion fields.

Finally, the bargaining concept includes the action of actors and their strategy development, and offers a very good justification framework for our understanding of the representation of interests as a socio-political process. For instance, beyond all legal norms we are also able to record the fact that before 1 May 2004 (that is the accession date of the 10 new members into the EU, and thus the acknowledgement of *acquis communautaire* as a *common* legal framework for the EU-25) there were European Works Councils in some companies, which incorporated – on a voluntary basis, that is only on account of the intention of the involved actors – representatives from CEE subsidiaries as full members (and thus even at an early stage further expedited the Europeanization process). In some companies CEE representatives possessed an observer status, whereas in other companies (and this was the majority) the accession date was initially waited upon in order to get started on the inclusion of CEE representatives in the EWC in accordance with the EWC directive. And furthermore, this approach can also explain the local site management's scope for action in the CEEC with regard to the development of industrial relations.

The Pressure of Change through Globalization with Respect to the Implementation of a New Labour and Production Concept and the Erosion of the Germanic Production Model

In Europe, nationally quite different systems of industrial relations have emerged in the last two centuries; these systems are confronted with extensive necessities for change. Two developments are especially responsible for this: the increasing globalization[1] of the economy and the implementation of new production and working methods.

An essential basis for industrial relations in the European countries existed in their respective national boundary. Despite all export orientation and international transactions, the national economy constituted the essential starting and reference point of the companies. The economic and social policy was only able to function because a relative compartmentation was given vis-à-vis the world market. The collective bargaining system as well as the works constitution (industrial relations scheme) and the corporate legal structure (corporate governance) were embedded

---

1   The term 'globalisation' is vague and quite controversial in the scientific and political debate. In the context of this work it is not necessary to differentiate the term. Here it means the considerable expansion of international economical transactions in conjunction with a change of corporate structures in the international context.

in this context. However, the supporting pillars of this system are now becoming hollowed-out with the increasing globalization.

The institutions of this internationalization are above all transnational corporate groups (but in the meantime also increasingly medium-sized companies) with several sites in various countries. These companies optimally attempt to organize production and distribution by taking advantage of different national circumstances. An essential condition for the company's subsequently increased possibilities of action is the deliberate politically expedited liberalization and deregulation of the global economy.

This increasing internationalization has far-reaching consequences. Deregulation expedited in many countries entailed manifold new rivalries and corporate lines of friction, which in their aggregate have decisively contributed to the weakening of trade unions and to the undermining of nation-state control possibilities. To strengthen the competitive ability of the industry settled in one's own country, a cost reduction competition between the nation states has been put into operation in the course of the conservative neo-liberal supply economic policy. The welfare state as well as many other political and ecological regulations is particularly becoming – in accordance with this interpretation – a cost factor that shall be reduced for promotion of the domestic economy. A downward spiral is being set in gear. At the same time, new intercorporate lines of friction are revealed in this constellation.

A prerequisite – and at the same time a consequence of these processes – is the increasing orientation of corporate actions towards criteria which are derived from the 'shareholder value capitalism' that has been discussed in the public realm. Orientation towards short-term profit and market values, essentially controlled through the interests of the investment funds and analysts, increasingly supersedes country-specific developmental models.

If one assumes that considerable pressure is already exerted on the industrial relations by the globalization trends, this is further strengthened through the implementation of new production technologies and the subsequently related new rationalization model. At the moment, a fundamental reorganization of business enterprises and companies is taking place on the basis of the comprehensive introduction of information and communications technologies. The objects of reorganization are not only single production stages, but the entire value added chain. A renunciation of Tayloristic rationalization paradigms is taking place, which primarily targets the effectiveness of single working steps through a further dismemberment of working processes in conjunction with an increasing utilization of technology. A guideline of the newly implemented paradigm is a 'systemic rationalisation', which is aimed at optimizing the entire production process, that is in particular also the interfaces between various production steps.

The practical adoption of the restructuring measures differs greatly from branch to branch, but also between various companies/business enterprises. For instance, popular keywords in this context are 'lean production', scaling-down the production depth or outsourcing. The aspect of cost reduction gains a significance that is not to be underestimated amongst the companies, which in turn is of paramount importance for the potential configuration options through representatives. In this context, one frequently speaks of a conquest of Fordist production structures, in particular mass production, and the transition to post-Fordist, flexible quality production. However, this characterization fails to appreciate the fact that the production forms to be implemented still concern mass production, and the flexible product configuration mainly relates to single components. For instance, in the car industry one can choose between cars with various equipment components (see the platform strategy at VW) so that in fact only a few vehicles are really identical. Yet the variation range of the single components themselves is limited, however.

This interindustrial integration commensurate with the modern production structures with their strategic corporate reduction to the core business, which first of all takes place on a domestic basis, is displaced through a strengthened international division of labour. At the same time, the integration of European markets plays a pre-eminent role for the export-orientated German economy.

The respective trade unions or the representatives on the site/company level are substantially affected by these measures.

> Reorganisation processes accelerate the trend towards the operationalisation of the representation and regulation of interests. This not only transpires because the implementation of new rationalisation paradigms call for "tailor-made" solutions specifically related to working processes. On the contrary, it turns out that attempts toward making the work organisation flexible inevitably have an effect on the regulation of working conditions, remuneration, working hours and so on (Doerre, 1995, pp. 158–159).

Insofar our survey is emphasizing the influence of the respective corporate strategies on the different types of industrial relations and vice versa.[2]

The German 'production model' (Streeck et al., 1995), as an expression of the interrelationships between business, social welfare system and industrial relations,[3] with the essential component of highly regulated industrial relations[4] is becoming more and more shaky and under political pressure (Doerrenbaecher, 2003, pp. 161–162). For this reason, it is also losing significance as a reference model for the development of industrial relations in the CEE subsidiaries of German parent enterprises. This could also be *one* explanation for the marginal influence measures of the German trade unions and works councils on the configuration of industrial relations in the subsidiaries of German parent enterprises in Central and Eastern Europe (this will be described below).

On the part of the CEEC there is a – virtually reflective – similar trend, even if partially due to other reasons: the decentralization as a core element of the formerly state-controlled planned economies led to a fragmentation of the economic processes

---

2   See Baccaro (2003), who examined theoretically the interdependencies between corporatism and interest representation system.

3   Industrial relations and welfare state are interrelated; see the survey by Brandl (2005), which is comprising 20 OECD countries.

4   The other elements of the German production model are a social market economy, a dual vocational training system, a considerable importance of banks in the system of corporate financing and control, as well as management that is more orientated towards (short-term) utilization of technology than financial objectives (see also Eberwein, 1990 and 1993 with regard to the latter).

and to a strengthening of the corporate level (Gradev, 2001, p. 16). This process of corporate acceptance signifies the free choice of foreign investors to arrange industrial relations according to their visions (which very often flows into the expansion of human resource management under exclusion of *collective* representation bodies). These trends have been strengthened even more through the partially difficult economic and social adaptation processes in the transformation societies.

In the aggregate, globalization, new production models and the specific evolution of the transformation processes in the former planned economies lead to a – decentralized – 'realignment of corporate strategies on the basis of new rationality and legitimacy visions and under primary reference to the global finance markets' (Kaedtler, 2004, p. 63), and from that point of view also challenge traditional collective representation bodies.

This decentralization/operationalization in the CEE societies is also expressed in the dominance of the corporate-related collective agreements. This aspect is possibly strengthened through the novelty in two of our three exemplarily selected CEEC (Czech Republic and Slovakia): with the introduction of a legally prescribed 'works council' the previously pure trade union representatives structures on the corporate/ site level will be modified. Poland is also on this path.

The Influence of Europeanization on the National Systems of Industrial Relations

The process of Europeanization is certainly also an element of the internationalization and globalization processes, but differs quite considerably due to the legal constitutionality of the European Union and the supporting economical, political and social alliances.

First of all, after the Second World War a West European Economic Community emerged – particularly due to the East/West system rivalry and the objective of a lasting peace that was elaborated in Western Europe immediately after 1945. At the latest in the mid-1980s, the increasing internationalization of the economy and the emergence of the triad (North America, (South)East Asia and Europe) particularly lead to a specific form of communalisation amongst European states. However, this is not synonymous with the emergence of a new supranational state, but rather leads to a specific coexistence of national, inter-governmental and supranational regulatory forms and authorities. Despite integration:

> an increasing unification of the national systems as a consequence of the Europeanisation of politics is out of the question. In the aggregate, one can ascertain that the communalisation of the political landscape in the member states can be more multifarious, and particularly in the states which have distinct national regulatory traditions, this leads to an increased complexity (Jachtenfuchs et al. 1996, p. 28).

A new quality of nationalism in Europe emerges in the course of this development, whereby 'the European level of nationalism changes not only in dependence on the national, but (...) as a 'central interface' assumes important functions with regard to the change of nationalism in Europe' (Ziltener, 1999, p. 202). As a result, in the past years a multilevel system of state regulation has emerged in Europe, which fundamentally differs from the system of international relations in the first decades after the Second World War (Marginson and Meardi, 2006, p. 54). If one considers the future development, neither a return to the all-embracing jurisdiction of the nation state nor dissolution in a new European federal state seems possible. Whereas the economic integration is far advanced and has led to irreversible structural changes in the national economies of the member states, vast state realms – in particular the socio-political and labour-political fields – are still nationally constituted in many cases. Differences of economic standards exist between the member states (especially after the EU enlargement on 1 May 2004), and at the same time there are also different structures of these systems based on traditions that are hundreds of years old. From that point of view it must be assumed that in the foreseeable future an intricate coexistence of national and European regulation remains extant in very closely related fields.

In relation to labour relations, this political-scientific approach under Europeanization is understood in much the same way as the existence of European Works Councils: on the European level they govern matters which can no longer be regulated through industrial relations within the boundaries of a single nation state.

In difference to the political-scientific application, the nation of Europeanization is understood in terms of sociological approaches under European integration of the reciprocal, horizontally proceeding interdependences and mixtures between the European societies (Dehley, 2005, p. 11), which are transnational (that is aligned to one or more societies), but not aligned to a common centre. Accordingly, 'Brussels' may well be a new political power centre, but is by no means a new society. More important are the connections *between* two societies among each other (for example between the French and German) as the smallest units, from which a European integration thus arises in a macro-sociological perspective (principle of horizontality). In relation to the Europe of the EU, this means that if the societies of the member states are closely intertwined with each other, then the *societal realm* is also no longer a sphere devoid of any relationship. In terms of the Europeanization of industrial relations this means that there had to be a close dependence leading to a mixture of industrial relations in different EU countries (that is a 'bottom-up' growth and not decreed by 'Brussels'); thus said, one could speak of a Europeanization of industrial relations. And such a 'bottom-up' process can only be configured by internationally active companies (or their actors) which have subsidiary enterprises in various EU countries. For instance, the industrial relations scheme of the pharmaceutical/ chemical concern Aventis Pharma SA was a typical example for the Europeanization of industrial relations: Aventis Pharma SA was established in December 1999 through the amalgamation of Hoechst AG (Germany) and the Rhône-Poulenc (SA), France. The corporate group's headquarters was Strasbourg, France. Insofar as the corporate codetermination and EWC are concerned, the industrial relations in the (French) parent enterprise were a mixture of the German and French models. They had been worked out after lengthy negotiations between the German and French shareholders, the involved trade unions and the works councils (meanwhile however, the Aventis Pharma SA has been in the possession of the Sanofi-Aventis SA with headquarters in Paris since 20 August 2004).

Taking this into consideration, a special feature of the socio-political integration has emerged in the course of the new integration strategy since the mid-1980s; Platzer has substantiated this with the technical term 'negotiated Europeanisation'.[5] This is a reference to the partial withdrawal of state or European institutions from the field of social policy and industrial relations – beyond the extent which is customary in many states; for instance, within the framework of free collective bargaining. For instance, the collective bargaining parties are granted opportunities within the framework of the evolving 'social dialogue' to adopt regulations, which (could) then gain legal validity by way of negotiation. It is disputed as to what extent the 'negotiated Europeanisation' will attain material significance. Some see an essential means for further development of Europe's social dimension in this. Others express themselves rather sceptically about their perspectives in view of the previously limited material results. Nevertheless, Platzer correctly explains that more far-reaching economic integration steps have always led to an examination of the European regulatory requirements in other political fields. Of course, up to now the socio-political regulations have always remained behind economic regulations in their scope.

> However, a development process of the 'social dimension' – partially 'out-of-phase' – takes place; this leads to expansion of material regulations (directives, decrees) and transfer-political control benefits, but is also expressed in an increase of 'soft' forms of coordination (reports, declarations, recommendations, outline directives and so on)' (Platzer, 1999, p. 181).

All in all, the development of industrial relations in Europe is not depicted as a European standardization. Strategies which explicitly or implicitly declare this as an objective must fail. To be anticipated is a development in which a differentiation is revealed with regard to retention of the dominance of the national regulatory level, whereby a supplementation of the various industrial relations systems will take place through European regulations as well as a change of the national systems themselves (in this regard, see also Traxler, 1995 and Traxler, Blaschke, Kittel, 2002).

But particularly in view of the 'negotiated Europeanisation' designated by Platzer, it always has to be taken into account that the utilization of the European regulatory level is always specifically linked with the prevailing national system of industrial relations. The effectiveness of European regulation can only be recorded under inclusion of this national linkage. Marginson and Sisson call this stage of Europeanization of industrial relations 'a glass half full as well as half empty' (2006, p. 81).

In political-strategic terms, the trade unions must find an answer to the question of how the subsidiarity principle can be specifically formulated for the field of industrial relations. And so it is a matter of deciding which regulatory contents should be negotiated exclusively on the European level, how the national systems must be further developed, how the relationship between the levels shall be organized, and

---

5   With regard to multilevel conceptuality, compare with: W. Lecher, H.-W. Platzer, S. Rueb, Weiner (2000).

which European regulations should be blocked to enable national regulations in the future.

For our research efforts it is also important that these 'third-state' influences on the industrial relations in the CEE subsidiaries of German parent enterprises depict a significant element.

Regarding Path (In) Dependence of Cross-Border Development Models in the Business Enterprise

The type of market economy and capitalism that nations rely on is very decisive for the development of industrial relations in the CEEC. For instance, whereas the American Sachs (1993) advocates the introduction of a pure 'Thatcher model' (and attempted to practise this in Russia), others argued – in a prominent position, the Schlecht (1994) – for the development of the German model of the social market economy as an optimal transformation strategy. The catastrophic effects – with the exception of Poland – of the so-called 'shock therapy' and the experiment of the 'one-to-one' transfer of other (Western) societal models on the transformation societies provoked deep criticism, especially from advocates of the theory of path dependency (Stark, 1994; Stark and Bruszt, 1998). Their theories emphasize the influence of historically deep-rooted structures, norms and mentalities on societal developments (as well as on industrial relations), and repudiate the idea that the collapses of the communist regimes have left behind a political and institutional vacuum. However, based on the background of other empirical studies, this theory can only be conditionally approved: in the case of Greenfield investments this represents dual path independence (irrespective of the industrial relations in the countries of origin, but also from those in the host countries of the investments).

If one includes the percentages of Europeanization of the respective national industrial relations – that is from third countries, then even three levels of path (in) dependence can be discerned.

This line of argumentation reveals that as a rule neither a 'one-to-one' transfer of Western production models and (Germanic) industrial relations nor the rigid insistence on linear-extended 'path dependence' (along handed down CEE lines, including 'transformation tripartism') render a solution, but rather a (to be verified empirically) 'hybridisation process' (Doerrenbaecher et al., 2000, p. 439): this process can appear in different characterizations as a mixture of:

1. Local conditions in the host countries (region, branch-specific, regional peculiarities, with Brownfield investments, specifics of the subsidiaries/sites, and so on)
2. Elements from parent enterprises (for example from Germany): in the following, we assume neither the theory of 'footloose' global enterprises (Altvater and Mahnkopf, 1996) nor that of the historically deep-rooted (nationally integrated) path dependency of industrial relations, also in globally active enterprises (Mueller-Jentsch 1995, Streeck 1995). Even the of the German system of industrial relations aim at a transformation beset with

compromise – but by no means in the sense of a dissolution scenario (Doerre 1997 as well as Doerre, Elk-Anders and Speidel 1997). Certain portions of the German system of industrial relations are already 'Europeanised' on the corporate level.

3. Influences of third countries or semi-governmental unions as external agents – such as the European Union or the CEE headquarters of German parent enterprises which are settled in Austria (Vienna), and (are thus able to) acquire specific (Austrian) influence on the arrangement of industrial relations in the CEE subsidiaries of German parent enterprises.[6]

Of course, this subsequently reveals a very inconsistent picture, and one feels inclined to quickly recall the 'corporate centralisation'. Nevertheless a few common interfaces between nation-state (under consideration of the heterogeneity within national 'models') and host country/third country influences[7] seem to arise in this connection: for instance, unified (industrial) trade union structures (such as in Germany) in their considerable significance for the organization of information, communications and with regard to representation of interests at branch as well as national level are only to be found as such in the Czech Republic and Slovakia, but not to this extent in Poland. However, this similarity between Germany and the two aforementioned CEEC is again diminished due to the fact that a considerable fragmentation occurs under the roof of the respective unified trade union, which partially does not even proceed along the lines of industry classifications.

The significance of collective agreements is quite different among the (German) country of origin and the three CEE host countries of FDI.

Because due to the dominance of *corporate/site-related* collective (in-house) agreements in the three CEEC the trade union representatives on the site/company level play a considerably different role than the works councils in Germany (which are not bargaining units, because in Germany collective bargaining normally is taking place on the supra-company – regional/sectoral – level).

In Germany, the treatment of industrial relations takes place in the broadest sense on different levels with corresponding divisions of labour: industrial and social law, collective agreements and industrial relations schemes on the company level. From that point of view the industrial relations scheme is only *one* component/element within an extensive mesh of institutions for handling and regulation of social conflicts (Braun, Eberwein and Tholen 1992, pp. 432–433). The effect of this institutional mesh consists of the fact that socially-conditioned conflict contents are desegregated, specified and differentiated, that is broken down, divided up and treated – depending on the different levels. Thereby conflicts are bereft of system

---

6   In November 2004, approx. 1,000 international companies had their Eastern Europe headquarters in Austria (in: *Welt am Sonntag*, no. 45, 7 November 2004); also among them the Henkel KGaA, which is also represented in our study sample.

7   With Doerrenbaecher (2003, pp. 151–155) one finds a broad account of the different theoretical approaches for an explanation of home country, host country and third country effects of investments, but which refrains from the terminology of different path (in) dependences preferred on our part.

overlapping explosive force and different partial solutions can be inserted as 'broken down problem complexes'. Within such an institutional mesh only such conflict objects which are able to be decided upon and implemented on this level can (and may) be aired within the framework of the industrial relations; in other respects, the EWC is similarly conceived in its interplay with the representative systems in the countries concerned.[8]

However, in the three CEE countries Poland, Czech Republic and Slovakia this division of labour between company/site, collective agreements and industrial/social law does not exist (or at least not in this characterization). In the practice of these countries these levels are strongly mixed with each other.

Insofar as the other side – the management/capitalism model (including the references to the form of conflict venue) – is concerned, the question emerges here as to whether the British understanding of management[9] would also be the more attractive (and perhaps also more practicable) model for German investors in the CEEC. Doerrenbaecher calls this the 'third country effect' (Doerrrenbaecher 2003, p. 165).

Therefore, under certain aspects the interesting possibility of comparison can arise between the British and Polish model one the one hand, and the German, Czech and Slovakian model (in which case there are considerable differences between the Slovakian and Czech model) on the other hand. The line of separation between EU-15 countries and the (new) eight CEEC members of the EU runs crossways to this 'model'. This new matrix is brought together through an evolving Europeanization of the industrial relations in all 'country types'.

In summary, the industrial relations dominating in the foreign-controlled CEE subsidiaries (and focused here on Poland, Czech Republic and Slovakia) can take on a more specific character through the following three factors:

- The unilateral path dependency of the host country of the investments dominates with regard to Brownfield investments, that is that the handed-down representatives system continues to exist in the plant.
- The process of the Europeanization of industrial relations in the EU countries with their important element of EWC can help to cope with the intransigent tripartism.
- It is equally valid for Brownfield as well as Greenfield investments that legal possibilities in the direction of a new form of representatives (works councils) are available in the companies/sites in both the Czech Republic and Slovakia; in Poland this was prepared by the government in 2004 with the objective of passing a law in 2005. However, this draft was already rejected in June 2005

---

8   However, the German 'model' of dual representation of interests has changed considerably; it is on the brink of considerable challenges (softening trends with regard to collective agreements – hardship case regulations, initiatives for more works council competencies with regard to companies softening of collective agreements, and so on).

9   In its practical implementation on the company level, the British understanding more closely follows the human resource approach – which emphasizes management dominance (dialogue with and codetermination through the workforce *without* collective intermediary) – than the German approach of co-management.

by a parliamentary committee; and it remains to be seen what significance the in September 2005 newly elected Polish parliament – and thus the new right-wing government – will have on the fate of this proposition.

If one assumes the fact that particularly in the SMEs hardly any trade union representatives exist (Gradev, 2001, p. 17), and one combines this fact with the 'union-free' zones already existing with regard to the Greenfield investments,in many cases, such representatives on the site/company levels can certainly close a gap – especially if one perceives from the general suspicion of trade unions in the CEEC that the trade union representatives on the site/company level shall be expunged with the establishment of a works council.

Formulated in concrete terms, these different path dependencies will be strengthened by a process that Doerrenbaecher (2003, p. 155) describes as a 'cross-border transfer of multinational companies', and which in turn – also at this point of argumentation that is not yet supported by specific empirics – strengthens the hypothesis of corporate-related nature of the effects of direct investments by Western companies on the industrial relations in the CEEC.

With the application of path dependency theories we primarily refer to the specific forms in the respective parent enterprises and subsidiaries. These are naturally embedded in the respective nation 'models' of industrial relations. In summary, the industrial relations in the CEE subsidiaries/investments can be energized from:

- the internal corporate group practices and visions of the parent enterprise
- the handed-down industrial relations in the Brownfield investments
- the political creative will of the actors in the CEEC
- the legal fundamentals in the concerned CEEC, and
- third-country influences.

Chapter 3

Investments by West European Companies and Industrial Relations in Poland, Czech Republic and Slovakia as Underlying Study Conditions

The investments of foreign companies in Central and Eastern Europe encounter formal (among others, legal) and informal conditions of industrial relations, which are then retained or changed in the further course of development. As far as that is concerned, in the following we will cast a brief glance at

- the general significance of investments by foreign – particularly German – companies in Central and Eastern Europe, especially in Poland, the Czech Republic and Slovakia, as well as
- the prevailing FDI industrial relations as underlying conditions of further development.

Extent and Significance of Foreign Direct Investments in Central and Eastern Europe Regarding the Extent of FDI in the CEEC

According to the UNCTAD World Investment Report for 2003 (UNCTAD, 2004), the worldwide FDI (inflow) declined for the third year in a row. After the CEEC defied this worldwide trend only a year beforehand, the inflow of investments in the CEEC now also declined in 2003 with 21 billion USD (in comparison, 2002: 31 billion USD). This decline was particularly conditioned through the movements in the Czech Republic and Slovakia (UNCTAD, 2004, p. xix). This decline in the FDI recorded in 2003 – particularly in the Czech Republic and Slovakia – is above all to be explained by the fact that the privatization of the industry as the main cause of earlier FDI there was almost completed in 2003 (Podkaminer et al., 2004, p. 16).

However, for 2004 the UNCTAD again reported a substantial worldwide upswing of inflow investments (648.1 billion USD) – mainly conditioned through a positive trend in Central and Eastern Europe and in the industrial countries (UNCTAD, 2005a, Tables I.3, 15; and UNCTAD, 2005b, Annex Tables B1, 303).

The annual fluctuations of the inflow investments are partially enormous and also dependent on major investments transacted in certain years.

Let us take the example of Slovakia: in 2006 the country is one of the most imports automobile producers in Europe with 850,000 units produced per year; whereas

Table 3.1   Foreign direct investments, inflows (in billion USD)

Countries/Regions	1999	2000	2001	2002	2003	2004
CEEC which became EU members on 01/05/04, *among them*:	18.6	20.3	18.4	22.6	11.5	18.8
Czech Republic	6.3	5.0	5.6	8.5	2.1	4.5
Poland	7.3	9.3	5.7	4.1	4.1	6.2
Slovakia	0.4	1.9	1.6	4.1	0.7	1.1
Total world, *of which*:	1,086.8	1,388.0	817.6	716.1	632.6	648.1
Germany	56.1	198.3	21.1	36.0	27.2	38.5

Source: *World Investment Report (2003) (UNCTAD, 2004, p. 72),*[1] *World Investment Report (2005) (UNCTAD, 2005b, Annex Tables B1, 303)*

there had not been any independent automobile production whatsoever there until 1991. In 1991, VW took over a small Škoda parts manufacturing production facility in Bratislava and expanded this facility into a high-volume producer (a turnover of 5 billion USD in 2004; 8,200 employees produced 280,000 cars and 369,000 gear units).

In 2003, PSA Peugeot-Citroen decided to build an automobile production facility 100 km away from the VW factory, and commenced with investments in the very same year. The start of the production was 2006 (full production capacity will be 300,000 cars annually). Parallel to this PSA Peugeot-Citroen decided to build a second factory (production start will be 2010 with an annual production of 150,000 units). But on 18 April 2006 PSA announced to close its Peugeot 206 plant at Ryton, near Coventry, UK, with the loss of 2,300 jobs.

In the beginning of 2004, the Korean auto manufacturer KIA Motors Company (a daughter of Hyundai Motors Company) also decided to build a factory in the same region (in Zilina), which shall reach its full production capacity (200,000 cars) in 2008 – then 2,400 jobs will be created.[2]

The main time-related emphasis of these Greenfield investments lies after 2003, so the marginal inflow of investments for Slovakia in 2003 is only an 'intermediate stage' for a subsequent, rapid growth.

As far as that is concerned this development in the CEEC presents itself differently. For instance, since 2000 Slovakia has been among the top 'winners' – even with the decrease of 2003. In this case this also naturally lies in the historical development. Here the privatization process is also approaching its end, so that now further investments – as in all other former transformation societies – are usually Greenfield investments. Yet after 1993 Slovakia initially managed to attract correspondingly less FDI than other countries in the course of privatization. This was also particularly due to political reasons (Meciar regime). A catching-up process occurred here with the change of government and and the subsequent policy since 1998/99.

---

1   Unfortunately, the World Investment Report for 2004 is not extrapolating the Table 1 figures for 2004, see UNCTAD (2005a).

2   The region around Bratislava is called now as 'Detroit East' and is a typical example for a cluster. On the other hand, this region will be rather vulnerable in case of a crisis of the automotive industry.

Table 3.2   Manufacturing industry's share in all FDI (in percentages)

	1998	2002
Czech Republic	46	36
Poland	39	36
Slovakia	49	36

Source: Hunya (2004, p. 12)

Table 3.3   Extent of FDI/holdings in the manufacturing industry per employee (1,000 euro) in 2001

Czech R.	Poland	Slovakia	Slovenia	Hungary	Estonia	Lithuania	Latvia
10.7	10.6	6.1	5.8	5.4	5.2	3.0	2.9

Source: European Commission (1999a); European Competitiveness Report (2003, p. 184)

Investments were primarily made in the manufacturing industry in the CEEC, even with declining shares (see Table 3.2).

These declining shares of FDI in the manufacturing industry point to the second wave of FDI, which concentrated more on knowledge-orientated productions and thus increased the share of service sector investments to the disadvantage of investments in the manufacturing industry.

Even within the manufacturing industry the branch distribution of FDI is unequal; for instance, in 2002 and 2003 less was invested in the CEEC from the electrical industry, whereas the automobile industry invested more.

Despite this decline in the inflow of FDI in 2003 in comparison with 2002, the UNCTAD sees good medium-term growth opportunities for inflow investments, particularly for the CEEC (UNCTAD, 2004, p. 69; and UNCTAD, 2004, p. 15).

In 2004, the trend also continued in most investing companies to shift investments more in knowledge-orientated productions and to neglect such FDI which are labour-intensive and dependent on low wages – such FDI flows eastward.

If one considers only the manufacturing industry and procures the FDI in terms of the *employees*, then the Czech Republic and Poland are on nearly level pegging, followed by Slovakia (see Table 3.3):

These varying figures reflect not only the attractiveness of the different countries, but also their varying privatization strategies in different branches.[3]

Sixty-one per cent of all FDI in the CEEC stem from the EU-15. Germany is at the top of the single country comparison with 19 per cent of all FDI in the CEEC. The Netherlands, the USA and France subsequently follow.[4]

It is interesting to note, that Germany as the biggest investor in the CEE region is focused more on vertical investments compared with FDI inflows from France,

---

3   With regard to the FDI figures in the respective branches/CEEC, see in particular the European Commission (2003b, p. 184); European Competitiveness Report (2003).

4   With regard to the individual figures, see also the Manager Magazine study from October 2003, in: Stadtmann, Hermann and Weigand 2003, 7.

Table 3.4   Amount of direct and (via dependent holding companies existing abroad) indirect German direct investments in the manufacturing industry (in million euro)

	All Countries	EU-25	Poland	Czech Republic	Slovakia
2001	177,546	71,016	4,343	4,758	1,190
2002	167,775	79,876	4,439	4,986	1,674
2003	165,560	84,719	4,242	5,677	1,918
2004	166,795	84,159	4,999	6,498	2,221

Sources: Deutsche Bundesbank [German Central Bank] 2002: 6; Deutsche Bundesbank (2003, p. 6), 34; Deutsche Bundesbank (2004, p. 6), 38; Deutsche Bundesbank (2005, p. 6), 38; Deutsche Bundesbank (2006, pp. 6, 34, 35)

which are more horizontal investments (see vertical/horizontal FDI, Keane and Feinberg, 2005).

Regarding the Importance of FDI for the German Economy

The importance of direct investments in the direction of the CEEC for the overall German economy is estimable through Table 3.4.

If one considers only 2004, the importance of the (direct and indirect) investments by German companies in the manufacturing industries in the three countries of most special interest to us – Poland, Czech Republic and Slovakia – is thus emphasized: 11,837 (million) euros have been invested there – nearly 45 per cent of the corresponding investments in all reform countries (including China, Russia, ex-Yugoslavia, Bulgaria, Romania), 14.1 per cent of the investments in the EU-25 and still 7.1 per cent of the corresponding investments in all of the countries around the globe (except Germany).[5]

Regarding the Effects of FDI on the Host Countries

What could be the effects – in purely economical terms – of the FDI in the CEEC (also compare with Vincentz and Knogler, 2003, p. 70)?

Coming from the older works by Helpman and Krugman (1985) on the complex relations between FDI and foreign trade, we distinguish between corporate-external and corporate-internal effects. Here we will concentrate on the corporate-external effects, as in recent years new evidence showed that there are major differences across firms within sectors of their participation in international trade and FDI. For example, exporting firms are more productive than non-exporting firms and multinational firms are more productive than exporting firms that are not multinational (Helpman, Melitz and Yeaple 2004). The question whether FDI will increase the productivity of the mother companies/subsidiaries, could only be answered on the micro level and depends on the size of the investing company and its subsidiaries, the target of FDI,

---

5   Hungary is to be mentioned as a fourth important CEE host country of German investments (see in particular Buch and Toubal, 2003, p. 596).

and so on (Javorcik, 2004). Insofar we will outline the corporate-internal effects of FDI in Chapters 4 and 5.

As far as the *corporate-external effects* are concerned, there is an indisputable connection between transformation-related modernization in the CEE countries and the FDI (Mako and Ellingstad, 2000, p. 343; Moran, Graham and Blomstrom 2005) – it ranges from technology transfer to higher wages and qualification levels, and includes creation of jobs (see also in particular Kaufmann and Menke, 1997, p. 151).

In addition to the provision of financial resources for the host countries (about one-third of the capital provided through the FDI has been used for privatization, Galgóczi and Kluge, 2003), the decisive effects of FDI lie in positive external effects (spill-overs) in the recipient/host country (compare with Vincentz and Knogler, 2003, p. 70). These effects include technology transfer, marketing channels, better management and qualification of the workforce. One must compare these external effects with the normal procurement and marketing connections. Of course, FDI – much like any other investment – also lead to additional demand for primary products as well as new product offers, and from that point of view also have positive effects on the overall economy.

In quantitative terms alone, the foreign capital flows provide an essential contribution to a recipient country's investment total. For instance, in recent years the FDI in Poland amounted to approximately 20 per cent of the entire domestic gross fixed capital investments. As a result, they are an essential factor for the amount of overall investments. Even more significant is the share of foreign companies for the recipient country's foreign trade: in 1999, 51.6 per cent of Polish exports and 55.8 per cent of Polish imports were attributed to companies with foreign involvement (Polish Council of Ministers, 2001).

The major importance of FDI for the development of the national economies in the CEE countries emerges impressively from the figures in Table 3.5.

With nearly all indicators of the manufacturing industry in the three CEE countries the share of foreign companies is above 50 per cent, sometimes far above, whereby a considerable increase can be ascertained between 1998 and 2001.

The investments of *German* companies in the manufacturing industry of the eight new CEE EU member countries by the end of 2002 brought about the creation

Table 3.5   Shares of foreign companies in the manufacturing industry in terms of equity capital, employment, investments, turnover and total export turnover (in percentages)

	Equity Capital 1998 2001	Employment 1998 2001	Investments 1998 2001	Turnover 1998 2001	Export Turnover 1998 2001
Czech Republic	28.4 54.5	19.2 34.1	41.6 69.3	31.6 53.3	47.5 69.3
Poland	43.2 53.1	26.0 32.9	51.0 64.0	40.0 52.0	52.3 66.2
Slovakia	35.2 55.9	18.5 36.4	50.1 73.1	36.2 59.3	59.0 74.9

Source: Hunya (2004, p. 15)

of about 396,000 new jobs in the host countries of these investments (Deutsche Bundesbank, 2004, pp. 20, 34).

Despite all of these positive factors, it is only then justified to grant the FDI a central role in the growth strategy of the concerned host country if they provide a transfer of knowledge and technology exceeding the normal input-output connections (Vincentz and Knogler, 2003, p. 70). Therefore, greater significance of the FDI is only then justified if their returns would be greater than the returns of domestic investments.

For evaluation of the FDI in the European catch-up process – and perhaps also in the overtaking process – it is therefore crucial as to how large the positive external effects are on the recipient country's economy. Many things are particularly contingent on whether the economy is able to absorb the transfer of technology – including the logistical prerequisites and consequences. This depends on the qualification of the workforce, but also on the institutional and legal environment – including the industrial relations. In this context, Galgóczi (2003) rightfully emphasizes the changes on the 'micro' – that is corporate/site – level, and in particular also means the corporate culture.

Another empirical study comes to the conclusion that a clearer, more positive effect of the FDI is verifiable for East Europe in the time span 1990–1998 (Campos and Coricelli, 2002). Yet another study (Zemplerinova, 2001) for the Czech Republic comes to the conclusion that as a result of the FDI, much more is invested per job than through domestic investments. A further outstanding case study regarding Hungary describes the positive role of the FDI in the process of the globalization and modernization of the national economy (Mako and Ellingstad, 2000).

According to the literature and other empirical studies, in the aggregate the FDI assume a crucial role in the transformation process (among others, Deppe and Schroeder, 2002).

But in addition, it must be unequivocally noted that the privatization of the economy and the subsequently related FDI represent a historically unique event that will no longer come to pass in the foreseeable future.

These positive effects of the FDI will be discussed in close connection with the inclusion of local suppliers into the network of foreign-owned enterprises/sites in the economical as well as the socio-political discourse. This inclusion of local suppliers significantly determines the technology transfers and decides whether the danger of the evolution of a dual economy is realized or not.

However, quite often these corporate-related effects fizzle out in the *region* in which the direct investor's subsidiary is located (with regard to the studies on Japanese investments in England at the end of the 1980s, which are also informative for the CEEC, see Elger and Smith, 1998a, p. 602).

Moreover, a study of a Hungarian region revealed that the investing multinational corporations advance the state of technology as well as provide qualifications and equipment to also make their subsidiaries operational, but that nevertheless these effects in the region were observed to be more sporadic than systematic on account of weak multipliers (Mako and Ellingstad, 2000, p. 358). And another study regarding the strategy of the multinational corporations in the CEE countries corroborates this trend, and maintains that the investing companies can only be successful if they organize alliances and investments so that they also benefit the regional and national actors of the host countries as 'win-win' arrangements (Rondinelli and Black, 2000, p. 85).

Diagram of Industrial Relations in Poland, Czech Republic and Slovakia in Relation to Germany

In the following section, the commonalities and differences among the industrial relations in the three host countries of the investments shall be presented briefly, since their institutional circumstances define framework conditions on which the West European companies make their investments. While doing so, we primarily refer to the corporate/site level, since the greatest changes take place at this level. The (as still planned in Poland, and already effected in the Czech Republic and Slovakia) introduction of so-called works councils on the site level in addition to trade union representatives on the site/company level could be of great importance for the West European, esp. German parent enterprises insofar as similar structures are already in existence in Germany. German works councils (which – in comparison with the trade unions – have a greater institutional influence on the arrangement of the industrial relations in the CEE subsidiary enterprises – which they do not use) often complain that they did not find any corresponding contact in the subsidiary enterprises. This previous shortcoming would also partially explain the practically marginal influence of the German works councils (and the trade unions anyway) on the arrangement of the industrial relations in the CEE subsidiary enterprises (see details below).

The essential elements of the industrial relations in Poland, Czech Republic and Slovakia are schematically compiled in Table 3.6.[6]

If one evaluates this tableau, the following summarized commonalities and the differences of the industrial relations in the three CEEC can be established:

---

6   Important detailed presentations are to be found in the presentation by Kohl (2003) (presentation of the realms of collective industrial law, company-focused industrial relations and representatives, sectoral industrial relations and collective agreement as well as industrial relations and tripartism on the national and regional level in the eight new CEE EU member countries); in Marginson, Sisson, Arrowsmith 2003 as well as in Tóth (2003) (here the main emphasis lies on the latest developments of industrial relations on the *company* level); Welz and Kauppinen are describing industrial action and conflict resolution in the new Member States (2005); in the writings of the IG Metall to trade unions and representatives on companies' level in the new EU countries (IG Metall, 2002, pp. 1–3); in Gradev 2001 with his CEE country reports (especially regarding the connection between representatives and FDI); Carley 2002 with his comments regarding collective agreement coverage and trade union membership; Vatta 2003 with a detailed presentation of employers' organizations (including chambers of industry and commerce) in the CEE countries; the reports of the Friedrich Ebert Foundation, 'Trade Union Cooperation Project', Warsaw (and in particular here the report from July 2003 concerning the status of Polish trade unions) and Budapest; as well as the progress report from this project regarding 'EU Enlargement and Labour Relations: New Trends in Poland, Czech and Slovak Republic' (Tholen, Cziría, Hemmer, Mansfeldowá, 2003). The following brief diagram refers to this literature.

Table 3.6   Diagram of industrial relations in Poland, Czech Republic and Slovakia

Levels/Countries	Poland	Czech Republic	Slovakia
Level 1: Form of conflict regulation	Conflict tripartism	Consensus tripartism	Blocked tripartism
Level 2: Organizational form of trade unions	Pluralistic variety of trade unions/3 large industrial unions, + smaller uions (partly crafts unions)	Unified trade union/ mainly industrial unions	Unified trade union, but fragmented/industrial + some crafts unions
Level 3: Trade union density in % (approx.)	15	30	40
Level 4: Relationship between the trade union and workplace representation	Monistic/hybrid dualism (since April 2006): • Trade union in the company/site **or** • facultative works councils	Monistic/hybrid dualism: (since 2001) • Trade union in the company/site **or** • facultative works councils	Monistic with a tendency towards dualism (since 2002): • Trade union in the company/site • Works councils
Level 5: Collective bargaining	Company/shop (approx. 8,000 contracts) Region/branch (17 contracts) National level	• Company/shop • National level	• Company/shop • National level
Level 6: Collective agreement coverage in % of all employees	40	25–30	48

- Trade unions and employers' associations have evolved from very different starting positions, and are in various stages of development.
- The rate of unionization is relatively marginal (especially in the *SME* realm), and is also still lacking at present – though trade unions in CEEC remain the largest voluntary organization in a largely passive civil society (Thirkell, Petkov and Vickerstaff 1998).
- The employers' associations are very weak and partially fragmented; collective bargaining is decentralized to a great extent, with a main emphasis on the corporate level.
- Traditional monistic structures (trade union representatives) prevail on the site/company level; however, in the Czech Republic and even more so in Slovakia with a recently legally prescribed dualism (establishment of 'works councils'); the establishment of works councils in Poland had been in the state of legislative procedure since 2004 – but this was stopped in June 2005. After the new elections for the Polish parliament on 25 September 2005 (with the consequence of a right-wing populist government) on 7 April 2006 a new law 'Information and Consultation of the employees' passed the two houses of the Polish Parliament. This law is more or less a copy of the respective Czech law.

- The governments have a very strong position in the definition of industrial relations by virtue of the instrument of tripartite organization, which is also partially attributable to the weaknesses of the two social partners. This transformation tripartism partially deludes both social partners into a purported importance in the society, which does not really exist, and leads to complacent paralysis – we call this 'the sweet poison of tripartism'. In addition, the open question emerges as to whether the transformation tripartism is compatible with the EU's self-understanding of social dialogue that emanates from bipartism (that is without the state actor).[7]
- In principal, a contradictory process between deregulation of the industrial relations and the social welfare system on the one hand, and the process of regulation prescribed through the *acquis communautaire* on the other hand, is determinable in the new EU member states. In our estimation, the direction in which the industrial relations in the three CEEC will proceed is only evident in outline.

But now to the single levels of industrial relations:

The Association Level

A large-scale fragmentation of the trade unions prevails in *Poland*:

There is the Solidarnosc [Solidarity] with approximately 850,000 members/ employees. It features a regional and industrial-sector structure; however, the regional organizations dominate (38 regions, approximately 17,000 works committees, 15 industrial-sector secretariats).

In addition, there is the All-Polish Trade Union Confederation (OPZZ) (established in 1984) with approximately 600,000 members (without pensioners) (status March 2006). The OPZZ is a rather loose confederation of 99 industrial-sector trade unions in 12 branches which have a considerable degree of autonomy.

Solidarnosc and OPZZ for a long time were rather hostile to each other for some reasons (OPZZ was accused to be a child of the communist regime in the 1980s, which had forbidden and persecuted Solidarnosc). So Solidarnosc blocked for a long time every attempt by OPZZ to become a member of the European Trade Union Confederation (ETUC) – only on 14 March 2006 OPZZ succeeded in its attempt.

Furthermore, there is also the Trade Union Forum Poland (FZZ) (established in 2002) with approximately 400,000 members.

In addition, there is the independent, self-governed 'Solidarity 80' trade union ((NSZZ) Solidarnosc 80) with approximately 150,000 members (1997, according to their own statements).

Moreover, there are roughly 180 autonomous, regionally or nationally active trade unions; most perceive themselves programmatically as apolitical, and concentrate on the representation of the interests for their respectively small-scale clientele.

---

7   An interesting practical insight into tripartism in Poland is provided by the Friedrich Ebert Foundation Warsaw (2004); see also Mailand, Due (2004).

There are essentially two employers'/business enterprise associations in Poland: The Confederation of Polish Employers (KPP) – which encompasses 51 (private-sector and state-organized) employers' associations, 1,500 individually-owned enterprises as well as 26 sector organizations as members – and the Polish Confederation of Private Employers (PKPP), which has 2,276 (mostly private and *SME*) enterprises as well as 18 industrial-sector organizations as members. In addition, there are two other (smaller) employers' organizations.

In the *Czech Republic* there is no such trade union fragmentation as in Poland. There are 34 industrial-sector trade unions with 772,000 members (without pensioners) unified within the Confederation of Bohemian-Moravian Trade Unions (CMKOS). The CMKOS, which was established in 1990 as a reformed successor organization to the former communist union, was able to assert its dominant position despite several attempts at splitting up. There are also other partially crafts/professional, partially regional unions without major importance.

Much the same as in Poland, the employers in the Czech Republic have two organizations. First of all, there is the Confederation of Industry and Transport in the Czech Republic (SOCR) with 1,700 enterprises and 31 sector organizations as members; and secondly, the Confederation of Employers and Entrepreneurs, which encompasses the seven national confederations as members.

In *Slovakia*, the trade unions are similar to and yet at the same different from those in the Czech Republic.

Here the trade unions are similar because there is also only *one* umbrella organization – the Confederation of Trade Union Federations (KOZ SR). The trade unions are different because – with 37 KOZ membership trade unions (approximately 655,000 members in 2001) – a considerable degree of fragmentation exists within the KOZ SR, whereby in some industries several single trade unions exist at the same time.

In contrast to Poland and the Czech Republic, till 2004 in Slovakia did only *one* employers' organization exist – the Federation of Employers Association of the Slovak Republic (AZZZ SR), which had been established in 1995 and covered 37 member associations (19 of them industrial-sector associations). However, a fragmentation of the employers' associations in Slovakia also occurred in April 2004: employers, who were no longer in agreement with the AZZZ SR, established the National Employers' Union (Republiková únia zamestnávateľov, RUZ). This new organization represents companies with in total 250,000 employees, and is politically quite influential and financially well-endowed. This fragmentation caused perplexities for quite a while regarding which of the two national umbrella organizations was allowed to represent the employer in the tripartite commission on the national level.

In *Germany*, there is one unified trade union featuring the Federation of German Trade Unions (DGB) as umbrella organization and eight industrial-sector trade unions. On 31/12/03 the membership amounted to 7,363 million workers, which corresponds to the union density (ratio of trade union members to employees) of approximately 25 per cent.

On the employers' side, there is a social association in charge for collective bargaining (Federation of the German Employers' Associations (BDA), with corresponding industrial-sector sub-classifications) as well as an industrial association (Federation of the German Industry (BDI) – also with corresponding industrial-sector structures).

The Level of Collective Bargaining

In *Poland*, the collective bargaining is usually organized on the site/company level, whereas the supra-company framework agreement on employment conditions governs general conditions. The coverage rate of the collective bargaining amounts to 40 per cent.

The *Czech Republic* is comparable with Poland in this respect: here the collective bargaining is also usually organized on the site/company level; industrial-sector collective wage agreements are merely outline agreements, whereby the corporate/ shops wage agreements may not establish conditions worse than the industrial-sector wage agreements. Fewer than 11 per cent of all employees are covered by the collective agreements concluded on the sectoral/regional levels. The degree of coverage of the collective bargaining amounts to approx. 25 to 30 per cent of all employees.

The situation in *Slovakia* is presented a bit differently: not only is the coverage rate of collective bargaining (nearly 50 per cent) higher than in Poland and especially in the Czech Republic, but the collective bargaining is concluded on the corporate/ site level as well as on the national (industrial-sector) level, whereby in contrast to the Czech Republic and Poland the industrial-sector orientation dominates.

In *Germany*, the regional industrial-sector collective bargaining dominates, even if the number of corporate/shop collective agreements continues to increase and there are many opening clauses for specified companies' situations in the sector/regional collective bargaining (catchword: 'breathing company/site'). In 2001, the industrial-sector collective bargaining in West Germany covered 63.1 per cent of all employees, and 44.4 per cent of all employees in East Germany (IAB, 2003, *Entwicklung der Flaechentarifbindung* [Development of collective wage commitment on sectoral/ regional level] 1995–2001).

The Site/Company Level of Industrial Relations

An 'eroding' monism of industrial relations prevails in *Poland*:

On the site/company level there is one trade union committee which is constituted on the basis of a resolution that must be passed by at least 10 people. The trade union or the respective committee on the company/site level is then judicially registered.

This monism is eroding for three reasons:

1. In case of mass dismissals, a new law from 13 March 2003 stipulates that in the absence of trade union representatives the rights to (obtain) information and consultation with regard to these mass dismissals devolves upon the workforce representatives, who must then be nominated in agreement with the management. This could be an initial juridical step in the direction of a dual representation of interest.

2. Due to the fragmentation of the trade unions – which also signifies weakness at the same time – some (large-scale) business enterprises have started with the establishment of voluntary works councils, which are then union-free.
3. A new trend emerged for Poland with the introduction of works councils planned by the previous government. In August 2004 the Labour Ministry presented a draft bill pertaining to 'Information and Consultation', which prescribes the establishment of works councils in business enterprises with 20 or more employees – but this draft was stopped by a Parliament's committee in June 2005. But in the course of 2005 the trade unions seemed to have come to terms with legally prescribed representatives on the site/plant level. They favoured the Czech model.

After the parliamentary elections in September 2005 and the establishment of the new (right wing) government, on 7 April 2006 a new law 'Information and Consultation of the employees' passed the Polish Parliament. This law is more or less a copy of the respective Czech law (that is the 'ad hoc' works council – see subsequent explanation).

In the *Czech Republic* and *Slovakia*, a dualism of representatives on the site/ company level has been introduced by lawmakers against the will of the trade unions – albeit with different nuances.

The (monistically-characterized) trade unions within the company/site traditionally prevail in both countries.

In particular, they alone retain the right to negotiate collective agreements with the employers for all employees on the corporate level (that is also de jure for non-union members). Therefore, there is no difference between collective agreement on the supra-company level and in-house agreement, but merely between company/site-focused and industrial-sector collective agreement (and then on the national level) – much the same as in Poland.

A supplementation to the labour law code has been undertaken in the two countries to the effect that a 'Works Council' can also be elected independently of the trade unions. However, serious differences exist between the two countries as far as the significance of these two representative bodies is concerned:

In the *Czech Republic*, a law pertaining to an 'ad hoc works council' entered into effect on 1 January 2001: if the formation of trade union groups on company/site levels does not evolve in accordance with the revised labour law, the employees of works with at least 25 employees can elect representatives on the site/company level. However, the right of trade union representatives to conduct collective bargaining was not transferred to the works councils in this case. In addition, some important information, consultation and participation rights remain exclusively with the trade union representatives (for instance, information pertaining to wage development, consultation regarding the economic development of the business enterprise, job development, and so on).

As far as that is concerned, the works councils retain the sole right to notification and hearing.

However, if a works trade union body is established (by only three individuals) in the same business enterprise after the election of a 'works council', this entity assumes the rights and obligations of the existing works council; the latter entity is then dissolved. We call this Czech variation a 'hybrid dualism'.

A new comprehensive Labour code has been put into force on 1 July 2006, which is confirming the priority of primary trade union organization over the 'works councils' – we call this the continuance of the hybrid dualism.

Slovakia has taken a similar approach with respect to 'works councils' as the Czech Republic but was more consequent in the end. There as well, from 1 April 2002 employees are allowed to elect representatives on the site/company level as long as trade union groups within company/site are not existing. The works councils only have the right to information and consultation but not for bargaining on a site/company level – that is similar to the Czech Republic. Works councils are elected in companies with at least 50 employees for a period of four years. If the company only employs five to 49 employees one individual is elected as representative.

But for Slovakia there are two significant differences with regard to the aforementioned law in the Czech Republic:

- In Slovakia, the corporate managements have the obligation to allow the employees to elect works councils in case of the absence of a trade union representatives in the business enterprise. This obligation then emerges if at least 10 per cent of all members of the workforce call for (in writing) the election of a works council.
- A dualism is possible in Slovakia since the autumn of 2003 – that is the simultaneity of a trade union works committee *and* a works council. If the majority of the 'works council' decides to do so, a representative of the trade union works committee can take part in its sessions. Moreover, the works council has the right to negotiate all matters which are not covered by the collective (in-house) *wage* agreement (between management and trade union representatives).

Until now, it is not yet clear how this nascent dualism will continue to evolve in practice.

In *Germany*, there is a dualism with regard to the representation. The works council legally represents the employees on the corporate/site level: 52.5 per cent of all employees work in corporates/companies/sites with a works council (in the following, compare with IAB, 2004). Yet there is a distinct differential between small, medium and large-scale business enterprises: the larger the business enterprise, the greater the degree of dissemination of works councils is. 93,5 per cent of all German companies with 500 and more employees have a works council, whereas on the other side of the size categories only 26 per cent of the companies with a workforce ranging between 5 and 49 employees have a works council.

Only the trade unions have the capacity to be a partner in the process of collective bargaining. However, works councils and works management can conclude collective (wage) agreements on the basis of industrial-sector collective wage agreements in order to take special features into consideration. But these company/site-centred collective agreements may not define any deterioration for the employees in comparison with the conditions stipulated in the supra-company (regional/sectoral) collective agreements. However, in recent years company's specific opening clauses have been increasingly adopted in the sector/regional collective agreements, which also allow wage reductions and prolongations of working hours without wage compensation (up until September 2005, 25 per cent of all collective wage agreements have made use of this). But this flexibility can certainly be defined as a strength of the German system of collective bargaining that permits 'breathing companies/sites'.

Chapter 4

The Views of the Actors on the Supra-Company Levels: Results of the Expert Interviews in the Countries of Origin and Host Countries of Investment and on the EU Level

The expert interviews on the supra-company level with representatives of trade unions, employers' associations and employment/economics ministries in Poland, Czech Republic, Slovakia and Germany as well as on the EU level were one of the main emphasis of the empirical work. In light of comparability aspects, the study is restricted to the manufacturing industry. Within the manufacturing industry we selected the metal and electrical industry (including automotive industry), the food processing industry and the chemical and energy industry.

These various viewpoints and experiences with regard to the effects of German direct investments on the industrial relations in Central and Eastern Europe will be presented in the following.

The Role of Associations in the Accompaniment of Investment Processes

National associations (trade unions and employers'/corporate federations) do not normally play any role worth mentioning in the accompaniment of direct investments on the supranational level.

However, the political, economical and social upheavals in Central and Eastern Europe since the beginning of the 1990s was of such dimensions that additional requirements were increasingly imposed on trade unions and corporate federations, particularly in the western part of Europe: considerable transfers of know-how from West to East were necessary to newly establish and/or to reorganize the necessary institutions in Central and Eastern Europe. These transfers were also concerned with conditions and processes as they were established through the direct investments of West European and – in particular here – German companies in the transformation societies. The importance of these investments for the economical and social renewal of the CEE societies has already been stated further above.

In the following it shall be clarified as to what extent the western – and in particular the German – associations also posed (or were even able to pose) this problem in reality.

At the same time, it is to be noted that in practice there has always been a mixture between 'institution-building' as the normal transfer from West to East and the – case-by-case – accompaniment of single corporation investment processes.

To anticipate the result: there are only very sporadic efforts – if any – on the *national* level as well as on the level of the EU associations (employers' and trade unions) to actively accompany the investment processes of western companies in the CEEC. Usually such efforts are actually left up to the single companies, that is the management and – if available – the representatives on the site/company level.

This renders an additional advantage to the employers' side with the fulfilment of arrangement options pertaining to industrial relations in Central and Eastern Europe: because of their interests and their instruments of power the employers are very interested in leaving negotiation processes within the scope of the business enterprise and in surrendering as few competencies as possible to higher-level authorities – that is associations. In contrast, employees are strongly dependent on their organizations and the principle of solidarity. They continue to lose more and more if:

1. arrangement possibilities are only opened on the corporate level,
2. and at the same time collaboration only takes place – if at all – sporadically on the supranational level for accompaniment of single economic organization processes.

The results in detail follow.

Industrial/Employers' Associations in Germany

Let's start with the industrial/employers' associations in Germany.

The BDI does not play an active role in the accompaniment of investment processes. Its activities in this connection are restricted to specialist conferences, information exchanges, and so on. For example, it accompanied conferences regarding privatization of industry in Poland.

The BDI has good relations with the employers' organizations in Poland and the Czech Republic, but their relations with such organizations in Slovakia is somewhat vague (because of the Meciar government's after affects). But in Poland the situation is a bit more complicated, since there are two umbrella associations as employers' organizations here. The Polish Confederation of Private Employers (PKPP) is an associated member with UNICE (full member effective May 2004), whereas the Confederation of Polish Employers (KPP), which rather represents the old industry, is not a member. Therefore, this fragmentation of the Polish employers' associations very closely resembles that of the Polish trade unions.

Insofar as the food processing industry is concerned, there are no corresponding activities in Central and Eastern Europe – from neither the German employers' associations nor industrial associations. In the opinion of the German employers' associations, one reason for this is the weakness of the corresponding associations in the CEEC, which hardly makes such activities possible (representative of the Federation of the German Food and Drink Industry (BVE)). On a general level, the BVE – as well as the other associations – has assisted with the build-up of corresponding leading associations in the CEEC within the scope of the EU Business Partnership project. The leading associations have been members of the European trade association, Confederation of the Food and Drink Industries of the EU (CIAA), since May 2004.

The employers' association '*Nahrung* und *Genuss*' ['Food and Consumption'] has similar marginal relations with the partners in the CEEC; however, more efforts have also been undertaken from the German side since 2003. In 2004, connections only existed with the Czech Republic and Estonia. On the German side, complaints are heard that there are no fixed structures in the CEEC and one frequently encounters different organizations which work side by side.

The German employers' association in the metal sector (*Gesamtmetall*) describes the collaboration as incipient. Additional difficulties crop up due to the fact that in the CEEC there is no separation between employers' and industrial associations (parties to collective bargaining) such as in Germany, and so consequently the discussions between East and West are difficult due to the different scale of responsibilities. Gesamtmetall has good relations with the metal employers in Hungary and in Estonia, whereas there are practically no relations whatsoever with the associations in Poland, Czech Republic and Slovakia (in the three countries which particularly interest us). Even existing relations have repeatedly petered out since the CEE associations restructured themselves. In addition, the CEE associations are fully utilized through daily political requirements, so that they have not even arrived at their other tasks (such as strategy, arrangement and corresponding contacts with EU-15 associations). Later we will also hear similar assessments regarding the *trade union* collaboration between East and West.

On the chamber level, German chambers of industry and commerce implement joint benchmarking seminars with their CEE partners to increase the efficiency of the employment of FDI on a general level ('institution-building'). But even in this connection there are not *continuous* bilateral contacts, but merely sporadic and ad hoc – as the representative of the Polish Chamber of Industry and Commerce reported from his experiences with the German Chamber of Foreign Commerce in Poland.

Insofar as the collaboration between investing companies and their associations as a basic prerequisite of the concomitant investment action of associations in the East and West is concerned, a distinction has to be made between large companies on the one hand and SMEs on the other hand: whereas large companies do not reach out to their associations because usually they have their own resources, the SMEs are frequently dependent on the support from their (industrial/employers') associations as well as the chambers of industry and commerce. However, there is a very vague perception as to which of these institutions can and should help whom, because there is a rivalry between industrial associations on the one hand and employers' associations on the other hand, and thus the perception is insufficient: this rivalry between the respective headquarters and regional institutions of these associations continues transversely. Such a constellation in Germany also impedes contact on the supra-company level with the corresponding institutions of the CEE host countries of the FDI.

On top of this is the fact that as a rule, the employers'/industrial associations on the part of the host country of the FDI are very weak: because in the transformation phase the build-up and expansion of employers' associations were neglected in favour of building up chambers of industry and commerce. For instance, an employers' association in Hungary was only able to be established through the initiative of the Hungarian Economic Chamber in August 2003 – after a three year project in the Hungarian food processing industry (financed by the EU). This means that – even if employers'/industrial associations from the EU-15 also wanted to do this and were able to do so in terms of capacity – no adequate contacts were available in the CEEC.

Trade Unions in Germany

But what do the intergovernmental contacts look like on the part of the trade unions?[1]

Here, similar to the employers' organizations, there has to be a separation between a general political level (institution-building) and the ad hoc cooperation between the associations in the East and West for accompaniment of investment processes.

Regarding general, continuously organized transfer levels ('institution-building')
On this – political-diplomatic – level there are relatively good relations and close communications via the international and other departments (this applies to IG Metall as well as to *IG Bergbau-Chemie-Energie* (Industrial Trade Union for the Mining, Chemical and Energy Industries, (IG BCE)) and the '*Nahrung-Genuss-Gaststaetten*' (Food, Consumption and Restaurants Trade Union, (NGG)) as well as via regional associations.

For instance, the IG Metall (Bavaria) district serves the entire CEE region (Czech Republic, Slovakia, Hungary, Romania, Bulgaria and the now independent countries of the former Yugoslavia); initial contacts were made as early as 1992. The trade union coordination of collective bargaining in the metal sector in Germany, Austria, Czech Republic, Slovakia, Hungary and Slovenia represented a positive approach with the Memorandum on Interregional Collective Bargaining Policy from 25 March 1999 in Vienna (IG Metall Bavaria, 1999). From today's point of view (2006), this type of cooperation on the level of the full-time apparatus is without reservation good; the work is authentic and there is a continuity of individuals. In contrast, the site/company levels are increasingly more difficult for trade union access. An increasingly divergent development conditioned through FDI is also determinable within the national economies of the CEEC; this also has considerable – negative – consequences for (trade union) representatives in the companies of the new EU member states.

The IG Metall district Berlin/Brandenburg – which had only very sporadic contacts with Polish trade unions on the site/company level until 1995/96, and which is now responsible for the cooperation with Poland – has since the start of Poland's negotiations for accession to the EU employed a full-time union officer with the task of maintaining contacts with Polish trade union officials on the industrial-sector

---

1   A general view of the transnational cooperation among labour unions is given by Gordon (2000)

level. As a result, Polish trade union officials have been systematically trained at the IG Metall training facility in Berlin.

The *IG BCE* does not have any regular contacts with the Czech chemical trade unions, but things are different between the IG BCE and the Czech energy trade union. There are very good contacts between the IG BCE and the Slovakian chemical trade union, whose chairman is simultaneously vice-president in the International Chemical Workers Trade Union.

In the realm of the food processing industry, the NGG trade union attempted to establish contacts above all with the transformed former communist trade unions; the contact with the new (reform) trade unions founded after 1991 were difficult. But also here the relationships are different from country to country. And so, among other things, the 'Train the Trainer' programme failed due to the fact that the participating Czech trade unions had to relinquish a large portion of the former trade union assets and did not have to take care of new companies. Certain agreements had not been complied with by the Polish trade union (OPZZ), and the contacts have broken off at present. The Solidarity industrial-sector trade union is too weak to maintain contacts. For a long time there were hardly any contacts with Slovakia. But an improvement of continuous transfers has emerged since a seminar from the NGG trade union and the Slovakian industrial-sector trade union on 'Strategy of Multinational Concerns' was held in 2000.

Regarding the intermittent (ad hoc) *level of the accompaniment of single corporate investments*
On this level there are only sporadic efforts on the part of trade unions in the countries of the parent companies (here: Germany, France, Switzerland) to accompany cross-border investment processes. This has several reasons: one is certainly to be found in the labour-division system of representations of interest between site/company and the supra-company levels. First of all, the works councils in Germany possess the essential information, which – again, for many reasons – is not completely forwarded to the respective trade unions on the supra-company level.

Moreover, according to a European federation representative's assessment, the supra-company's trade unions from the FDI countries of origin in the EU-15 hardly had power to convince the parent company's own representatives of the necessity of a cooperative collaboration between all levels of representations of interest.

Some practical examples of *ad hoc* cooperation:

The IG Metall district Berlin/Brandenburg held a corporate-related international seminar of the Gillette concern with representatives from Poland, the Czech Republic and Germany. This is surely a good approach to accompany cross-border investment processes on the trade union side.

Another practical example has been able to illustrate how information and communications channels could be organized with the inclusion of both levels of representation of interests (trade unions and works councils). During a conflict in a Czech site of the Robert Bosch GmbH, the representatives turned to their trade union headquarters in Prague, which for their part informed the IG Metall board chairman in Frankfurt/M. about this. He in turn forwarded this matter to the IG Metall's responsible local administrative office, which on their part informed the

Bosch concern works council. The Bosch concern works council notified the Bosch concern management about this conflict (up to this point the latter had learned nothing about this), and subsequently the concern chairman and concern works council of the Stuttgart-based Bosch headquarters travelled together to the Czech Republic to solve the conflict there. This created a long information chain, which principally indicated a proper and important method for the internal corporate exchange, but nevertheless is very susceptible to misunderstandings and erroneous information at the same time.

Difficulties regarding the transfer/accompaniment of investments
A major obstacle of these transfer services on the part of the West European/German trade unions lies in the (for them) confusing number and structure of CEE partner organizations. This partially makes it very difficult to find the right partner for the problem to be solved. For instance, in Poland the 'deliberate confusion and the constant balancing out between Solidarity and OPZZ' (representative of the IG Metall executive board) obstructed the build-up of lasting contacts with IG Metall on the executive board level, and the IG Metall's danger of wearing itself to a frazzle in the internal Polish quarrel is considerable. As far as that is concerned, since 2000 there have been very few inquiries on this *level* from Poland for German assistance. The West European reference trade union is now the Swedish metal worker's trade union, although most of the investments come from Germany.

For instance, with regard to the steel industry as a special partial division of the metal industry, a project with the Polish steel industry (so-called 'coupling for exchange of views on the corporate level') failed. 'It degenerated into nothing but tourism', says the IG Metall secretary responsible for this sector. There will also be no new attempts of this kind as long as the privatization of the Polish steel industry is not fully completed.[2] Up to now there have not been any projects such as this for the Czech Republic and Slovakia. Contacts on the supra-company level between trade unions in the East and West can only be established in this sector within the framework of the EMF (steel committee) and on the level of European Works Councils.

Furthermore, the experiences of German trade unions in their continuous transfer of services are characterized by the fact that the CEE trade unions are to a great extent organized in a company/site-centred manner (not only in Poland, but also in the Czech Republic and Slovakia). And so, for instance, the regional level – in its essential function of practical, bur nevertheless supra-companies' orientated concern with problems of FDI – is almost entirely lacking.

On the CEE side there is also the obstacle of cooperation – that in some countries the respective national government attempts to prevent an open dialogue. For instance, the Polish trade union Solidarity was only able to organize a meeting –

---

2   In the spring of 2004 large portions of the Polish steel industry were sold to the Indian-British consortium LMN/ISPAT. In 2005, LMN/ISPAT merged with the US concern 'International Steel' and was renamed after its owner as 'Mittal Steel'. In 2006, Mittal Steel with a turnover in 2005 of 28.1 billion euro is succeeding to buy Arcelor with a turnover in 2005 of 39.7 billion euro.

against the greatest resistance from the Polish Ministry of the Treasury – between them and the new owners of a portion of the Polish steel industry (LNM/ISPAT – now Mittal Steel) together with the western trade unions, *before* the signing of the purchase agreement.

Political foundations with close relations to trade unions
So it is frequently left up to political foundations with close relations to trade unions to organize at least the initial enthusiasm for collaborations between trade unions in the East and West. For instance, in 1996 the Friedrich Ebert Foundation – as a political foundation of the Social Democratic Party of Germany – invited (together with the German Trade Union Confederation (DGB)) participants to Budapest for an initial conference with all democratic and reformed trade union federations of the (at that time) potential 10 CEE member countries (including Romania and Bulgaria). 26 confederations, which ultimately came, represented a very broad spectrum of organizational structures and self-images (Friedrich Ebert Foundation Warsaw, 2003, p. 2).[3]

And in September 2003 the working group of the works councils and trade unions of the Danube region's mineral oil industry sat in conference for the third time at Semmering in Austria. This conference originally emerged as an initiative of the Friedrich Ebert Foundation, the European Mine, Chemical and Energy Workers' Federation (EMCEF) and the trade union of the Hungarian mineral oil concern MOL with participating trade unions from 11 CEEC, including Russia. Representatives from Bulgarian, Romanian, Serbian, Croatian and Austrian companies/sites – in particular Lukoil and OMV – attended thereafter. Trade union representatives of the Polish mineral oil concern PKN Orlen participated in this third conference for the first time in 2003 at the invitation of the Friedrich Ebert Foundation (Friedrich Ebert Foundation Budapest, 6/2003).

The seventh Volkswagen/Friedrich Ebert Foundation seminar for the representatives on the site/company levels of all Central and Southeast European sites of the VW concern was held at the Hungarian Audi site in Gyoer. After intensive groundwork by the then FES regional coordinator, the consolidation process was able to be concluded with the admission of representatives from the Bosnian VW works in Sarajevo. In terms of content, the network deals among other things with the comparative analysis of collective agreements, social security systems, problems relating to occupational health and safety, codetermination and the work of the EWC at VW (Friedrich Ebert Foundation Budapest, 6/2003).

In November 2003, the working group of the Central and Southeast European Siemens sites' representatives was established in Vienna. The meeting was organized by the Confederation of Austrian Trade Unions (OEGB) and the Friedrich Ebert Foundation with the involvement of IG Metall. The exchange of views among the works councils and trade unions also led to the realization that the management in many south-east European business enterprises does not always operate in a manner friendly way to trade unions. Due to the lacking legal framework conditions, the

---

3   There was and is a vast number of corresponding seminars, of which the confederations introduced here are merely a part and mentioned by way of example.

consensus-orientated social dialogue in the Siemens concern or in their respective CEE subsidiaries in many places does not always come about (Friedrich Ebert Foundation Budapest, 6/2003).

The Social Partners on the European Level

On the European *level*, the 'Eurofederations' (European industrial-sector trade unions) as well as UNICE as the European employers' association (there are no branch associations in this connection) have a fundamentally different function than the associations of social partners on the national level.

Of course, on the trade union as well as the employers' side (most) relevant CEE associations are members in the European associations, but nevertheless Eurofederations as well as UNICE emerge at any rate as 'indirect intermediaries'.

Insofar as *common* activities among trade unions and employers' associations on the European level are concerned, the cooperation of 'Eurochambers' with the European trade union in the Office for the Exchange of Information and Technical Assistance (TAIEX)[4] actually constitutes the exception. For instance, UNICE very rarely cooperates with the European Trade Union Confederation (ETUC) with regard to East/West European matters.

Regarding the European employers'/industrial associations
UNICE (Union of Industrial and Employers' Confederations of Europe) with its 34 member associations, which comprise 16 million business enterprises, has repeatedly emphasized the important role of social partners with regard to the build-up of market economy structures and democracy in the CEEC (UNICE, 2000). Of course, UNICE also emphasizes in its policy the importance of bilateral contacts between employers' associations in the East and West, but also additionally (even if hesitantly) relies on the EU's PHARE (Poland and HungaryAssistance for the Reconstruction of Economy) twinning projects for promotion of social dialogue in the CEEC. UNICE itself has been very involved in various sectors (Vatta, 2003, p. 8), namely:

- Through the involvement in the 'Business Support Programme' – which takes place within the framework of the EU's PHARE programme and has the strengthening of employers' organizations (in addition to UNICE, European Association of Small and Medium-sized Craft Enterprises (UEAPME)and Eurochambers also participate), including the chamber entities in the CEEC as an objective. Since 1998 (up to and including 2002) a total of 37 million euro have been appropriated for 17 subprojects from the EU Commission (Vatta, 2003, p. 7);
- Through the 'Industrial Forum on Enlargement' that is coordinated through 'Mouvements des entreprises de France' (MEDEF) and the GD Employment and Social Affairs of the EU Commission. This is an instrument for the exchange of information and definition of solutions of Acquis-relevant

---

4   Office for information exchange and technical assistance.

problems. This forum develops recommendations for the governments and the commission;
- Through the Conference of Social Partners regarding matters of EU enlargement and the annual 'round table talks' of the employers' organizations of the EU-15 and the new EU members (since 1999).

Moreover, UNICE has – in accordance with the annual progress reports of the EU Commission regarding matters of enlargement, which have been drawn up since 1998 – prepared its own reports for every candidate country in 2001 and 2002 (UNICE, 2001; UNICE, 2002). The reports from members of a task force group on EU enlargement (UFTE = UNICE Task Force on Enlargement) were the empirical basis for these reports. This task force pointed out abuses in the candidate countries (for example corruption, overpowering bureaucracy, ignoring national minorities) and provided recommendations (for active labour market policy, qualifications measures, privatization, and so on).

All of these activities are not able to – and do not intend to be – a replacement for investment accompanying measures; UNICE leaves these measures more to the actors on the micro level – that is the enterprises.

But in addition to UNICE there are still other industrial associations on the European level, such as the European Association of Small and Medium-sized Craft Enterprises (USEPME), the very influential European Roundtable of Industrialists (ERT), the European Organisation of National Chambers of Industry and Commerce ('Eurochambers') – and last but not least, the Industrial Forum on Enlargement (IFE): however, they all leave an (*ad hoc*) accompaniment of investment processes up to the pertinent enterprises, although particularly the SMEs require urgent assistance.

In summary, the following can be said about the activities of the employers'/ industrial associations as well as the chambers of industry and commerce on the European level:

- Despite the rapid build-up of chambers of industry and commerce in the CEEC (in comparison with the employers' organizations), and thus also a reliable partner, the Eurochambers and their EU-15 member organizations have only partially managed – and on a more general basis – to accompany European investment processes in a promotional capacity (insofar as outline conditions are concerned).
- The EU-15 employers' organizations were very hesitant before 1 May 2004 to open up membership to CEE members. As a result, the EU-15 employers' associations for the most part retained their exclusivity with regard to definition and organization of training programmes for the CEEC, which was rather obstructive to the promotion of mutual understanding.
- On the other hand, the current situation of the employers' organizations in the CEEC (perhaps with the exception of chambers of industry and commerce) also gives rise to doubt in an effective and equal share in such training measures, and perhaps also later in investment accompanying measures.
- The quite remarkable degree of lacking knowledge and the not yet so far advanced preparations of the domestic CEE firms with regard to the

requirements, but also the opportunities with respect to the EU enlargement, clearly illustrate the very large gulf between the local/domestic CEE companies on the one hand and the FDI affiliates of western companies in the new EU member states on the other hand. Here the western FDI have a structural lead which they obviously expand repeatedly. This also has repercussions on the structure of the national economies in the CEEC – since innovative, export-orientated activities are then increasingly concentrated on the FDI and the (still very large) remainder of the domestic firms start to fall back on the internal markets and less innovative industrial sectors.

Regarding the European trade unions/Eurofederations
On the EU-15 level, the European federations and their national members have been working for several years on consistent strategies and the necessary build-up of action competencies, such as the development of formulas for a gradual standardization of collective bargaining policy demands and international cooperative agreements with regard to the representation of trade union members in a different EU-15 country.
For instance, the European Mine, Chemical and Energy Workers Federation (EMCEF) has developed future discussion emphases for three industrial sectors in which the CEE member trade unions are also expressly invited:

- in the energy sector this is 'social dialogue',
- the main emphasis in the plastics sector is on the 'European Professional Certificate',
- in the chemicals sector: the 'promotion of workplace attractiveness' (because the attractiveness of this sector is very marginal for the workforce).

On account of this complexity, the EMCEF with its 127 member organizations and 2.6 million members has radically changed (and had to change) its information policy since 2000: not every member will be informed about everything, but through the installation of a website with consistently up-to-date information and various sectoral access authorizations on their part the member organizations will be obligated to collect the information. The continuous transfer service regarding the structure of institutions could be additionally strengthened through the establishment of a branch office in Budapest and through the introduction of sponsorships (for instance, the Spanish and Italian member trade unions take care of those trade unions from the VISEGRAD countries in this manner). Nevertheless, quite a few deficiencies remain, particularly in the institutional realm. For instance, in June 2003 out of a total of 20 presiding committee members only two came from the CEEC. In the case of FDI, EMCEF establishes the contacts if the investments are foreseeable. But if they do not accompany these contacts on account of their special role and for reasons of capacity, this remains left up to the national unions.

The European Federation of Food, Agriculture, Tourism Trade Unions (EFFAT) (covers three sectors: agriculture, food processing and tourism) perceives their main task as establishing the connections between the representatives in a company in the various EU-25 countries. According to the EFFAT officer, however, there is a frequent lack of initiative on the part of the representatives in the CEE subsidiaries as well as in the parent enterprises from the EU-15.

That's why EFFAT's main emphases are:

- the support of representatives in transnational companies, especially in European Works Councils,
- the development of social dialogue,
- representation vis-à-vis the European institutions,
- assistance within the framework of EU enlargement.

For instance, EFFAT organizes regular meetings for accompaniment of the enlargement process and develops annual work programmes for the CEE member trade unions.

Just like the EMCEF, the EFFAT also maintains an office in Budapest with the specific task of supporting the CEE members under the special conditions of the EU enlargement.

The three main emphases of the *EMF* (which encompasses the European metal and electrical industry) are the:

- European collective bargaining policy,
- European industrial policy (for instance, leadership concepts were developed together with the employers for the aerospace industry as well as for shipbuilding),
- corporate policy (all instruments of involvement on the corporate level will be used in this connection).

The working methods were redefined by the EMF Executive Committee on 12 June 2003 in Prague (EMF, 2003). There is the central instrument of the three political committees (which respectively deal with the three main emphases), then the sectoral committees and furthermore the horizontal committees. In addition to the horizontal committees 'Equalisation Policy' and 'Training and Extended Vocational Training', there is also the committee on 'EU Enlargement' (which is of particular interest to us), which handles matters of EU enlargement transversely to the political and sectoral committees.

Even before 1 May 2004 the EMF also once again pressed very strongly for equality of the members from CEEC at the EMF congress at Prague in June 2003. But despite these trust-promoting measures, the EMF also did not manage to quash the general deficit of trust between EU-15 trade unions and those in the new EU member states in certain fields. In the event of relocations from West to East many EU-15 trade unions refuse the passing-on of information to the trade unions in the CEE sites. Furthermore, – often against the will of their own trade union – quite a few EWC from western parent companies baulked at a (up until 30 April 2004 still voluntarily granted) membership of representatives from the CEE sites, which in turn led to a loss of trust between the trade unions in West and East on the supra-company level.

By this it once again becomes clear that only a coordinated procedure between representatives on the site/company level and industrial trade unions (supra-company level) was/is a necessary prerequisite, not only for a meaningful transfer from West to East for build-up of (trade union) institutions in Central and Eastern Europe in this historically unique situation, but also for the *ad hoc* accompaniment of investment processes.

Investment Accompanying Measures from the Viewpoint of Social Partners in the Three CEE Countries

Czech Republic

There are no specific efforts to accompany the investment between the trade unions in the Czech Republic and Germany. The situation on the part of the employers' associations is similar – with the exception of Japanese investments. In the opinion of the chemical industry employers' association in the Czech Republic, this 'reticence' is also explained by the fact that such concomitant measures are not decisive for the investments. The foreign companies which want to invest in the Czech Republic already establish their own contacts beforehand; moreover, many companies wiling to invest have set up offices in the Czech Republic as the basis for their future investments.

Slovakia

In the metal industry, the trade union OZ KOVO speaks of very good contacts with IG Metall, which for their part requests information from the works councils of Germany companies willing to invest, and then provides this information to the Slovakian trade union. On the employers' side, organizations in this industry have contacts with the metal employers' association in Bavaria.

However, the metal industry is also the exception; because neither in the chemicals sector nor in the energy branch nor in the food processing industry do trade unions and employers' associations speak of such contacts. For instance, the trade union OZ Chémica speaks of the fact that only they alone have expressed the desire for such contacts.

The employers' associations in the chemical, energy and food processing industry leave corresponding contacts up to the single companies.

Poland

In Poland, only the trade unions – and not the employers' associations – have contacts with the future investor. This is concurrently corroborated by both social partners, whereby such contacts are also not concerted on the part of the employers' associations.

Insofar as the contact between the trade unions in Poland and Germany regarding FDI is concerned, the metal trade unions from Solidarity and OPZZ agree that these concomitant investment contacts may well be necessary, however, they have not come about to date.

The situation appears somewhat differently with regard to *Solidarity Chemicals* and *Solidarity Food processing industry*: according to information provided by the respective secretariats, corresponding initiatives have already come about here – but more sporadically, however.

Conclusion regarding the role of CEE trade unions in the active accompaniment of investment processes

The CEE trade unions are on the brink of a hardly solvable dilemma: because on the one hand they have long since shared all of the objectives as they are developed by European Trade Union Confederation (ETUC) and the single Eurofederations and practiced for the EU-15. But on the other hand, the rapidity and the complexity of the transformation processes – and at the same time the European integration processes – force many trade unions from the CEEC into an overemphasis of their protective function, and thereby to a neglect of their organizational function (besides, they do not have this professional full-time apparatus like the German trade unions do). Based on mere principle, many trade unions are thus unable to cope at the moment; they are not even able to use the arrangement of the European level to reach a systematic cooperation with the trade unions from the countries of origin of investment (Friedrich Ebert Foundation Warsaw, 2003, pp. 11–12). For instance, only the Czech metal workers' trade union is represented in the EMF task force; the Polish and Slovakian trade unions are not participating due to financial reasons (status: Spring, 2003); and at the same time one has to take into account that *only* the Polish Solidarity and *not* the OPZZ is a member in the EMF.

However, there are also exceptions here: for instance, the metal trade unions of the VISEGRAD countries (Poland, Czech Republic, Slovakia and Hungary) try to establish common positions among one another and then to also make them socially acceptable throughout Europe via the EMF.

What Could a Common Arrangement for Accompaniment of European Investment Processes Look like in the Future?

The latter-mentioned example could provide hope for the application of the 'zipper principle': First of all, every actor (trade union, employers' organization) develops their own strategy and an action plan that subsequently builds on a sustainable collaboration. At the same time, it did not have to be completely open (in being sector and country-specific) as to whether such a collaboration initially extends to only *two* countries (East and West) or also encompasses several or even all countries, and whether the initiative and initial accompaniment then emanates from the respective *national* organizations or from the *European* organizations. If these two sides of the 'zipper' are conceived, then a common policy of trade unions *and* employers' organizations can evolve – that is the jacket (symbolically spoken) would thus zip itself up.

Industrial Relations and Management – Management Concepts, Management Behaviour and Autonomy of Subsidiary Enterprises in Central and Eastern Europe

Among other things, foreign companies provide not only capital, technology, organization and market strategies to the host country of their direct investments, but also the underlying notions of management style, management concepts, human resource policy, and so on. To what extent these notions are realizable in practice – or whether other notions prevail – is one of the cognitive objectives of the project.

With respect to foreign direct investments (FDI), we asked to what extent the implementation of a different management concept occurs, how considerable is the local management's autonomy vis-à-vis the corporate group management, and about the recruitment of in-patriates for the local management.

The Notions of Managers from the Western Parent Enterprises in the Initial Development Phase of the FDI Subsidiaries

First of all, foreign managers – so-called 'ex-patriates' – bring a different kind of thinking and action into the CEEC. Of course, the question refers to what extent this has also prevailed.

In essence, there was no management concept in the CEEC at the beginning of the transformation period (regarding the concept of management in planned economy business enterprises: Eberwein and Tholen, 1994, p. 42 as well as Eberwein and Tholen, 1997, p. 46). As far as that is concerned, the parent companies attempted to completely change the management side in their CEE sites (as a European Trade Union Institute (ETUI) representative noted), which also led to resistance in the initial period (according to a representative of the Polish Solidarity).

In addition, there was also a somewhat unfortunate dispatching policy of the western (German) parent enterprise: there is a rapid rotation process for managers in major German enterprises. The managers are transferred after a maximum of four years in Germany (and a bit longer in foreign countries). At any rate, as a German manager (indeed, usually as a plant manager in the beginning) this is too brief to build up a bond of trust with regard to the workforce and the representatives in the CEE subsidiaries.[5]

On top of that is the fact that even in Central and Eastern Europe the major German enterprises have initiated an intensified process of detachment in recent years. These detached corporate elements and the transformation into legally unaffiliated firms are now managed above all by younger managers from the parent enterprise, who were particularly active in the USA beforehand and so the German cooperation-orientated management culture is no longer necessarily the model in the CEE subsidiaries.

Moreover, in the past it was not always the best managers who were sent by the German parent enterprises to their CEE subsidiaries for the build-up and expansion of industrial relations. Because the technology-orientated philosophy of German enterprises entails that the best managers were dispatched to the immediate core areas (technology, organization and at any rate finances). As a result, those whom the executive board considered as expendable were represented in the personnel realm of the CEE subsidiaries – with the exception of Greenfield investments.

In view of these difficulties and the impediments with regard to optimal staffing of management positions in the CEE subsidiaries, it is quite astounding that a truly successful business management was usually able to emerge.

---

5   But from the viewpoint of the expatriates, four or even six years abroad is a very long time, and under circumstances can certainly block a successful 're-acclimatisation' in their home country.

*The Second Development Phase of the FDI Subsidiaries – the Notions and
Methods of the CEE manager*

In general, there is a 'historic' succession of staffing with regard to the management
positions in the development of the FDI subsidiaries, which also had an influence on
the autonomy of the FDI business enterprises vis-à-vis the parent enterprise and the
application of management styles.

A very close connection of the subsidiaries to the parent enterprises – in terms of
personnel as well as leeway – followed in the start phase of the FDI. The managing
director came from the parent enterprise; the staff was predominantly comprised of
locals.

After the parent enterprises brought along their own management style in the
first phase at the beginning of the 1990s and their CEE subsidiaries hardly had any
autonomy, this changed in procedural terms – intertwined with the altered personnel
composition of the management crew for the subsidiaries.

As a result, the leeway of the local plant was enlarged, but with differentiations.
Locals ('in-patriates') took over as managing directors (however, quite often a
manager from the parent enterprise remained as deputy plant manager, but he was
not always on the scene in the subsidiary): locals were/are often chosen as personnel
managers because they know best about the local conditions like national labour
law, language, mentality, and so on. Because the personal sector in a business
enterprise is deeply-rooted – like no other sector – in the local context (Hummel et
al., 2005). Under this aspect, this management position constitutes the bridge to the
social partners in the companies/sites in general and especially to the trade union
representatives. Both actors (local management and representatives) are staffed with
local personnel and have paramount importance as intermediaries.

In this second phase, the technical boards of directors were also comprised of
locals, whereas the financial boards of directors quite often remained in the hands
of managers coming from the parent enterprises. These local specialists are to a
great extent trained by the parent enterprises in the fields of technology and labour
organization to accompany the modernization process from Brownfield investments.

On the whole, it can be maintained that the personnel composition of the
management personnel for the FDI subsidiaries gradually changed, and thus also the
autonomy vis-à-vis the parent companies. Of course, the dominance of the structures
in the parent companies is also emphasized here, at least in the initial period of the
investments. This dominance was also engendered by the fact that in the Brownfield
investments there was no independent 'management culture' in the western sense,[6]
and the Greenfield investments were rearranged in all sectors.

Parallel to this, the western managers in the CEE workforces who embodied
the western-capitalist management styles were an absolutely positive alternative.
Because local managers in the CEE subsidiaries partially prove themselves to

---

6   The term 'western' corporate culture and management style is to be differentiated.
Differences between the western countries of origin of the companies as well as the managers
give rise to a quite differentiated image (see the summary of this chapter for a more precise
rendering).

be very radical in the application of human resource policy: due to the absolute dearth of suitable management personnel in the CEE countries in the beginning of the transformation period, many of the old cadres were retrained and partially even 'involuntarily' recruited for staff departments in the FDI plants. Under the old regimes, these cadres were often promoted in their positions for political reasons and were not professional suitable for this purpose.[7]

In the beginning, this caused quite a few irritations, and not just because these now retrained cadres had retained their traditional qualifications of 'deception and muddling about' (that is all of the things that were usual in communism, when it was a matter of course to grab as much personal leeway as possible), as many EU-15 enterprises had feared in the beginning. Instead, they now believed – popularly spoken – as 'converts' that they must profile themselves through 'rigid appearance as manager capitalists'.

This management style was particularly evident in the small and medium-sized subsidiary enterprises from (also larger) western parent enterprises. Incidentally, this strong authoritarian-paternalistically characterized management style is frequently found in SMEs in West Europe. It is not very open vis-à-vis cooperation-orientated industrial relations.

But the authoritarian-paternalistic management style not only refers to the old cadres, but also partially to the new, young managers from the CEEC, who – in exaggerated demarcation from the planned economy times – seek their role models in the 'radical nature' of certain market concepts (Domanski, 2001, p. 47 and Deiss, 2003, p. 43).

This means that as a result of the increasing recruitment of local managers, a solution and cooperation-orientated management style – which included the participation of the employees and thus also rendered a more successful management style – did not necessarily arrive on the scene in the FDI subsidiaries.

In a survey of 167 managers in seven CEEC, Edwards (2003) ascertained that in principle the managers in these countries are structurally overburdened (in comparison with EU-15 managers), since they:

1. have been continuously confronted with transformation problems, which are actually a unique historic event, and
2. had to solve quite normal capitalistic problems at the same time.

We would like to add that the local managers:

3. must come to terms with their own personal past and that of their home countries, since they – differently than the Western managers, and irrespective of their age and their professional positions up to 1989/90 – grew up in 'loser societies'.

But a hybridization process also occurs in the realm of corporate culture and the individual management value system (Doerrenbaecher et al., 2000), in which the

---

7   Srubar (2003) calls this "status inconsistencies".

elements of the management culture prevailing in the business enterprise are adapted to the conditions of the recipient country of FDI and vice versa – that is a process of reciprocal learning.[8]

Regarding the Autonomy of the FDI Subsidiaries Vis-À-Vis their Parent Enterprises

The profit expectations of the investing business enterprises are also among the immediate questions pertaining to the autonomy of the FDI subsidiaries. Is an immediate profit expected from the CEE subsidiaries? Or is the strategic development (market development, and so on) in the foreground, that is will losses be tolerated in the first years?

First of all, the answer to these questions depends on the *objective* of the FDI: First of all, losses are also planned-in with regard to the strategic objective of market development; on average, profits are expected after two years. Here, the local management has a certain degree of leeway vis-à-vis the parent enterprise. But there is also an exception in sites with comparably greater autonomy insofar as collective bargaining and settlements are concerned. The specifications of the parent enterprise still dominate here – since the often observed alliances of the local management with the representatives in the CEE subsidiaries also provide little help.

With regard to investments for (wage) cost reasons, the specifications of the investing company are much more rigid for the CEE subsidiaries, and not merely in temporal perspective. Here the autonomy of the local management is comparably less.

But a differentiation also has to be made here: the profit expectations from business enterprises are very often also *sector-specific* with regard to their CEE subsidiaries. In accordance with the almost identical statements from our interview partners, it can be said of the following industries (which are not completely listed here, but which cover the industries on which we attach special empirical importance) that:

- no immediate profit expectations exist: energy industry, pharmaceutical industry, steel industry, and metal processing with the focus on the car industry. Typical for these industries are the partially very high investment sums, which make an immediate 'return of investment' impossible right from the beginning.
- immediate profit expectations exist in the tyre industry, retail trade (supermarkets), information technologies (mere transfer and not development) and financial investments.

---

8   But these procedural changes of management concepts and also the recruitment policy of local managerial personnel in the CEE subsidiaries are not CEE-specific. Apart from the desire of many parent enterprises 'just not wanting to take over any old cadre without scrutiny', and thus also to preclude planned economy elements (including individuals) in their CEE subsidiaries right from the beginning, the representative of the European trade union confederation EMCEF can certainly be concurred with that 'there is no difference vis-à-vis the EU-15. If the result tallies, then the local management everywhere has a certain degree of leeway'.

Furthermore, the size of the *business enterprise* naturally also plays a role. As a rule of thumb, it can also apply here that large business enterprises do not entertain any exaggerated profit expectations on account of their strategic alignment and very high investment sums in the initial years.

On the other hand, small-scale enterprises in particular must generate immediate profits, namely because their equity position is much too short to be able to cover long-term losses. This compulsion is also strengthened through the behaviour of the banks to grant only 'safe' credits in anticipation of the credit guideline 'Basel 2' – to the disadvantage of the soliciting SMEs. Small enterprises are just not able to undertake a diversified calculation as is true with the major investors.

A Summary of Influence Factors on Management Actions and Concepts

However, the aforementioned statements must also be put into perspective with regard to influence factors, namely:

1. *With respect to the type of production* if the subsidiaries merely represent an 'extended workbench', the autonomy of the subsidiary is very marginal.

   On the other hand, if the FDI expand a specific product range, the autonomy is relatively large (example Siemens). In this case, the parent enterprise makes a fundamental strategic decision with regard to the FDI, and thus defines the basic conditions. Under this "umbrella" the subsidiaries then have a considerable degree of autonomy – but only if the overall corporate objective is achieved.

2. *With respect to the size of the investing business enterprise* the SMEs assert to a much greater extent their own management notions and corporate culture in their CEE subsidiaries.

   But also large-scale enterprises from the EU-15 (and first and foremost here from Germany) not only brought along their technology and organisation, but also attempted in the first phase – also in matters of industrial relations and corporate culture – to assert the notions of the parent enterprise. However, in a second phase they gradually adapted to the conditions of the host country and the respective region. The recognition of the significance of mentality issues for corporate policy was and is linked as a result.

   One can only concur with Galgóczi and Kluge (2003) in his argumentation (which is first of all only empirically restricted to Hungary), and expand this argument to the relationships in the new Central and East European EU member states – that the multinational concerns had a positive influence on the corporate culture in the respective host countries with their FDI in the CEEC. In particular, the human resource policy has a considerable influence on the corporate culture and thus also on the industrial relations of the CEE subsidiaries. According to Galgóczi in a concluding evaluation, the most significant function of such a creative human resource strategy is the evolution of the business enterprise into a 'learning organization' based on the principles of social dialogue and the respect of the interest of the other respective actor.

3. *With regard to the country of origin of the FDI* the perceptions of the representatives from the CEEC are interesting, since they have better possibilities of comparison with regard to the differentiations among western management styles.

This is how a representative of the Slovakian trade union KOZ presents a ranking of foreign management concepts with regard to their (practiced) interpretation of social dialogue in their respective CEE subsidiaries: Accordingly, the investors from the EU-15 solicit a dialogue with the trade unions, US-American companies entirely disregard any dialogue whatsoever, and firms from South Korea even implement their traditionally dismissive attitude vis-à-vis trade unions in their Slovakian subsidiaries. A representative of the Polish Chamber of Industry and Commerce adds that in the FDI from major US-American business enterprises in Poland 'the people are supposed to function like little cogs in the wheel, and all important decisions are made in the head offices'.

Galgóczi and Kluge (2003) adds that the uncompromising transfer of management cultures from the countries of origin would be typical for Asian FDI enterprises. US-Americans prefer effectiveness first and foremost, and the corresponding corporate culture transports this objective. The most important thing for them would be the 'corporate identity' and the loyalty of the employee vis-à-vis the company. In particular, German firms had an innovative interpretation of corporate culture,[9] which then procedurally becomes an adaptive behaviour, however. German parent enterprises do not normally force their model on their CEE subsidiaries; they rather prefer more flexible structures.

But there are also differentiations within the EU-15 management 'models'.

Direct investments from Romance (EU-15) countries – and especially France in this case – have much greater difficulties building up participatory structures for CEE trade unions within their subsidiaries than German and Scandinavian investors, because in last-named countries of origin there is already a distinct culture of codetermination.

4. *With regard to the corporate-specific strategy of the individual business enterprise* irrespective of the size of the business enterprise and other factors, the autonomy of the FDI subsidiaries vis-à-vis their parent enterprises also depends on the respective corporate culture and the strategic alignment of the investment, which can be very different from company to company.

Corporate culture is also influenced by the subjective-individual perception of the management role by the single managers. Managerial behaviour, career orientations, the shaping of HRM, and so on (see also Hodson, 2005; Martin, 2005). Following Parsons (1939); Luhmann (1964) and others, the internal company/subsidiary constellation is made up of a complex working together of different influences. Internal company mechanism of mediation take their force

---

9   Galgóczi differentiates between an *adaptive* behaviour pattern orientated towards the circumstances of the FDI host country and an *innovative* approach preferential to the corporate culture of the country of origin.

from the constellation of partial interests, competencies and real possibilities of influences; from the conflicts, alliances and competition arising from these and from the necessity to maintain and to legitimate one's authority.

The studies by Doerr and Kessel (1999) have provided good examples for this: A new product concept was developed by Volkswagen/Škoda on account of strong pressure on the part of the Czech partner; accordingly, this also comprised a different management concept. A new factory was built by Audi (a brand from the VW concern) in Gyoer/Hungary within the framework of the internal corporate group combine. This did not mean that the factory management board in Gyoer adopted the Audi concept on a one-to-one basis, but the management policy in Gyoer had to be oriented to a stronger extent on the 'European management style' (see Doerre 1997 for more details pertaining to this term). With its Hungarian FDI Audi pursued a globalization/Europeanization strategy which – other than with regard to VW/Škoda – integrates the single factories into one production combine.

On top of that is the fact that business enterprises – even in the same size class and within one industry – prefer different models of hierarchy and centralization. For instance, the head offices from General Electric (USA) and Philipps (the Netherlands) show a very powerful, centralist-authoritarian organized position within the respective enterprise as a whole, whereas Siemens pursues a more decentralized approach.

New Forms of Representatives in CEEC as a Challenge for German Investors and CEE Actors

German parent enterprises with their investments in Central and Eastern Europe encounter conditions such as laws, deep-rooted norms and political processes which (can) have a considerable influence on the arrangement of industrial relations in their subsidiaries. For instance, tripartism defines the allocation of roles between the state, employers' associations and trade unions not only on the central political level, but also in the realm of collective bargaining policy. Since the trade union representatives on the site/company level – if extant – in the CEEC also has the right to conduct collective bargainings, this tripartism also essentially affects the industrial relations on the site/company level.

The new laws (passed in 2002/03) in the Czech Republic and Slovakia regarding introduction of 'works councils' – that is representatives initially independent of trade union representatives in the companies/sites – can also open up new opportunities for arrangement of industrial relations.

The introduction of works councils planned by the government also reflects a new trend for Poland. In August 2004 the labour ministry presented a draft bill for 'information and consultation', which prescribed the establishment of works councils in companies with 20 or more employees.

As a result, Poland could have taken a similar path with regard to the establishment of an additional system of interest representation *alongside the trade union* representatives on the site/company levels, as the Czech Republic and Slovakia have already done – even if this is against the gradually reticent resistance of the trade unions. However, since June 2005 – and in particular after the parliamentary election in September of the same year und the new right wing (minority) government – the process of the introduction of a 'works council' in Poland seems to at least have slowed down.

These statutory initiatives in the three CEEC have been essentially advanced through the EU directive from March 2002.[10] As a result, the EU obligates the member countries to creation of statutory fundamentals for the establishment of information and communications bodies on the corporate/site level by 2007 (with transition deadlines for the new EU members). Briefly summarized, this directive confers representatives similar information and communications rights such as European Works Councils. This could create a considerable improvement for countries without prior corresponding legislation, and certainly means only a minimum standard for countries with well-developed rights of participation on company/site level (such as Germany).

In the following, we intend to examine the example of the new 'works councils' in the Czech Republic and Slovakia,[11] insofar as these institutions offer perspectives regarding further development of industrials on the site/company level and insofar as these institutions could also be of interest to German parent enterprises with their investments in these countries.

In many companies/sites in the CEEC trade union representatives are dwindling. Numerous SMEs in Greenfield investments do not have any trade union organization. This leads to the fact that trade unions and workforces are neither able to obtain reliable information about management plans, nor are they able to conduct collective bargaining. Some managers in the 'trade union-free' companies/sites also lack a legitimized workforce contact. The election of 'works councils' has been enabled through amendments to the labour laws in the Czech Republic and Slovakia to establish the prerequisites for information and consultation of the employees in companies/sites. In Poland the eroding monistic (trade union) representatives in the company/site, but because of the new law from April 2006 it is temporally limited (see above).

How they behave with regard to the new institutions and what the introduction of a dual system of representatives could boil down to is a crucial question for the future of the trade unions in these countries.

Evaluation of Literature

Challenge for the trade unions
The former monolithic trade union landscape in the CEEC during the communist period has been replaced in the meantime through a distinct pluralism. Most

---

10   Directive 2002/14/EC/ of the European Parliament and the Council from 11 March 2002 establishing a general framework for the informating and consulting employees in the European Community.

11   As in Poland the new law passed the parliament only on 7 April 2006 our empirical fieldwork could not consider this new development.

studies conclude that the situation is dramatic from the trade union standpoint. The emergence of a private economic sector has been accompanied hand in hand with a far-reaching erosion of trade union representatives (Weiss, 2002). In view of their loss of importance in the CEEC, the CEE trade unions must render proof of their future capability and innovative ability vis-à-vis the employees. 'This is only possible if they also show creative power in addition to their necessary protective function. This necessitates increased presence and an appearance that can be experienced by the individuals in the daily operational routine' (Kohl (2002, p. 414). An elastic system of the division of labour between trade unions and by the whole workforce elected representatives has developed in most EU-15 countries. For such a formalized participation of worker representatives in the workplace in addition to the trade unions on supra-company level it seems very likely 'that management is normally more willing to cooperation with elected representatives – particularly if the election of theses representatives is urged to cooperation by law – than with an organisation that as a collective agreement party always forcibly threatens with the ultimatum of labour dispute and also has to employ this measure' (Kohl 2002, p. 414).

Polish works councils in the 1980s
With regard to the trade unions in the three CEE countries Poland, Czech Republic and Slovakia, the resistance against the introduction of a dual system of representation on the site/company level is predominant. In Poland this has led to the fact that the actors (government, trade union and employers' association) very lately have agreed on a compromise – under the heavy pressure by the EU directive from 2002.

From a western viewpoint this is insofar unintelligible, since particularly in the 1980s (that is after the prohibition of Solidarity and the imposition of martial law in Poland) there was a close connection between the 'underground' Solidarity and the 'works councils' existing at that time in Poland. Of course, part of the Solidarity union considered these works councils as part of the communist regime, but on the other hand these works councils were elected by the workforce and the Solidarity representatives were quite often the winners of these elections. A similar situation also emerged in the beginning of the 1990s (that is after the defeat of communism, but before the beginning of the privatization of the national economy). An empirical study in the Warsaw region showed that there was a strategic alliance between works councils, the Solidarity leaders and the works directors – the OPZZ was excluded from this alliance (Kozek et al., 1995).

And so it is by no means correct that works councils in Poland were exclusive vicarious agents of the dictatorship. Despite these thoroughly mixed and – insofar as that is concerned – also positive experiences, Solidarity (or their respective leaders) considered these works councils as typical for the state-planned economy and as not useful for a privatized national economy (Weinstein, 2000).

Only slowly – under the pressure of the inevitable – did the Polish trade unions deal with the new 'works councils' and while doing so they favoured the ad hoc works council according to the Czech model. Under the umbrella of the new Polish Government (established in the autumn 2005, re-organized as a right wing coalition in June 2006) on 7 April 2006 a new law 'Information and Consultation of the employees' passed the two houses of the Polish Parliament. This law is more or less a copy of the respective Czech law.

Protests in Slovakia

In Slovakia the trade unions vehemently opposed an introduction of the dual system in the debate concerning amendments of labour law. Among other things, in 2002 the KOZ organized a three-day protest in front of the labour ministry. Despite the involvement of the ILO, no agreement on the role of works councils could be reached, and so the amendment of the law was passed without the consensus of the social partner (Tóth and Ghellab, 2003, p. 42).

The brief period since the creation of statutory fundamentals for the election of works councils in the Czech Republic and Slovakia does not enable any detailed overview concerning the number and functioning of this new form of representatives (Tholen et al., 2003). Neither the responsible labour ministry in Slovakia nor the Slovakian employers' association AZZZ were able to provide reliable data on the introduction of works councils. Interview partners from the ministry and the employers' association were not able to name any firm (with the exception of a few large companies) which had a works council.

As far as that is concerned, up to now the attempts in the new EU member states to create another (perhaps second, but perhaps also under exclusion of the trade unions the sole) channel for information and consultation of the worker by means of works councils remained merely limited to paper form, with the exception of Slovenia and Hungary.

Counter-example: Hungary and Slovenia

In the counter-example of Slovenia and Hungary it becomes clear that in post-socialist trade unions there are good reasons for the affirmation of the dual system. For instance, in contrast to the Soviet-model trade unions, the Slovenian trade unions did not have any institutional rights at the workplace. That is why they saw works councils not merely as a way to safeguard the representation of employees' interests, but also as a means to anchor the trade union organizations in the company/site (Tóth and Ghellab, 2003, p. 46). Perhaps the former 'self-management' in Yugoslavia provided important inspiration for affirmation of the dual system in Slovenia as a successor state to Yugoslavia.

The example of Hungary shows that works councils also function in companies/ sites in which there are (even different) trade unions.

In Hungary there were also initial conflicts with the trade unions during the establishment of works councils. But arrangements have been worked out in the meantime. In 1992, the works councils there were created by the government as a counter-model to the post-communist trade unions. Nevertheless, the trade unions have survived and accepted the works councils. Eighty per cent of all works councils in Hungary are nominated by the trade unions (status 2004).

A study by the Hungarian Consultant Service for Interest Protection (ÉTOSZ) comes to an essentially similar assessment. The evaluation of qualitative interviews with Hungarian trade union leaders, works council chairmen and employers comes to the conclusion that 'in the practice of the past 10 years, the willingness (of trade unions) to engage in stronger cooperation has increased considerably. However, to this day the trade unions have neither a theoretically sound assessment of this new institution nor a uniform strategy for the relations with the works councils'. Most trade union leaders describe the works councils as one of their most important channels for procurement of information.

> The majority of trade union leaders assess the existence of works councils as an advantage for the *joint* representation of employees. What is interesting is the reference that the works council can be a connective fixture between trade unions, where there are several competing trade union federations (Friedrich Ebert Foundation Budapest 3/2003, 12).

The study comes to the conclusion that the activity of works councils and trade unions has interlocked to such an extent over the course of a decade that one can hardly imagine how a works council can function without trade union backing.

However, the Hungarian works councils are met with lacking recognition amongst Hungarian managers, whereas the German managers (as managing directors of subsidiaries from German parent companies) work just as well together with the works councils in Hungary as in Germany (Boehlert, 2004, p. 66). But in the event of the existence of several works council bodies in *one* (large-scale) enterprise, there is a frequent lack of communication between these works council bodies (ibidem). All of this is indicative of the fact that all points out that the dual system has established itself in Hungary, but is nevertheless only at the beginning of development.

Trade unions have also successfully assimilated 'works councils' in EU-15 countries such as France, Spain and Italy. The question is posed regarding a long-term strategy for the new EU countries vis-à-vis the works councils. Otherwise there is the danger that with continuation of the trade union blockade the works councils unilaterally introduced by legislators (and partially also employers) weaken the trade unions instead of opening an additional path for information and consultation of the workforce.

It is not yet discernible whether a pragmatic adaptation process in Hungary as well as in the Czech Republic and Slovakia (and from April 2006 also in Poland) can over the course of a longer development overcome the distance and scepticism of the trade unions and lead to a 'unionisation of the works council entity' (Brigl and Matthiass, 1926) – especially not in which forms such a process could come to pass. Historical reasons as well as the special conditions of the transformation societies speak against a simple transfer of western models. For instance, in the EU directives regarding industrial relations, Weiss (2002) actually sees the encouragement for the CEE countries to enter together with the EU-15 states into a learning process on the search for a best practice and to push flexible procedures instead of recommending the introduction of a specific institutional model.

Results from the Expert Interviews

Our study corroborates the scepticism of the CEE trade union representatives against the introduction of a dual system. The worry about a detrimental rivalry of the works councils with the trade unions predominates. None of the polled trade unionists referred positively to the historic experiences in their own country or to the example in Hungary.

On the other hand, based on their own experiences, German trade union representatives appreciate the elasticity and the information opportunities of the dual system, but on condition that works councils are linked to trade unions. They advise the CEE trade unions to implement an integrative strategy vis-à-vis the works councils.

The representatives of the European trade union federations emphasize even more unequivocally that the future of the CEE trade unions necessitates a modified approach towards the 'works council' institution.

To be emphasized is the fact that the employers' representatives in Germany as well as on the European level explicitly spoke out in favour of the election of works councils in the CEE countries, but partially with the express reservation that these bodies should not be dominated by trade unions.

The results in detail follow.

Opinions from German and European trade unionists

German and European trade union representatives view the sceptical attitude of many CEE trade unions vis-à-vis the new regulations for establishment of dual structures with concern. In their opinion, the decline of trade union representatives in the companies/sites threatens to lead to a rapid loss of effective trade union power.

The representatives from German trade unions assess the experiences with the dual system as positive on the whole, but on the condition that works councils will be integrated in trade union strategies. On this condition they think that with a dual system of representatives the challenges of the further transformation and European integration will be more effectively overcome than with the previous monistic system. But they admit that at the moment the establishment of works councils are first of all an 'expression of the hybrid transition situation'. A developmental direction is hard to make out. Škoda in the Czech Republic is mentioned as a positive example. There the trade union representatives on the site/company levels are de facto 'works councils' and thus outstandingly linked to the trade unions.

Furthermore, the difficulties of trade union integration of possible 'works councils' in previously union-free Greenfield investments are recognized.

For German trade unions it is open, whether the existence of trade unions representatives on the company/site level – that is in Brownfield investments – will allow the formation of works councils, and thus a dual representatives system. Because the previous legal basics only provide for such a dual system of representation (trade union representatives in addition to a works council elected by the overall workforce) for Slovakia.

With the respondents from European trade union federations the future of CEE trade unions is even more clearly linked with a modified attitude towards the works councils than by trade union representatives from Germany. The rejection of works councils in the Czech Republic is naive and stems from the ignorance of the actual mode of operation of the German dual model (EMF representative). In the Czech Republic and in Slovakia the legislators have only legalized what exists in reality anyway. It should be the task of the trade unions to win over the works councils for themselves. The representative of another European trade union federation expressed himself in similar fashion.

The risk complained about by the CEE trade unions, that works councils might become management stooges, principally also exists with regard to *trade union* representatives on the site/company levels. Works councils are also linked to the company in Germany. This is a structural characteristic that on the other hand also constitutes the elasticity of the German system (according to the EFFAT officer).

Employers in favour of representatives on the site/company level
We only received a few comments from the employers' side in Germany and on the European level due to the lack of sufficient knowledge concerning the works councils in the Czech Republic and Slovakia. But these individuals speak clearly in favour of building up a dual system in the CEEC. At first glance the transfer of the dual system according to the German model appears to be a model certainly worth following. A virtually emphatic praise of the German works council system stems from the mouth of an interview partner from the Research Institute for German Business in Cologne (affiliated to the employers' associations), who in the long term predicts the installation of representatives on the site/company level in all CEE countries:

> The German works council system is an export sensation, the German works council a production factor. The corporate executive boards had to hurriedly send the most eligible people (from departmental manager to foreman) to the works council, because the works council represents a very significant hinge in the business enterprise. The establishment of a works council system also means that a genuine competitive advantage emerges for German companies, because now they can deal with similar structures in the CEEC, just like at home.

Although this evaluation may also be much exaggerated, it certainly indicates that the importance of the works councils as partners for social dialogue is highly regarded among German companies. This also entails the emphasis which now allows us to take a more precise look: because in the opinion of employers there is a risk with regard to the installation of works council structures in CEE plants if a preponderance of trade unions comes about. In the CEEC there would be a clear trend away from trade union dominance towards representatives on the site/company level. That is to say that the employers gladly favour a works council structure without trade union integration – consequently, a monistic system without trade unions.

Summary of Opinions from the CEE Countries

Opinions from the Czech Republic
Neither among trade unionists nor employers is there a considerable interest in the introduction of works councils. In accordance with the law, works councils do not have the right to collective bargaining. The Czech trade unions fear that in a different case they could evolve into 'yellow' rival trade unions, pocketed by the management. The employers see in the works councils a more adequate form of workforce representation than in the trade union representaatives, because works councils represent the entire workforce. Their installation could have a positive

influence on the representatives of employees, since membership in the trade unions is continuously declining. Overall, the employers look upon works councils a little bit more positively than the trade unions. On the other hand, the Czech trade unions openly criticize their colleagues in Germany in their efforts to help the dual system achieve a breakthrough in the Czech Republic:

> The trade union organisation in companies/sites has two roles, that of the trade union and that of the works council. This is a bone of contention with the German IG Metall, which simply does not want to understand this. According to the intention of the new labour law, the new works councils shall come under the thumb of the employer (representative of the Czech trade union KOVO).

The negative attitude of the trade unions is strengthened even more through the extremely marginal (known) number of new works councils: only two new works councils – both appointed by management – came to a conference of the Czech organization for collective bargainings (AKV) in August 2003. Even the Czech labour ministry knows nothing about the existence of works councils, although a representative of this ministry can imagine a positive influence of the new works councils, especially in case of union-free Greenfield investments.

Opinions from Slovakia

The introduction of works councils is contentious. They are often seen by trade unionists as 'yellow' trade unions, pocketed by the management. Particularly predominant is the worry that the installation of works councils helps the employers 'to keep the trade unions out of the companies' (representative of the Slovakian trade union umbrella organization KOZ). However, the Czech Trade Union of Metal Workers (KOVO) and members of the food trade unions meanwhile accept the fact that the 'works councils' as a German model of representatives on the corporate level will be introduced. On the other hand, the food trade unions understand the new works councils as an approximation of an EU model to safeguard information and consultation rights for all employees. The opinions of the employers' representatives are also different, depending on the branch: from the perception that works councils enable a better workforce representation than the trade unions to the opinion that works councils are unnecessary where the trade unions function well. The time span for a well-founded evaluation of the institution 'works council' is still too brief overall. A monitoring of the implementation processes would be useful (one of the conclusions from the PHARE project concerning the development of bipartite social dialogue in Slovakia).

Opinions from Poland

All interview partners accepted the necessity to implement the EU directive from March 2002 concerning information and consultation in the enterprise/site, but it did not appear to make sense to them that works councils are the suitable institution for this purpose. Trade unionists feared that works councils could become a tool in the hands of the employers. Nevertheless, due to the stronger political pressure, the willingness (at least with Solidarity) to accept the Czech 'model' of a works council increased since spring 2005 – consequently, a works council which could be replaced by trade union representatives. Insofar it was not a surprise when under the umbrella of rightist-populist government (supported by the Solidarnosc) a law was passed on 7 April 2006 to introduce 'works councils á la Czech'.

The employers understand the necessity to consult the workforce in a modern management scheme. As a result, even before the new law voluntary works councils had already been installed by some companies: 'They serve as a "safety valve" in large firms to ensure efficient management and binding regulations' (interview with the federation of industrial enterprises at Gorzow in Poland).

Nevertheless, the federations of industrial enterprises in Poland are also uncertain as to how such a process of establishing a dual system of representation could look like. The topic 'works councils' is open in the practice and thus offers leeway for future developments.

Conclusions

Whether an integration of the new forms of representatives on the site/company level comes about in trade union strategies may be of crucial importance for the development of industrial relations in the CEEC. As a result:

1.   the fragmentation of trade unions could also be countered on the site/company level; and
2.   the large number of companies/sites in which there are no representatives whatsoever at present could be reduced.

Our study has revealed that at the moment there is massive resistance against such a strategy on the part of the trade unions in the three CEE countries. This trade union resistance feeds itself on the fear of detrimental competition, but also on the undeniable intentions, particularly the CEE employers, to eliminate the trade unions. The degree of influence which the positive evaluations of trade unions (especially German) and the European trade union federations could evolve in the direction of a dual system is not discernible at the moment.

On the one hand, the rationale of the CEE trade unions against the introduction of a second level of representation (that a rival institution would be created) appears quite plausible from their point of view and current weakness – which hardly leaves any leeway for the integration of works councils in the trade union organizations.

But on the other hand, the company's production model on the whole (of which international relations are an essential element) is also internationally weakened with regard to its considerable importance for international competitive ability, since the comparative/competitive advantage of the internationally active German parent enterprise vis-à-vis their most important competitors could be lost as a result.

The European Works Council (EWC) could play an important role with in view of a possible pragmatic learning process. At any rate, in order for it to even be able to develop its role as an information and consultation organ, the interaction with representatives on company/site level is imperative; however, this phenomenon is only very seldom to be found in the CEE plants.

The Perspectives of European Works Councils Regarding Mediation between East and West

The establishment of European Works Councils plays a stalwart role in the development of a European system of Labour Relations that also incorporates the new EU countries. The Europeanization of industrial relations is understood here as the emergence of a complementary level (Hoffmann, 2001, p. 2) which does not replace the national systems. On the contrary, the functioning of national industrial relations represents an important prerequisite for the emergence of a system of European industrial relations. Experiences of European Works Councils show how initiatives regarding cross-border information from countries of origin and host countries of direct investments grasp at thin air if no representatives on the site/company level exist in the CEE sites. Therefore, it will have to be examined how the increasing orientation towards European standards and norms (Gradev, 2001) has an impact on the development of national industrial relations in Central and Eastern Europe, and which opportunities and difficulties are discernible on the single fields of Europeanization (collective bargaining policy, social dialogue on the site/company and supra-company level, role of European Works Councils, information and participation of representatives in European public companies (SEs)).[12]

But for this purpose it is necessary that we first of all take a look at the previous functioning of the EWC in the general framework of the Europeanization process of industrial relations in the EU-15.

As Kotthof/Kruse emphasize, the European situation of representatives is still open with regard to configuration. The dynamism of development depends – not only in the case of European Works Councils, but also on other fields – more on voluntary action forms than on the completion of predetermined institutional action parameters (Kotthoff, Kruse, 2002, pp. 4, 28). That is why the attitudes of the respective actors (employers' associations, national trade unions, European federations and institutions) acquire considerable importance for the form of European elements of industrial relations.

Up to now, the Europeanization of industrial relations with the European Works Council is the most advanced in comparison with collective bargaining policy and the European public company.[13]

---

12   An informative overview of the literature regarding the various instruments of the Europeanization of industrial relations (status 2002), such as:
1. Europeanization of the actors,
2. European social dialogue,
3. employment policy,
4. coordination of collective bargainings,
5. European Works Councils, and
6. European public company

is offered by Hoffmann, Hoffmann, Kirton-Darling, and Rampeltshammer'(2002).

13   There is still not much empirically substantiated material available on the European public company (EU Directive 2001/86/EC, which governs the participation of the employee in European public companies (SEs). Only a few companies like the European largest insurest company (Allianz AG, based in Munic), decided in 2006 to become an SE.

A considerable potential with regard to the development of European industrial relations, and thus also as a bridge to the EU-10 countries, is attributed from the employers' side as well as on the part of the trade unions. However, the opinions are also very strongly contingent on the respective national perspective of the observer: for instance, on account of his German perspective (determined by strong, also legally prescribed codetermination bodies), Wolfgang Streeck arrives at the opinion that the construction of the EWC resembles neither that of a works council nor is it European (Streeck, 1997). In contrast to this, British observers arrive at a very optimistic view of the potential effect of the EWC, since there are no such institutions of this kind whatsoever in the English system of industrial relations (Wills, 2000).

However, together with other authors – such as Lecher, Nagel and Platzer (1998); Hyman (2000), Marginson (2000), and Marginson and Meardi (2006) – we perceive the EWC's developmental process as considerably more open with regard to configuration.

The evaluation of the dynamism and the EWC's real chances in this bridge function continue to be strongly contingent on the assessment of its prior development since the coming into effect of the directive (22 September 1994) regarding the implementation of a European Works Council. Therefore, we will first of all cast a glance at studies on the practice of the existing EWC:

- After an 'establishment boom' in the period immediately before the commencement of the directive in 1996, the further establishment of European Works Councils occurred only hesitantly. There is a by far not yet exhausted potential here.

- Various types can be differentiated in the EWC's practice, which range from a rather 'symbolic' EWC with a far-reaching formal participation in the annual meetings to a dynamic, developing body. By its actual role – information and consultation – the last-named type begins to work out surpassing, common, community-wide, coordinated standpoints, action programmes and agreements (Lecher, Nagel and Platzer, 1998, pp. 84–86).

- In addition, the strained relationship between national and European interests – including the trade union cultures – constitutes a complex and partially quite contradictory action parameter for the EWC (Eberwein, Tholen, 2002, pp. 158–159).

- Among the frequently mentioned problems for the development of the EWC into a dynamically functioning body are: the management attitude towards the EWC and the overall industrial relations in the respective company, difficulties with regard to the linguistic understanding and the development of intercultural competence, problems with regard to the cooperation with

---

Moreover, the anchored transfers of employee shares through the drafts of the EU merger directive (see the proposal of the EU Parliament and the EU Commission regarding "Cross-border mergers of companies with share capital – general approach (15315/04) from 26 November 2004 (called '10th EU Directive') and the EU Takeover Directive (S.I., 2006/1183, which came into force on 20 May 2006).

supra-company trade union bodies and in the communication and information between the EWC and representatives on company/plant level.

The previous practice of the EWC is determined through the rights and obligations predetermined in the EU directive and the national implementing laws as well as the subsequently influential social role of the EWC:

In general, the EWC (regardless whether restricted to the EU-15 or encompassing the new CEE member states) defines itself through a three-sided reference system (Eberwein, Tholen, 2002, p. 83): accordingly, the EWC adopts a suspenseful boundary position in the intersection of expectation attitudes of different actor groups – representatives and workforces, management and trade unions.

These connections are illustrated in Figure 4.1.

This strained relationship is further complicated by the fact that differentiations could be made on the management side regarding corporate headquarters and sites, and among trade unions with regard to European federations and national associations. Indeed, the latter are also by no means uniformly structured in all countries. Furthermore, differentiations could also be made between the (in turn, nationally quite differently institutionalized) representatives and the workforces in the respective countries, whose entitlements and expectations also do not have to be automatically identical.

But these differentiations shall not be traced here. However, it is clear that the EWC finds itself in a complex position and situation. The EWC is also institutionally provided with a relatively marginal degree of self-authority. As a result, it can only develop an effective (political) practice if it demonstrates an acceptance on the part of its interaction partner, associated with the possibility of sufficient information and has a concept of its own activity at the same time. The development of an independent self-understanding as the EWC, the EWC's coming to terms with its own internal aspects, but also external communications and information problems as well as the development of a strategy which can guide its practical actions are pertinent on this score.

If this independent profile does not develop, the EWC also cannot play an independent role in the communication and the balance between East and West.

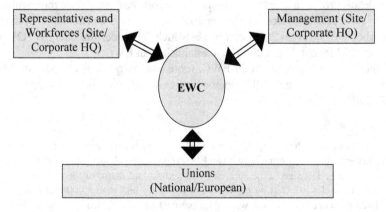

Figure 4.1   The EWC and its interaction partners

Further problems of the EWC work are:

- Since the institution framework of the EWC activity is less focused, the personal commitment of individual representatives acquires a special role for the development or stagnation of the European Works Councils. This particularly applies to the integration of CEE workforce representatives in a European system of industrial relations. We call this the 'subjective factor', of which more will be subsequently spoken.
- The requirements of the European Works Councils have further increased with the accession of the EU-10 countries in May 2004, which especially pertains to the intercultural competence and the capability to integrate other traditions and industrial relations.
- A special problem also emerges in the fact that a trade union presence is lacking on the site/company level in a considerable number of CEE companies, and therefore contact partners for the EWC are difficult to find or not even able to be found at all.

Assessments of the Development of European Works Councils up to Now

EWC new establishments – a potential that is not yet exhausted

It is difficult to obtain accurate figures concerning the extent of existing European Works Councils (EWCs). Corporate fusions, restructurings and closures have effects on the number of existing European Works EWCs. As in the case of the amalgamation of Aventis Pharma and Sanofi in 2004 (as a rule) one body emerges from two previous EWCs during fusions of two enterprises.

On the other hand, new EWCs continue to be established in EWC-eligible enterprises, but this process has slowed down considerably after the initial establishment boom (IG Metall, 2004a, p. 6). More than half of all agreements made concerning the installation of an EWC came about in 1996 alone (immediately before the effective date of the directive). Since then, about 40 other agreements are made every year (European Council for Economic and Social Affairs, 2003, p. 4). That's why EWC figures are always only 'snapshots' which lag behind the real development. With this restriction the follows details provide a reference to the not yet exhausted potential for representatives and trade unions. Figures from December 2005 (that is under consideration of the new EU member states) reveal 2,204 companies which fell under the directive. Of those companies, 772 (about 35 per cent) have established an EWC.[14]

Of the 737 companies with an EWC, more than two-thirds (69 per cent) have subsidiaries in the 10 new EU member states (European Trade Union Institute (ETUI), 2006, p. 38).

---

14   In December 2005, the 2,204 EWC-eligible companies employed a total of 23.6 million workers. The 772 companies with an EWC represented about 61 per cent of these 23.6 million employees. The size of the company is the important factor of the compliance rates: among the companies affected by the Directive that have less than 5,000 employees in the EEA only 23 per cent have EWCs, while 61.3 per cent of the affected workforce larger than 10,000 employees have EWCs (ETUI, 2006, pp. 28, 33).

The distribution of CEE subsidiaries from EWC-eligible companies which have their registered office in the EU-15 reveals the following picture (in parenthesis, the respective number of companies *with* an EWC): in Poland there are 819 (425),[15] in Hungary 662 (334), in the Czech Republic 636 (333), in Slovakia 340 (199), in Estonia 181 (101), in Slovenia 185 (108), in Lithuania 162 (87) and in Latvia 15 (8,478) subsidiaries of EWC affected parent enterprises from the EEA (ETUI, 2006, p. 37).

The EWC degree of coverage in companies which are active in the eight CEE EU member countries is with more than 50 per cent still significantly greater than the corresponding proportion in *all* EEA countries (35 per cent).

And so, purely based on the number, European Works Councils represent a weighty factor for the development of bridge functions to the MOE countries.

But what is interesting that though the coverage rate is higher in CEE countries than in EU-15 member states, the integration of representatives coming from CEE countries, is lagging behind: only 166 companies that have EWCs and that operate in new member states (including Malta Anc. Cyprus) are effectively integration representatives from these countries. This is 15 per cent of the companies operation in the new member states (ETUI, 2006, p. 41).

How does the previous work of the EWC now stand?

Considerable differences in the development of the EWC
The European Council for Economic and Social Affairs, a body comprised of European employers' associations and trade union federations, sees in the European Works Councils until now a 'decisive step in the development of an actual community-wide social dialogue on the corporate level.... The positive role of European Works Councils in the improvement of social dialogue and the information/consultation within the company (is) acknowledged by wide circles' (European Council for Economic and Social Affairs, 2003, p. 7). '(The EWCs) thereby ensure an exchange and a handling of procedures beyond cultural boundaries, which is one of the most conspicuous and essential phenomena of social Europe' (European Council for Economic and Social Affairs, 2003, p. 5). In contrast to this very optimistic survey, other empirically substantiated studies portray a more realistic picture of the EWC's role and function, which is particularly characterized by information and communication deficiencies between the EWC and the representative systems in the different countries concerned (see the case studies in Eberwein, Tholen, 2002, pp. 81–156).

Various developmental types of EWC
The conference that was held on 25 and 26 November 2002 at Aarhus (Denmark) and organized by European Trade Union Confederation (ETUC) together with Danish trade unions offers abundant experience material concerning the practice of European Works Councils. Approximately 350 European Works Councils met with representatives of national and European trade union associations, training institutes and EWC consultants. It turned out that serious differences exist even in

---

15   See for further information Meardi (2004).

EWC activity – information and consultation – designated by the EWC directive as central. A rough classification reveals four EWC gradations (see also Stirling and Tully, 2004):

- Some EWCs receive only very limited information, which has already been published. A consultation does not even take place.
- Another EWC group is quite well informed, but it not consulted.
- A third, rather small group is satisfactorily informed and consulted. But very few of them are able to bring forward their viewpoints regarding cross-border corporate decisions.
- Only some EWCs are able to take a step further and enter into a discussion with the corporate management, which sometimes led to negotiations on European agreements (LO [Danish Trade Union Confederation] et al. 2002, 12).

A comprehensive study conducted in 2001/02 by the European Foundation for the Improvement of Living and Working Conditions presents the results of 41 EWC case studies in five countries (France, Germany, the UK, Italy and Sweden): there is a broad range of EWC characterizations, which do not allow a uniform picture or even the forecast of a certain developmental direction. In several cases the existence of the EWC can promote a 'harmonisation' of (nationally) different industrial relations within the respective enterprise. And the EWC can even stimulate the establishment of representatives in (CEE) subsidiaries. But on the whole this study ascertains that in most companies the EWCs play only a relatively insignificant role in the coordination of trade union measures and their scope for action is for the most part restricted to defensive measures (European Foundation for the Improvement of Living and Working Conditions, 2004, p. 103).[16]

On behalf of the European Trade Union Confederation, in 2005 Jeremy Waddington conducted a survey on the views of Works council representatives in 24 countries (Waddington, 2006).[17] The main results partly confirm the older surveys, partly going beyond:

- less than one-third of the EWC representatives report useful 'information and consultation' on all the issues mentioned in the EWC Directive;
- especially issues like health and safety and environmental protection are reported by about one-third of EWC representatives to have appeared on the agenda of the EWC, but – in contrast – such sensitive issues like trade union

---

16   A study sponsored by the European Commission and supported by ETUC as well as Spanish, French, Dutch and British trade unions underscores that many European Works Councils repeatedly have to fight for the right to obtain sufficient information on time. It is even more difficult to anchor a genuine consultation process. Only in a few cases, above all in the automotive industry, was the EWC able to gain a role as negotiation partner (CCOO de Catalunya et al., o.J, 23).

A comprehensive overview of the contradicting meanings of academics and practiotioners about EWC could be found in Fitzgerald (2004).

17   This survey is a kind of panel study, as Waddington carried out a previous study of the views of EWC representatives from six countries, Waddington (2003).

rights, working time and profit sharing/financial participation are reported by more than half of the EWC representatives as having not appeared on the EWC's agenda: and more than half of the EWC representatives report that the issue of 'trade union rights' had not even raised at the EWC, though (or because) in this sample only less than half of the EWC representatives (46.9 per cent) reported that all employee representatives on the EWC were trade union members;

- Only 0.8 per cent of EWC representatives think that the EWC is 'very effective' as a 'means' to influence management;
- Support from the national trade unions is regarded by the EWC as the most useful;
- There are considerable national variations in the views of representatives towards the EWCs: partly these variations come from the characteristics of the labour relation systems with which is respondent is familiar and how EWCs 'fit' in with this system. Partly the corporate management is influencing the nature of EWC agreements according to the conditions in the country of origin: f.e. agreements with companies based in Anglo-Saxon countries tend to place more restrictions on employee representatives than agreements concluded by companies based on continental Europe.

But if the share of those EWCs whose actions go beyond the role as passive information recipient would increase, a significant dynamism of European industrial relations would already be anticipated as a result. A prerequisite for this would be the development of a collective self-understanding of the EWC. A prerequisite for the development of independent (for the most part independent of the corporate group management) structures and procedures despite the origin of systems of different industrial relations would be 'that the EWC representatives are union organised and anchored in the national system of representatives. But above all – just like the trade unions – they must relinquish their self-understanding as a national-bound representatives open themselves to the notions of a European – an international solidarity beyond the sites' rivalry' (Zimmer, 2003, p. 625).

These results, which emphases the more subjective factors of the involved actors, are corroborated through a study (conducted in 1999) regarding the influence possibilities of Danish EWC representatives (Knudsen, 2004). Accordingly, it was less the formal determinations and the resistance of employers, which construed the relatively marginal influence of the EWC, but rather the passive attitude of most EWC representatives – starting with the inadequate communication among one another and leading to a general – very prejudiced – contempt of the potential EWC possibilities (Knudsen, 2004, p. 218).

Can European Works Councils Play the Role of Pioneers in the Integration of Employees from Central and Eastern Europe?

In view of the described problems in the previous work of the European Works Councils, an assessment such as that rendered by IG Metall for the industrial sectors metal, textiles and clothing, wood and plastic sounds very optimistic:

Through the EWC we have the opportunity to more rapidly improve the working conditions in the new EU countries – at least within the company (IG Metall 2003, 10).

The EU Directive 94/95/EC concerning the European Works Councils had been cast in the national law in all new EU member states in Central and Eastern Europe by no later than 30 April 2004. None of the acceding countries had applied for transitional arrangements. And so the directive had to be applied directly.[18]

Although not legally prescribed before 1 May 2004, representatives from the CEEC had also been previously integrated in existing European Works Councils in many cases. The willingness to do so varied quite strongly from company to company and from branch to branch. In the multinational companies of the EU-15 which had sites in CEE countries in 2002, 84 members or observers came from the CEE countries (Kerkhofs, 2002, p. 65). According to a study by the Polish Solidarity trade union, Czech as well as Polish companies/sites were represented in nearly 50 EWCs in 2002 (LO (Danish Trade Union Confederation) *et al.* 2002, 18).

According to the 'eiroonline news' (European Industrial Relations Observatory from September 2004), in 2003 there were 51 Czechs as EWC members in EU-15 multinational corporations (of which 24 were full members and 27 were observers); Poland had 59 members in the first half of 2004 (of which 32 were from Solidarity, 10 from the OPZZ and at least 11 had been sent by management); eight representatives came to the EWC from Slovakian subsidiary enterprises; the appropriate preparation had been made in two others on 1 May 2004 (EIRO, 2004).

The status of CEE representatives before 1 May 2004 ranged from full equality with the representatives from the EU-15 (for instance, with VW and Opel) to mere observer status. Even where CEE trade unionists had not yet been integrated in the European Works Councils before 1 May 2004, solid working contacts with West European colleagues had nevertheless been developed in many cases. And so the view of the CEE representatives in the multinationals had expanded beyond one's own site. As a result, the competence which results from the manifold cooperation, including international training courses, grows. For instance, the experiences are usually positive where there are Polish representatives in the EWC. They feel as if they are taken seriously (Domanski, 2001).

IG Metall complained that sometimes the CEE representatives were denied the right to an interpreter and the translation of documents during meeting (before the accession date 1 May 2004). They could only practically participate if they had a good command of one of the EU-15 languages (IG Metall, 2003, p.17).

The inclusion of CEE representatives in *all* existing EWCs was met with resistance in some companies before 1 May 2004. For instance, at General Motors it lasted four years and took considerable pressure on the part of the EWC until the management was willing to include CEE representatives in the EWC (CCOO de Catalunya et al., o.J, 19). On the whole, there were a multitude of inhibitory impediments on the part of the management, but also from single EWCs (problems of contact with partners from the CEEC; fragmentation of trade unions; lacking trade union representatives on the site/company level; doubt in the EWC with regard to being able to solve the additional problems in the integration of CEE representatives (additional languages and further cultural diversity)).

It is not to be disputed that the European Works Councils are on the verge of new challenges with the integration of workers from countries whose employer-employee relationships and wages differ considerably from the West European level. They must also keep an eye on how the representatives from the new EU members have been selected. In the CEE subsidiaries the inferior degree of trade union organization has a negative effect on the democratic legitimacy of the EWC members. The aforementioned Solidarity study asserts that in the 'union-free' companies/sites the EWC representatives are often 'not proper representatives, but sales department staff, quality controllers and so on, who have been selected by management without the trade unions or the workforces having been asked' (LO [Danish Trade Union Confederation] et al., 2002, p. 18).

Moreover, EWCs themselves – in those multinational corporations in which they managed to hire full-time experts for the coordination of EWC work (EWC secretaries or managing directors) – can feel as if they have taken on too much with the additional task of mediation between East and West.

Especially on the part of the CEE trade unionists, it is expected from the membership in the EWC that they obtain better information from the corporate management. In addition, the symbolic value of the EWC and the possibility to exchange information with other employees from other sites in other countries is also emphasized. Ultimately, the fact that the EWC contributes towards dismantling double standards in the companies is also considered as a possible perspective (LO, Danish Trade Union Confederation *et al.* 2002, 18).

It may be doubtful whether such expectations in the EWC's work and functions are also realistic.

Indirect Effects of European Works Councils on Industrial Relations

The evaluation of six case studies of Polish subsidiaries of multinational companies from different countries provides a reference to the actual effects of the EWC (Meardi, 2003). The study describes the direct effects of European Works Councils on Polish industrial relations as negligible – similar findings to the analyses concerning the activity of European Works Councils in the EU-15. But the study identifies two indirect effects:

1. A so-called 'information effect', that may not directly influence the corporate decisions, but contributes towards an altered atmosphere – 'a change in rhetoric' (Meardi, 2003, p. 12) – between management and representatives; this is a factor that can influence negotiations, consensus and mobilization of the workforce.
2. A 'legitimation effect' that exploits the possibility of new and surprising alliances within a company. Sometimes Polish trade union representatives and managers of the corporate group headquarters have engaged in a joint

cause against the local Polish management. This concerned cases in which the trade union representatives complained in the EWC about the conduct of local management. They succeeded in moving the top management – which feared the negative publicity and repercussions in the West – to curtail the autonomy of the local management in Poland. This may not be a general trend in all of the multinational companies operating in Poland. However, the EWC's perspective of direct connection to corporate headquarters by circumventing local management to be able to positively refer to the western model of social relations should also not be estimated as too insignificant.

High potential of European Works Councils – results from the expert interviews
For the most part, the participants in our study estimate the potential of the European Works Councils in the establishment of a European model of industrial relations in the CEE countries as high. But the assessment of the EWC's role varies, depending on how the previous work of the EWC in the EU-15 countries is seen. There are considerable differences between the industrial sectors with regard to the establishment of the EWC as well as the assessment of their work. The German union IG Metall (metal sector) representatives express themselves relatively optimistically, whereas the IG BCE (German union for the minging, chemical and energy sectors) assesses their role more cautiously. The NGG (German union for food processing and restaurants) sees the branch as confronted with special difficulties on account of the situation, and is rather at the beginning with regard to the utilization of the EWC as an intermediary between representatives from (German) parent enterprises and (CEE) subsidiary enterprises.

The representatives of the European trade union federations also emphasize an important bridge function of the EWC. But due to the previous practice there is no exuberant optimism for the fact that European Works Councils could quickly become a stable support mechanism amongst the representatives in the enlarged Europe.

The employers think ithat perhaps the EWC could play an intermediary role in the integration of the new EU members. However, they also see the increasing tasks for the EWC and the complexity of the topics as too much for the EWC to handle.

Particular results from the expert interviews
Our interview partners from IG Metall emphasized the EWC's important role as a bridge for development of industrial relations in the CEE countries. The EWC is seen as the most important field for information and communication, more important than the collective bargaining coordination among the associations. The EWC can generate pressure for compliance with minimum standards in the respective companies; for instance, it has the right to inspect the company's balance sheets (which the industrial trade unions do not have); the company pays many costs (for translations, meetings, and so on).

The interview partners from the German trade unions warn against an exaggerated expectation of the EWC's role: because after 1 May 2004 the EWC in Central and Eastern Europe would play a similar role to the EWC in the EU-15. In the beginning there is the acquaintanceship phase – the general understanding of the structure of an information network, up to and including formulation of political fields.

The EWC's developmental potential is underscored by our interview partners from the European trade union federations, but here there is also a certain degree of scepticism in light of the EWC's previous difficulties. Strictly speaking, the EWC would be an ideal instrument for mediation between East and West. But it is not clear at the moment whether they are taking advantage of these great developmental possibilities as well as their opportunity.

Our interview partner from the ETUI sees the balance between the single sites of multinationals as a future field for the EWC. With many multinational companies the productivity of their sites in the East is just as high as that of their sites in the West, but the wage ratio was 1:3 or even 1:4: 'One must talk about this'. The EWC can also provide impulses for collective bargaining. Another example for a future EWC intermediary role could lie in finding a balance between overtime work in the East with simultaneous short-time work in the West. But there has been relatively little 'good practice' with the previous EWC.

Examples were also mentioned for the problem regarding lack of contact partner in the CEE subsidiaries. In one case, a Polish representative was supposed to become – according to the intention of the German corporate group management – a member in the EWC. The responsible Polish trade union was not able to comply, because there were no trade union representatives in the Polish subsidiary, since the Polish plant manager had previously prevented its formation (according to an IG Metall representative).

Among the interviewees from the German employers' organizations there was only a rudimentary knowledge of the status of the European Works Councils. Insofar as our interview partners were informed about the existence of the EWC, they corroborated the considerable differences amongst the single companies.

The employers also think it is likely that the EWC can play an intermediary role in the integration of the new EU members. The EWC is still developing. However, the EWC's are overloaded with too many topics, and so the subject matter is too complex for individual EWC members. Many representatives in the EWC do not speak any English. The costs for the EWC further increase as a result (esp. translation costs). That is why the German employers are also not currently in favour of a revision of the directive in the sense of an expansion of the EWC competencies and the frequency of meetings.

Summarizing Opinions from the CEE Countries

Czech Republic
If there is a European Works Council in the company, the domestic trade unions have contact with it. Wherever trade union officials were previously integrated in the EWC, they emphasize the improved information possibilities concerning the company's plans and intentions. The employers are not effectively informed about the European Works Councils, and consider the EWC as a matter of the trade unions.

Slovakia
The respondents from the energy sector consider an intermediary role of the EWC as possible. In the metal industry, the employer representatives appraise the

personal contact as the most important element of the EWC activity. The trade union representatives consider the EWC to be a useful channel for obtaining information about the company's development and plans. The social partners in the food processing industry appraise the role of the EWC in a similarly positive manner. They also think that an influence on the manager behaviour is possible. The respondents from the energy sector also think that the importance of the European Works Councils will increase even more in the future.

Poland

The general opinion of the European Works Councils is quite positive due to the previous experiences of Polish representatives. Solidarity is particularly interested in the EWC. EWC's are appraised as an instrument to improve the cooperation amongst the various national representatives in the companies, to obtain information about the corporate plans, and to become acquainted with and discuss differences among themselves. It has been critically remarked that management could attempt to manipulate the EWC in its meaning, and that not all information could be passed on to the trade unions due to the confidentiality requirement. Sporadically, a danger is also seen in the fact that in the EWC the workers identify with the concern to such an extent that this undermines the solidarity with the workers from other companies.

The Polish employer representatives have little knowledge of the institution 'European Works Council'.

In all three CEE countries the trade union representatives positively assess the information possibilities concerning corporate strategy and plans that have been improved through the EWC. The cooperation with West European trade unionists and the establishment of a supranational discussion culture is seen as an important step for integration in a greater Europe. It is also taken into consideration that the European Works Councils could have a positive influence on the behaviour of local (CEE) managers. The fact that local employers/managers have little knowledge of the EWC institution and frequently regard the EWC as solely a matter of the trade unions appears obstructive to an expansion and strengthening of the European Works councils in the CEE countries. The language problem continues to be seen as an obstacle for the development of the EWC. But the 1 May 2004 accession date is generally seen as the commencement of the full integration of CEE representatives in the European Works Councils of western companies, so that – if one adopts this point of view – there are hardly any experiences regarding the actual function of the EWC in Central and Eastern Europe (see also EIRO, 2004).

Upshot: Opportunities and Problems of the European Works Councils through the Admission of the Eight CEE Countries into the EU

In general, an important role in the development of European industrial relations is attributed to the European Works Councils. They are perceived as the most tangible action perspective with regard to the Europeanization of industrial relations. Surveyed trade unionists and employer representatives concur with this. But among trade union representatives there is a preponderance of voices which warn against excessive expectations. Only in a minority of West European EWCs has it been possible up to now to develop functioning networks of representatives and to develop the inception of a supranational 'European' consciousness. In view of the serious differences in the wage and salary structure and the menace of the relocation of sites away from West Europe/Germany into the CEE countries, the further development of a supranational action model may not be easy. In positive cases, the European Works Councils will initially provide a contribution – just like in the previous EU-15 – towards mutual acquaintanceship, better understanding of different trade union cultures and exchange of information. Hopes that European Works Councils can contribute towards a rapid levelling of differences with regard to social standards may not come to fruition. If considered in terms of tendency, there could be effects for a modified atmosphere between management and representatives in the CEE countries through the existence and activity of the EWC. Several examples show that CEE representatives in the EWC managed to resolve conflicts with the managers of subsidiary enterprises with the help of the EWC and the central corporate management. As far as the EWC representatives from the CEE subsidiaries are concerned, the direct connection to corporate management signifies a gain in prestige and tends to expand their action possibilities. The lack of representatives in a growing number of CEE sites is a problem for the expansion of EWC activities in the CEE countries. In this case, West European EWC representatives plainly lack legitimized contact partners. Furthermore, the scepticism of the surveyed CEE trade unionists vis-à-vis the (for them) new institution of the works councils represents an obstacle. The extent to which European Works Councils can contribute towards development of representatives on the site/company level in the CEE subsidiary enterprises – and thus towards development of more stable elements of a social dialogue as a prerequisite for mediation between a company's West and East European sites – would have to be examined during the course of further development. The experts surveyed on our part – particularly on the European level – saw this rather sceptically.

This scepticism relates to the EWC's degree of dissemination as well as the assessment of the previous practice.

The accession of the CEE countries to the European Union on 1 May 2004 represents (-ed) a major challenge for trade unions, existing EWCs and the respective representatives in the different countries. Will this challenge lead to a new drive of the development of European Works Councils? As already argued above, there is great potential for further new establishments. However, it is also clear which tremendous tasks are in store for the representatives with the accession of the 10 new EU countries. The warning of employers against expecting too much of the EWC cannot be dismissed. That is why in the discussion surrounding the revision of the EWC directive it would also be a good idea to think about the structure and size of the existing bodies as well as a clearer definition of the rights of representatives to information and consultation. But it is also not to be precluded that particularly the major challenges which are associated with the accession of the EU-10 countries can lead to a vitalization of the existing EWC and to impetus for further EWC establishments.

**The Influence of German Parent Enterprises on the Industrial Relations
in their CEE Subsidiaries – Solution-Orientated and Corporate-Centred
Approach**

Foreign enterprises frequently play a pioneering role in the CEE countries with regard
to the modernization of production. As a rule, they implement the most progressive
technology in their subsidiary enterprises and revive the organization of labour and
the management culture. But to what extent do the foreign enterprises also import
their forms of industrial relations? The answer to this question is less uniform. There
are distinct differences between the countries of origin among the parent enterprises,
but also between the enterprises with corporate group seat in the same country. The
nature of the direct investment (Brownfield or Greenfield type) also has an influence
on the different form of the industrial relations in the subsidiary enterprises.

Overall, the question is posed here as to whether the Germanic 'production model'
(Streeck et al., 1995) – if there is even such a model in reality (Doerrenbaecher, 2003)
– will be transferred from the parent enterprises to their CEE subsidiary enterprises.
Here we intend to concentrate on the industrial relations at the corporate/site level.

In Germany, the handling of industrial relations takes place in the broadest
sense on different levels with corresponding divisions of labour: Labour and social
legislation, collective bargaining, works constitution act and co-determination act
from 1976 (industrial relations scheme). As far as that is concerned, the works
constitution (that is the industrial relations on the corporate/site level) is only *one*
component/element within an extensive interweaving of institutions for coping with
and settlement of social conflicts (Braun, Eberwein, 1992, pp. 432–433). The effect
of this interweaving of institutions consists of the fact that socially-conditioned
conflict contents are desegregated, specified and differentiated. As a result, conflicts
are deprived of their explosive force that threatens the general social system. Within
such an interweaving of institutions, only such conflict objects can (and may) take
place within the scope of industrial relations, which can then be decided upon and
implemented on this special level.

However, this operational division of labour – collective bargaining, labour law
and social legislation – does not exist (or at least to this extent) in the three CEE
countries. In the practice of these countries, the levels are strongly mixed with one
another. Commensurate with the assessment of the High Level Group on Industrial
Relations, 'in most candidate countries, collective bargaining is very weak at the
main intermediary levels (sectoral and regional), entire economic sectors and
categories of workers are not covered by collective bargaining.... A balanced mix
of national, sectoral, regional, local and workplace collective bargaining is needed'
(2002, p. 29).

Evaluation of Literature

In his case study of Hungary, Doerrenbaecher (2003) comes to the conclusion that
as a result of the German direct investments in Hungary the German 'model' of
industrial relations has been 'exported' to a lesser extent than the technology and
organization of labour:

It turned out that only larger German enterprises and those smaller enterprises which allot their Hungarian subsidiary enterprises a strategic role in the overall corporate group had a stronger reproduction of their domestic industrial relations (p. 167).

With regard to the characterization of participative industrial relations, Galgóczi and Kluge (2003) see the western employers as 'reluctant missionaries'. Accordingly, the business enterprises – in particular the Anglo-Saxon enterprises – are not interested in strong, well-(trade union) organized employees who could emerge as negotiation partners. 'All they do to optimise the existing structures is: As much socially responsible behaviour and cooperative corporate culture as necessary, but also as much adaptation to (weaker) local conditions as possible' (Galgóczi, Kluge and Voss, 2003, p. 42).

But even in those cases, where MNCs have come from home countries where f. e. Works councils are an institutional feature like in Germany and Austria, these MNCs have often been able to avoid union recognition, esp. In Greenfield investments (Rainnie, Smith, Swain, 2002).

Galgóczi makes a distinction between two main approaches of foreign enterprises with regard to the arrangement of industrial relations: the 'adaptive' approach, 'in which the management adapts its relations with the employees to the traditions and the legal framework of the respective country and merely complies with the minimal conditions while doing so', and the 'innovative' approach. Here, the management attempts to transfer the corporate culture of the parent enterprise to the subsidiary. And so not only are corporate organization, management style and the organization of production fundamentally changed, but also the industrial relations (Galgóczi, 2004, p. 19).

Depending on the country of origin, the investments pertaining to various transfer models are clearly determinable. According to Galgóczi, Asian enterprises more likely tend to a rigid transfer of their indigenous culture. Efficiency is the utmost priority for American firms. If this objective seems expedient to a cooperative corporate culture, then they accept this, but without making any effort towards an introduction of such systems. By contrast, European – in particular German enterprises – tend towards an 'innovative' approach (Galgóczi, 2004, p. 19).

It must be analysed to what extent foreign direct investments contribute to the limitation of collective bargaining on company/site level in the CEE countries (neglecting the supra-company levels). There are no inspirations emanating from the foreign enterprises with regard to establishing a system of collective bargaining. Western trade unionists thus fear that any further pressure on an undermining of the collective bargaining in the western EU countries could emerge.

Katharina Bluhm contradicts this pessimistic view in her company-related study. Of course, it is clear that – especially in the labour policy – few direct central guidelines emerged on the part of the parent company (Bluhm, 2003). Nevertheless, the labour methods and policies of the country of origin spread to the CEE (Polish and Czech) subsidiaries. They form the (positive as well as negative) background experience of the German business managers who now manage the CEE subsidiaries, and function not the least as an orientation variable for the local actors in the respective host countries. The results are different (company-related) models of selective perception and adaptation. Bluhm emphasizes that 'the German works councils, in conjunction with the trade unions, are still strong enough to assert cross-border reorganisation' (Bluhm, 2000, pp. 12–15) – an assessment that we do not necessarily share on account of our empirical experience. According to Bluhm, the more cooperative behaviour in very large companies is 'attributable to the very strong position of the works councils and the trade unions in large German industrial enterprises, and to their ability to organise the cross-border exchange on their own.' Bluhm comes to the conclusion that until now the German companies have not used their foreign direct investments in the CEE countries to disable the German regime of industrial relations.

But on the other hand, 'any hope, especially in the case of German enterprises, that their cooperative corporate culture was transferred and that they function as a missionary for the European social model turned out to be illusory' (Bluhm (2000, pp. 12–15).

As a consequence of the transformation of the production structures in the CEE countries in the direction of greater added value, Bela Galgóczi anticipates a greater tendency towards cooperative corporate cultures in the European trans-national enterprises, as well as the assumption of corresponding EU directives, a consolidation of the labour market and the implementation of competition laws. The possibility of more short-term gain in profit through the exploitation of lower standards would be increasingly reduced as a result. Employment participation itself would become a productivity factor (Galgóczi, 2004, p. 22).

In the following section, it shall be examined as to what extent these empirical approaches are also reflected in our results.

Results from the Expert Interviews

As a rule, the multinational companies implement the most progressive technology in their subsidiary enterprises in the CEE countries. The representatives of the employers' associations and trade unions we interviewed were largely in agreement in their assessment. The evaluation of the FDI effects on the industrial relations was quite inconsistent. A change of the corporate culture and in the case of European – particularly German – companies, also a tendency towards more cooperative forms of industrial relations is perceived in relative accord.

The Results from Germany and the EU Level in Detail

The transfer of the most modern technology and newer modes of working can lead to the fact that the subsidiary enterprises partially show a higher degree of productivity than the enterprises in the country of origin. With Greenfield investments the enterprises strive toward a blueprint with which they then show a greater degree of efficiency than the parent enterprise in Germany.

In all three fields (technology, organization/management, industrial relations) the companies may initially bring along their own ideas from Germany, but in relation to the industrial relations this transfer is much less characterized than in the other fields.

Alongside our research hypothesis it seems meaningful to make a differentiation depending on the type of the investments. With Greenfield investments the companies frequently orientates themselves neither towards their experiences made in Germany nor towards the handed-down industrial relations in the host countries of the investments. In concrete terms this means that there are frequently no trade union representatives on the site/company level. With Brownfield investments the foreign investors must get involved much more strongly in available structures and norms.

Some of our trade union interview partners from Germany also assume that the business enterprises perceive their CEE subsidiaries as an experimental field for deregulated industrial relations.

The role of the *works councils in the German parent enterprise* with regard to the build-up of industrial relations in the respective CEE subsidiaries (transfer service) is seen quite differently: whereas some underscore the role of the German works councils for the form of the industrial relations in the CEE subsidiaries ('Where they are active, things function in the CEE subsidiaries. But only there' – EMF representative),[19] in other cases the passivity of German trade unionists and works councils in relation to influencing the industrial relations in the CEEC is lamented.

The case studies will be able to provide further insight into the role of the works councils during the composition of CEE industrial relations.

National Specifics from the CEEC

Czech Republic
The form of transfer varies from case to case, and depends on the respective company. Technical standards are adopted, but this does not apply as a rule for the corporate culture. However, the new owners bring along – at least in the beginning – a better quality of industrial relations.

Slovakia
The assessment of the interviewed social partners does not essentially differ. They both agree that European companies normally accept or adopt the domestic norms. However, the fields and extent of the adaptation differ from branch to branch. With respect to technical standards, the interview partners were of the opinion that in Slovakia these standards comply with the EU norms, and that is why German investors seldom had to implement their own standards until now. In the chemicals industry the foreign companies pay special attention to occupational health and safety, quality assurance and environmental protection. In the realm of management structures and organization of labour there was a growing trend towards introducing the systems of the parent enterprises in the subsidiary enterprises. The fact that the positions in top management are usually filled with managers from the parent enterprises was also a contributory factor. With respect to the industrial relations, it was emphasized that the foreign companies respect the domestic legislation. The

---

19   See Müller-Jentsch, 2001 with regard to the increasing importance of the works councils in Germany (in comparison to the trade unions) in relation to the status as well as to the functions and influence.

corporate representatives thought that the foreign companies would even implement the labour legislation more straightforward than the indigenous companies. However, there are clear differences between the countries of origins of the investments:

> The foreign business enterprises respect the local laws. In general, they support the trade unions in order to have a partner for the social dialogue – with clear differences between German, French, and Italian companies on the one hand, and those from the USA and the UK on the other hand (representative of the KOZ, Slovakia).

In the metal industry, the German management strives towards using the experiences and the creativity of the indigenous labour force to develop new types of procedures and techniques on company/site level that are more effective and comply with the regulations of the domestic legislation.

Poland

The prevailing opinion among the interview partners is that a mixture of various technical and organizational models exists in Poland. The industrial relations in the Polish subsidiaries of foreign investors are subject to a transformation process beset with compromise. The Polish labour legislation established the framework for the investors, which they had to observe – even if they did not always gladly do so. In general, foreign direct investments are welcomed, and their role in the modernization of the industry is acknowledged. However, the evaluation of the foreign multinational companies differs, depending on the industry. Trade union respondents from the metal industry and the food processing industry think that in the final analysis the foreign companies ultimately did what they wanted. All interview partners evaluate the system of industrial relations in Poland somewhat critically. The waning influence of the trade unions with the inadequate status of the employers' associations does not allow any genuine social dialogue and collective bargaining on a supra-company level. The problems from the field of industrial relations emerging in connection with foreign companies will not be solved in one coordinated process. They are more subject to a company/site-centred process that depends quite strongly on the respective management and its willingness to negotiate and to solve the problems. At the same time, the trade union representatives appraise the Polish managers very critically. They would cause more difficulties than they facilitate the cooperation with the investors.

Conclusions

Altogether, the responses point in the direction that technology, organization of production process and labour and partially also management concepts may not always be transferred on a one-to-one basis, but have been nevertheless transferred to a great extent from the German parent enterprises to their CEE subsidiaries.

This appears somewhat differently with regard to the industrial relations on the corporate/site level. Certainly, our empirical findings reveal that there is a general tendency in the CEE countries towards establishment of a culture of negotiation solutions as the main method for regulation of industrial relations (see also Gradev,

2001, p. 16), and that the German investors also prefer this solution and cooperation-orientated method. However, our study also corroborates the results of the studies from Kluge and Voss as well as Doerrenbaecher, who ascertained a 'selective transfer' for the industrial relations overall (Kluge and Voss, 2003, p. 67/Doerrenbaecher, 2003, p. 167). Even German companies are very reluctant to transfer their positive experiences with the co-management model to their CEE subsidiaries.

In their transfer of industrial relations, German companies particularly avoid legally established agreements for regulation of this 'cooperation orientation'.

This 'reluctant' commitment of German companies regarding general transfer of their experiences in German industrial relations to the CEE subsidiary enterprises is also expressed in the fact that as a rule, no efforts have been made in the Greenfield investments to establish (juristically secured) institutions of workforce representatives – despite the subsequently related difficulties through the absence of a corresponding collective bargaining partner on the part of the employees.

Under these general determinations, there is no general model for the arrangement of industrial relations in their CEE subsidiaries that would be identifiable on account of their specific strategies obtained from German parent enterprises in the manufacturing industry (we explicitly preclude business services and the retail trade here). Of course, there are nuances between the branches of the single companies (such as between the chemical, energy, automotive and food processing sector). Furthermore, the size of the parent enterprises play a role; as a rule, medium-size and large-scale companies in Germany feature a works council (which could then theoretically exert influence), whereas in small companies this is often not the case. Investment reasons (market developments or reasons of cost) now and then have a certain influence on the arrangement of industrial relations.

But on the whole, all of these independent variables do not construe any general explanatory model in the sense implied above. For instance, the existence of a works council in the German parent enterprises does not automatically signify the possibility, the will – or even the attempt – to establish representatives in the CEE subsidiary enterprises with respect to Greenfield investments. Yet another example for this is the very different attitude of German works councils towards the integration of CEE representatives in the European Works Council (if available) before 1 May 2004 (accession of the eight CEE countries into the EU). And in this overall context it must be asked to what extent the works councils in the German parent enterprises are even included in the investment decisions in their respective company, and whether subsequently secured conclusions can be drawn about the influence possibilities of the representatives with regard to the set-up and structure of representations of interest in the CEE countries.

As the host countries of the investments, the (quite different) CEE countries also do not offer any explanatory model for different country strategies among the West European parent enterprises with regard to the arrangement of industrial relations in their subsidiary enterprises. In general, it is determinable that the companies observe the respective laws, which are of course different from country to country. But apart from this general determination there are no indications that historical, social, political and economical differences in the CEE countries lead to a country-specific, different strategy of the parent enterprises with regard to the organization of the industrial relations for their subsidiaries.

This all indicates that it particularly depends on the strategies of the *single* parent enterprises (including the position and the policy of the works council) – independent from industrial-sector affiliation, share of the wage costs in the total cost of the product, company size, and so on. We call this a 'corporate-centred approach' for explanation of the corporate policy[20] with regard to the development of industrial relations in their CEE subsidiary enterprises. This also includes the history of the business enterprise, the corporate culture, the size, the subjective behaviour of the acting corporate actors, and so on.

But this 'corporate approach' is characterized by the 'solution and cooperation-oriented' imprint, and thus also complies with the understanding of democracy generally prevailing in Europe. As far as that is concerned, with the notion of 'solution and cooperation-oriented corporate centralisation' we offer an explanation for a potential transfer model of industrial relations through German parent enterprises to their CEE subsidiaries.

The 'German production model' is not transferred in its entirety, but the basic assumption of this model (negotiation and cooperation on different levels with different radii of action) is also reflected in the industrial relations of the CEE subsidiary enterprises – albeit with many variations: from codetermined model with collective workforce bodies to human resource strategies which avoid *collective* representative bodies.

Here it will also have to be examined (through the case studies) whether the perceptions (and certainly also experiences) of our *supra-company* interview partners accurately reflect the company's/site's reality.

Based on our expert interviews on the supra-company level, it also turns out that the influences of the trade unions from the countries of origin of the investments – and even the works councils of the German parent companies, which are more powerful in this political realm – on the arrangement of industrial relations in the CEE subsidiary enterprises are rather marginally assessed (see also Rainnie, Smith and Swain, 2002).

They restrict themselves with their concentration on training courses/seminars more to (passive-reacting) information than to (active-acting) utilization of existing structures, such as corporate codetermination. However, in this case an industrial-sector differentiation is to be made: influences in the food processing industry are even weaker than in the metal, chemicals and energy industry.

This conclusion also has to be subsequently examined regarding whether it is merely due to the *specific* perception of the full-time trade union officers on the national and EU level or tallies with reality.

On the whole, we assume that the subsequent case studies are able to portray a differentiated picture of the possibilities of the institutions and actors of German codetermination for influencing the CEE industrial relations.

---

20   In his Hungarian case study pertaining to the effects of German direct investments on the Hungarian subsidiaries, Doerrenbaecher (2003) ascertains a 'strong heterogeneity in the internationalisation of business enterprises' (p.167).

Chapter 5

The Nine West European Multinationals: Different Patterns of the Impact on the Industrial Relations in their CEE Subsidiaries

In the following, the research hypotheses and the thesis of 'solution-oriented and corporate-centred approach' will be examined by using nine smaller case studies.

Document analyses and expert interviews with management and representatives in nine (mostly German) parent enterprises and their 21 subsidiaries in Poland, the Czech Republic and Slovakia have been conducted for this purpose.

The first criterion of the corporate selection pertained to the:

- Type of investment: while doing so, we decide between Greenfield and Brownfield investments on the one hand and between labour and capital-intensive investments on the other hand (decision criterion: capital-intensive means that the labour costs amount to less than 25 per cent of the overall costs of this business enterprise).
- Branch: the branches metal/electrical/automotive as well as chemicals/plastics/energy and food processing have been selected for two reasons: First of all, most of the companies which transact the direct investments in the CEE countries come from these branches (within the manufacturing sector) – our results shall also be more generalized as a result. And secondly, these branches comprise a support area of such (German) trade unions (IG Metall, IG BCE and NGG) which are all to a great extent very active on the European political scene.
- Moreover, we wanted to knowledgably represent a sufficient share of companies with subsidiaries in *all* three CEE countries in our sample. Comparability between subsidiaries from different host countries *within* one parent company was targeted with this selection.
- Furthermore, European Works Councils should be available in an ample number of companies: the adequate inclusion of parent enterprises which have an EWC allows conclusions regarding the proportions of Europeanization in the subsidiaries in the CEEC and the parent enterprises at the headquarters, and at the same time enables an (empirically substantiated) analysis of the interactions between the actors in the field of industrial relations in the East and West.

Table 5.1   Corporate selection

Company	Branch	Poland	Czech Republic	Slovakia
Volkswagen AG	Metal/automotive	X	X	X
Robert Bosch GmbH	Metal/car parts	X	X	
Siemens AG	Metal/electrical	X	X	X
RWE AG	Energy	X	X	X
Nestlé SA	Food processing	X	X	X
Dr. August Oetker KG	Food processing	X	X	X
Continental AG	Chemicals/car parts		X	X
Aventis Pharma SA (Sanofi Aventis SA after 20 August 2004)	Chemicals/ pharmaceuticals			X
Henkel KgaA	Chemicals	X		

Volkswagen AG – a German-Style International Enterprise

The Enterprise

The corporate group with headquarters in Wolfsburg (founded in 1938) is one of the leading car manufacturers worldwide and the largest automobile producer in Europe. The enterprise – with 4.984 million vehicles delivered worldwide in 2002 – achieved a car market share of 12.1 per cent. The West European market represented the largest sales area with 35.6 per cent, ahead of Germany (18.8 per cent), the Asia-Pacific region (16.1 per cent) and North America (12.6 per cent).

In Germany, the Volkswagen AG consists of the Volkswagen works in six sites: Wolfsburg, Brunswick, Hanover, Kassel, Emden and Salzgitter. It is the parent enterprise of all other Volkswagen group companies, which are owned either completely or via majority stake.

The concern's car business is subdivided into two brand groups: Audi (Audi, Seat, Lamborghini) and Volkswagen (Volkswagen, Škoda, Bugatti, Bentley). The concern has created four areas of responsibility/regions for regional control: European Union, North America, South America/South Africa and Asia-Pacific.

The state still exerts direct influence in the enterprise. The German federal state of Lower Saxony was the largest single shareholder up until mid-2005 with an 18.2 per cent stake. It is stipulated that the state of Lower Saxony can always send two representatives to the supervisory board. And no other shareholder can – no matter how many shares they possess – exercise more than 20 per cent of the voting rights. As a result, it is possible perhaps the representatives of the state of Lower Saxony and the trade unions'/works councils' representatives always have the majority in the supervisory board – this is also called the 'VW system'. It remains to be seen whether this will change, especially since Porsche became – effective October 2005 – the largest single shareholder with the acquisition of 18.5 per cent of the ordinary shares (status 8 October 2005).

In 2003, the Volkswagen Group employed 335,000 people worldwide, of which the majority (174,000 = 52 per cent) were in Germany.

Volkswagen produces at several respective sites in all three CEE countries in our study.

In Slovakia, Volkswagen acquired the majority stakes in the incorporated firm (joint-stock company) *Bratislavské automobobilove závody* (BAZ) in 1991. The joint venture was reorganized into VW Slovakia in 1999. Volkswagen has invested 1.175 billion euro here since 1991. Formally a Brownfield investment, the production site was virtually newly constructed from the ground up, so the acquisition actually has to be regarded as a Greenfield investment. On 31 December 2003, 8,566 employees worked at two sites (Bratislava and Martin). VW Slovakia produces the Passat, Golf, Polo, Bora, as well as transmissions and components for VW, Audi, Seat, but also for Porsche and British Leyland. The output of cars increased from 2,952 in 1993 to more than 281,000 in 2003. Ninety-nine per cent of the production is exported. VW Slovakia is the most important Slovakian exporter as a result.

In the Czech Republic, Volkswagen acquired – with the support of the Czech trade union – in 1990 the historic and famous Škoda firm in Mladá Boleslav with the support of the Czech trade union. The firm was established in 1885 and has produced cars since 1905. After 1989 the company sought strong foreign partners. Škoda Auto produces cars, engines and transmissions. In 2003, 437,554 cars were manufactured, of which a major portion were exported to a total of 58 countries. On 31 December 2003 a total of 21,506 people were employed with Škoda.

In Poland, Volkswagen Motor Polska in Polkowice Dolne produces engines for other VW works. Production started in 1999. The works is a Greenfield investment in a special economic zone which has fiscally facilitated investments. In 2004, the company produced 580,000 engines with 1,000 employees. The workforce is very young, with an average age of 28 years. A portion of the new recruits were trained in other European VW plants (of which most of them are in Germany) for three to six months, and then they passed on the acquired knowledge to colleagues. In the beginning, all key positions – including the 'shift master' – were staffed with German supervisors, who guaranteed a thorough training of the workforce in accordance with the concern's quality standards. On 31 December 2003, 5,336 employees were counted for all of the investments situated in Poland (also including the works in Poznań).

Two motives played the main role with regard to the investment decisions for the benefit of Central and Eastern Europe: the opening up of new markets with the expectation of growing markets, and the lower wage level in comparison with Germany. The wages in the CEE concern's sites/companies are considerably above the respective national average.

The German consensus model of industrial relations is no reason for the German management to undertake relocations – 'quite the contrary'. The high level of qualification in the CEEC facilitated the decision. Regions which have a good infrastructure and universities are preferred.

Industrial Relations

The institutional system of codetermination is extensively developed in the German companies/sites. Representatives occupy half of the seats on the supervisory board.

The works councils of the sites' level elect Joint Works Council of Volkswagen AG, whose works is organized in numerous subcommittees. On the next higher level a Corporate Works Council exists on a voluntary basis for the overall Volkswagen Group (comprising Audi), in which the works councils of the domestic corporate group companies are represented.

The supra-company collective agreement (regional, sectoral) sommon in Germany's collective bargaining is not the legal regulatory framework in the VW concern, but rather the in-house wage agreement concluded with IG Metall. In the past, the culture of a cooperative conflict resolution has led to a series of collective agreements regarding prevention of collective (mass) dismissals and closures of companies/sites.

In the CEE companies in our study there is a *trade union* system of representatives. In all VW subsidiaries there are trade union representatives which conclude collective agreements. At the same time, they are the management's contact partner in all other matters of industrial relations.

At Škoda, the OS KOVO has 12,000 members, and with the pensioners and trade union members in the sites Vrchlabí and Kvasiny 19,500 altogether. In addition, there is a small independent trade union, which for the most part consists of young workforce members who do not want to pay any high union contributions. The overall rate of unionization amounts to about 60 per cent. Several older (concerning age) top managers are also traditionally organized in the trade union. As a consequence of an agreement concluded with VW, the representatives also represent the suppliers companies insofar as they are located on the Škoda grounds. At the moment there are eight of them, and their (trade union) chairmen are members of the Škoda trade union committee.

Collective bargaining take place on the company (Škoda) level. In addition, the management is provided with a special fund, of which the allocation has to be negotiated.

At VW Slovakia, the trade union organization is a member of the branch organization metal, The Czech Trade Union of Metal Workers (KOVO). The rate of unionization amounts to about 70 per cent. The collective bargaining on the shop/company level take place within the framework of the sectoral collective wage agreement (= skeleton wage agreement), which only stipulates sectoral minimum wages. As a rule, the collective wage agreements at VW Slovakia exceed this minimum agreement.

As a rare exception in Polish Greenfield investments there is a functioning trade union organization at Volkswagen Motor Polska/Polkowice Dolne and a high rate of unionization (75 per cent). The exclusive trade union is the (Solidarnosc 80), Trade Union Solidarity 80 (Poland) (NSZZ Solidarity). The trade union organization was established with the support of the works management a year after the start of production. Contacts between Polish and German representatives strongly influenced the establishment of the trade union organizations in the companies/sites. The present (in 2004) trade union chairman was engaged as a football player for eight years with the German national league club VfL Wolfsburg, came into contact with German trade unionists there and learned a great deal about German trade union work. The overall trade union management was trained with the support of the Friedrich Ebert

Foundation. The German Volkswagen corporate works council also provided support through information, training and organizational assistance. At the start of the VW investments the workforce behaved quite indifferently vis-à-vis the initiative for establishment of a trade union organization. The union membership development proceeded sluggishly up to the first organizational elections, and quickly grew thereafter to 75 per cent of the workforce. Every new member of the workforce is now approached during the hiring process by a responsible trade union official.

In the meantime, there have been numerous negotiations (24 between 1998 and 2003) between management and trade union representatives on topics such as inflationary adjustment, bonus payments, and distribution of working hours (incidentally, such topics are also belong to everyday business for German works councils). The main object of the negotiations was the management's demand for introduction of a more flexible shift system and as a countermove the guarantee of appropriate bonus payments.

The trade union also attends to social improvements on other fields, for instance the transport of employees to and from work or the taking out of insurances at favourable conditions. While doing so, the generated money is used to support sports or other leisure activities, and thus also to develop a collective union life outside of working hours.

At the start of the investments in the CEEC the VW concern sent quite a few German managers – for top management as well as for middle management – to the subsidiary enterprises. According to statements from the management, as a rule the top management also continues to be deployed from the headquarters. An exchange takes place in middle management after further qualification. However, the concern also tries to place local managers in top management. According to statements from CEE representatives, VW first of all selectively deployed German personnel managers to introduce cooperative industrial relations. At first the Wolfsburg managers had quite considerable difficulties in managing the CEE sites in an appropriate manner (which could also be respected by the workforce). The group executive board used these difficulties and conflicts as an opportunity to further develop the training of its international management. Those VW managers who come from the CEE sites subsequently adopted the cooperative VW philosophy with few exceptions.

The respondents from the CEE plants corroborate a far-reaching change of management through the joint venture with VW. At Škoda, 'the entry of foreign investors signified a total revolution after 42 years in a different system'. First of all, the executive board was renewed, and thereafter an economic committee was formed, to which all executive board members plus assistants and trade union representatives belong. A greater transparency of management decisions was introduced. In 2004, five executive board members originated from Germany – in 2005 the German HR manager was replaced by a Czech for being accused of bribery. The middle management is mainly recruited from the Škoda-internal junior staff.

There are differing statements concerning the degree of independence vis-à-vis the German headquarters. The surveyed executive board members say that the Škoda management largely makes its decisions independently. The trade union representative believes that the decisions are made in Wolfsburg.

In Poland, the relations between management and employees are described on both sides as good, honest and open. The communication is orientated towards pointing out problems and their solution. The management expressed misgivings that the trade union might possibly make wage demands in the future which could jeopardize the company's competitive position. From the management's point of view the key question is asked as to whether the trade union is willing to take on responsibility for the company's economic position. In addition to the institutional cooperation, there is a daily, less formal exchange. This is used by management for greater flexibility with regard to working hours and for achieving a dependable product quality. In the eyes of the workforce, the managers are first-class experts – a phenomenon that could be described as positive professional authority. The communication is facilitated through the fact that many employees speak German. The company offers language courses in which almost 200 works employees participate per semester.

The concern's close system of coordination with constant contact between the specialist departments suggests that the local management's leeway is relatively limited. The budget is predetermined for the CEE companies/sites by the Wolfsburg headquarters. At Škoda, any expenditure that exceeds the budget by one million Euro must be approved by the corporate group headquarters.

At VW Slovakia there is also a continuous development of management. If possible, management is recruited from in-house junior staff. Otherwise managers come from throughout the VW concern, not just from Germany.

The greatest change in the management culture is unanimously perceived by all CEE representatives in the introduction of more open forms of dialogue between management and employees. It includes sufficient information and consultation on various levels.

The German management also perceives strong changes in the attitude of CEE trade unionists:

> The representatives from the CEEC first had to learn targeted conflict management.

This also applied to the means of strike. One example is an industrial dispute on wages at Škoda that – after a successful warning strike – led to a wage settlement. It is important that employees underwent such limited conflict experiences.

The concern pursues an internal competition among the sites with regular comparison of the results ('benchmarking'). The personnel managers from all Volkswagen group companies worldwide meet once a year, whereas the personnel managers of the European sites have an additionally meeting per year.

In the German companies/sites of Volkswagen, the works councils are already integrated in plans *before* the final decisions. Regular planning rounds, under inclusion of the Corporate Works Council, take place. According to unanimous statements from representatives and personnel management, the co-management in the parent concern is also considered as a guideline for industrial relations in the CEE subsidiaries. Company/shop collective agreements are concluded with the responsible trade union in the CEE plants. Just like in the German parent enterprise, frequent regular meetings of the representatives (in the case of CEE companies, the trade union representatives) with the personnel management take place. Just like in the parent concern, the work is organized in technical committees (for example for wage matters, working hours, occupational health and safety). Once a year, there is a meeting amongst all trade union representatives and the management. No VW site exists without representatives or being covered by collective bargaining.

Volkswagen tries to implement the parent concern's standards in the foreign subsidiary enterprises. This applies first and foremost to the technology, but then also to the industrial relations. The basic philosophy laid down in the company's corporate guidelines is to be implemented universally. The declaration on social rights, which – in accordance with the ILO standards – defines minimum standards, is valid in all VW works worldwide. Within this framework VW takes into account the respective national culture of the industrial relations and allows the subsidiaries creative possibilities. The cooperative relations between management and representatives in the German company have been largely transferred to the CEE companies/sites. Differences amongst the CEE companies/sites result from the different tradition. At Škoda, a distinct corporate culture existed before the acquisition through VW. Entire generations have worked in this company. According to the opinion of the Czech respondents, Škoda and VW reciprocally influence each other. In the Slovakian company the influence of the VW culture is more direct on account of the weak tradition of the works, just like in the Greenfield investment Volkswagen Motor Polska.

Institutional forms for information and consultation between management and representatives have been introduced in all CEE companies, according to the parent concern's model. The most important body at Škoda is the economic committee. It meets once or twice a month. In addition, there are joint committees (management plus representatives) for occupational health and safety, social matters, personnel and work organization. At VW Slovakia and Volkswagen Motor Polska, trade union representatives also take part in meetings with the management. There are regular meetings with responsible staff representatives as well as frequent contact between the meetings. Here there are also mixed committees for occupational health and safety, social matters and canteen provision.

The relations with the management are described by the CEE trade union representatives as open and characterized by reciprocal fairness. The management at VW Slovakia sees the trade unions as a constructive social partner. Communication takes place not only at common meetings, but also occurs through frequent discussions, the exchange of e-mails, and so on. According to our information, there have been no major disputes to date between management and trade unions at VW Slovakia.

There have been several industrial disputes (including strikes) at the Czech Škoda works in the past years. But all actions were for a limited period. In the opinion of the Czech interview partners, the conflicts were not very far-reaching. Until now, all could be resolved through negotiations.

The VW suppliers in Central and Eastern Europe, in which the CEE trade unions have difficulties in organizing the employees, represent a problem. In start-ups the management attempts – under exclusion of the trade unions – to form its own contact partners in the workforce. The VW AG's representatives in Germany takes countermeasures against this exclusion and thus advocates 'supplier parks' – a regional employment policy which has been developed in Wolfsburg. It provides that more VW suppliers are located.

Employee and personnel representatives from the Wolfsburg headquarters intervene if there are locally irresolvable conflicts between management and representatives. On the other hand, the parent enterprise's works council also exerts a moderating influence in the sense of cooperative conflict resolutions in the relationship with the foreign representatives.

There has been a European Works Council since August 1990. The impetus for its formation came from two directions:

1. From the experiences with international trade union work in the subsidiary enterprises in Brazil, Belgium and South Africa, in which trade union support work was provided in the 1960s and 1970s,
2. From the possibility of direct parallel production to German production sites after the acquisition of SEAT Spain.

In 2004, the EWC comprised 25 members. To keep the size of the EWC in a manageable framework, two additional committees have been established – one for Audi and one for the VW service enterprises. The speakers of both committees are members of the EWC. The EWC steering committee consists of 11 members. The president and general secretary come from Germany. The entire executive board of the VW AG and the personnel managers of all subsidiary enterprises participate in the EWC annual plenary sessions. The Volkswagen EWC is closely interlocked with other German codetermination institutions. There are no extraordinary EWC meetings. Current problems are handled in a continuous process of communication between management and representatives.

VW was also a pioneer in the formation of a 'World Works Council' (WWC) in 1998. EWC and WWC hold joint sessions; the entire plenum meets once a year, whereas once, only the presidium meets. A staff comprised of three members is available to the corporate works council in Wolfsburg for international relations.

Representatives from the CEEC were admitted to the EWC with full rights immediately after the CEE involvement by Volkswagen. In 2004, Škoda had two members in the EWC, and one of them is also a member of the WWC. The trade union chairman from Škoda is a member in the presidium of both bodies. The trade union chairman from Volkswagen Slovakia is also a member of both representative bodies. The trade union chairman of the Polish Volkswagen Motor works only has an observer status, since the regular Polish EWC seat is assumed by a trade union representative from the works in Poznań – without this being perceived as discriminatory.

The participation in the EWC or the WWC is considered by the CEE trade unions to be very useful for obtaining a broadened view of the concern's overall situation and its strategy. There are differing opinions as to what extent the obtained information can acquire practical significance. The Slovakian trade union representative thinks that such information could also be useful in negotiations with the local management. On the other hand, the Škoda representative thinks that it could not be of much use in the collective bargaining in the Czech Republic: every representatives body in the different countries defends their own interests, their own workplaces.

Even outside of EWC and WWC sessions there are developed connections between representatives in Germany and the CEE companies.

There is a reserved appraisal regarding the new (legal) institution of the works councils in the Czech Republic and Slovakia among the CEE respondents. Originally, the management from VW Bratislava examined the possibility to introduce a works council according to the German model. But since the Slovakian labour law did not allow works councils simultaneously, the management decided to support the establishment of trade union representatives. Based on the previous experiences, the management as well as the trade union representatives at VW Slovakia consider works councils in the company to be superfluous.

The trade unions work quite well with us (management representative).

On the other hand, the Czech and Slovakian trade unionists perceived the works councils in enterprises in which there are no trade unions as useful. Škoda suppliers in which the management resisted the establishment of trade union representatives are mentioned as an example. The election of works councils is the only chance for creation of a representatives body for these workforces. On the other hand, wherever trade union organizations exist the establishment of works councils would only undermine the position and the activity of the trade unions.

Summary
Volkswagen has a highly cooperative culture of industrial relations and transfers this to the CEE subsidiary enterprises. In fact, the representatives in the CEE subsidiary enterprises also assume the role of co-managers. But insofar as rights of codetermination and institutional representational bodies are concerned, the relations between management and representatives depend on the respective national legislation. Nevertheless, relations going beyond this are developed, for example regular local exchange between representatives and personnel management, as well as the organization of ongoing work in committees. The German model of industrial relations with its pressure and simultaneous offer regarding reaching a consensus is considered as a guideline in this connection.

In the corporate culture there are certain differences among the subsidiary enterprises in the various CEEC.

Škoda Auto belongs to the 'family silver' among the Czech enterprises. Due to its longstanding tradition and a distinct corporate identity it was necessary to establish a connection between the traditional system of industrial relations at Škoda and the influence of the parent enterprise. In the beginning 1991 this process did not proceed without difficulties and mistakes. For instance, immediately after the acquisition of Škoda through the VW group, the then (German) chairman of VW Škoda offered to provide the Škoda representatives a gratis 'tandem' from Wolfsburg for learning the specific VW working culture. The trade union representatives at that time rejected this offer, and thus displayed an identity that is necessary – especially in times of upheaval and uncertainty –to participate themselves in the arrangement of new structures, and not to place one's own fate entirely in foreign hands.

In the meantime, the industrial relations of the parent enterprise have prevailed at Škoda even without the 'tandem method' – that is under active involvement of the (Czech) trade union representatives. The Rhine-Alpine model of capitalism is highly appraised by both sides.

At VW Bratislava the corporate culture is more strongly influenced by the German parent enterprise. The workforce sees VW Slovakia as a German enterprise. However, the management endeavours to combine Volkswagen's corporate knowledge and culture with the indigenous culture, experiences and the creativity of the local employees. Although the Anglo-Saxon model also has quite a few merits in the opinion of the Slovakian VW management, it prefers the Rhine-Alpine model because it is based on a greater participation by the employees.

Volkswagen's unique role with regard to industrial relations in the CEEC is particularly evident in the case of Volkswagen Motor Polska/Polkowice Dolne. The formation of a trade union organization has been actively supported in this works by German trade unionists and works councils as well as by the management. Based on their previous experiences, the Polish trade unionists prefer the German model of industrial relations, which in their eyes leads to a greater identification of the employees with the enterprise. They describe this model as 'capitalism with humane countenance'. Up to now the cooperative model from VW has been able to prevent serious conflicts, although there was a momentary lack of orders/shortage of employment. It was bridged in accordance with the Wolfsburg model by means of an agreement on unpaid free days.

The model of cooperative industrial relations has prevailed in all three CEE subsidiary enterprises. Up to now this form of industrial relations seems to function without greater points of friction (even after initial difficulties at Škoda); although – differently than in the German parent enterprise – there is no dual system of representatives. The management maintains the same close relations (based on information, consultation and dialogue) with the trade union representatives on the site/company level as the management in Germany maintains with the works council. De facto the trade union representatives on the site/company levels at the *Czech*, *Slovakian* and *Polish* VW sites assume a role similar to that of the works councils in the *German* VW sites. At the same time there is a regular exchange in various committees. This model transfer is supported through the cooperation in the EWC, WWC and frequent bilateral contacts among the (different forms) of representatives.

Robert Bosch GmbH – Problems With Conflict-Orientated Trade Union Representatives

The Enterprise

Founded in 1886 by Robert Bosch in Stuttgart as a 'workshop for precision mechanics and electrical engineering', today the Bosch Group – measured in terms of turnover (2003: 36.4 billion euro) – is among the largest industrial enterprises in Germany. The company is distinguished through its corporate law constitution (stipulated in the company founder's last will and testament) in the form of an industrial foundation. The Robert Bosch Foundation possesses 92 per cent of the share capital in the Robert Bosch GmbH. The foundation uses its dividends accrued from the proceeds for charitable tasks. About 580 million euro has been provided for charitable purposes by the end of 2002.

Bosch is active in the following business fields: automotive technology, industrial technology, consumer goods and building technology. The company places a strong focus on research and development. In 2003, 2.7 billion euro were spent for this purpose (in comparison: investments in tangible (fixed) assets amounted to approx. 2 billion EURO). Bosch is considered as the second largest applicant (2,748 patent applications in 2003) with the German and the third largest applicant with the European Patent Office.

At the end of the nineteenth century the company became involved abroad. Today the company is internationally aligned. Of the total of 232,000 employees (beginning of 2004), more than half (123,000) work abroad. Bosch is represented in more than 50 countries with its 258 subsidiaries and holding companies. Of the 249 sites, 185 are located outside of Germany. In addition to Central and Eastern Europe, growth opportunities are seen above all in China and other Asian countries as well as in the NAFTA region.

The driving motive for direct investments is the presence on local markets. As an automotive supplier the company has to produce in the proximity of the most important customers. But the low labour cost level also plays an important role in other business sectors (for example household appliances). According to management statements, tax concessions are 'taken advantage of', but are not a driving motive. The existence of qualified local human resources has a considerable influence on the choice of location. At the same time, the increasing competition among companies for qualified human resources leads to the fact that Bosch went into the Czech Republic, Poland and Hungary, and here deliberately not in booming regions, because there were no longer enough highly qualified human resources there. This investment policy counteracts a gap of development in various regions. The management emphasizes the surprisingly fast learning process in the CEE subsidiaries. Up to now the highly complicated start-ups of new productions were only carried out in Germany. Works in Hungary and the Czech Republic took over this control unit function for the first time in 2004.

Brownfield as well as Greenfield investments have been transacted in the CEEC. But Greenfield investments are always targeted to be able to build up the production and select employees according to the company's own visions.

The working conditions in the CEE subsidiaries do not show any essential differences with those in comparable companies in the respective regions. But the total income – for instance, in Jihlava, the Czech Republic – among the wage earners lies about 15 per cent above the other firms in the region (mainly domestic companies).

The wages in the Polish Mirkow (near Wrocław (Silesia)) are higher than in the comparable regional average, even if the workforce expects higher wages than the local Bosch management is willing to pay.

Bosch was already active in the Czech Republic (then part of the Austro-Hungarian Empire) at the end of the nineteenth century. In 1920, the company opened up a business in Prague. The 44 years of interrupted relations were resumed in 1989. In 2004, Bosch employed approximately 8,500 people in three Czech branch establishments. Bosch Diesel in Jihlava (approx. 6,000 employees) is the largest business among them. The company was established in 1993 as a joint venture between the Robert Bosch GmbH and engineering works *Motorpal*. Bosch acquired all shareholder stakes in 1996. Formally, this concerns a Brownfield company, but in reality the company has developed like a Greenfield investment. Bosch took over only one production hall under construction and only a portion of the qualified workers. From 1992 to 1996 it was fruitlessly attempted to instal a trade union organization. This only succeeded in April 2002 with the help of KOVO. As a result, the overall influence of traditional structures on the new company was marginal. The wages lie above the regional average, but are considerably lower than in the Bosch works at České Budějovice.

In Poland, 1,370 workers were employed at various sites in 2004. We are particularly interested in the Henkel Bosch Uklady Hamlcowe (Henkel Bosch Braking Systems) at Mirkow, which in 2004 had 560 employees, achieved a turnover of 60 million euro and manufactured 10 million auto brake components for the overall European market. Formerly a part of the state concern in Twardigóra, Bosch built a completely new factory in Mirkow and took the entire machinery there – including the (highly qualified) workforce – in 2003. From that point of view this factory is not a typical Greenfield investment. High-ranking guests from the realm of politics and the church came to the inauguration of the establishment.

Industrial Relations

In addition to the corporate and joint works councils in the German parent company/ sites, there has been a European Works Council since 1998; according to information provided by employees, this was long struggled for. At the request of the corporate management it is called the 'Europa Committee' (EC), because the management did not want any expansion of the 'works council' institution beyond the German borders. But de facto the EC has considerable latitude. The German Joint Works Council chairman presides. The EC is dominated by German members. But they are making an effort to form a partnership on an equal basis with the representatives of the other countries. For instance, the Germans gave up a few EWC seats in favour of France and Spain to relinquish a mandate to each of the competing trade union federations there and thus to end the conflicts between the rival trade unions. Italy has developed a rotation system for representation of the various trade unions. The personnel managers from the subsidiary enterprises also take part in the plenary sessions. The EC's steering committee plays an important role. It meets four times a year and the corporate management informs the steering committee in the event of supranational decisions. On a given occasion the steering committee invites representatives from various sites from different countries to hearings, among them also non-EC members. The EC sessions are working sessions. The semblance of tourism junkets are to be deliberately avoided. The EC also undertakes visits to the different production areas; this includes subsequent discussion with works councils/ trade union representatives from the corresponding site. The still large rift between the EWC institution and the respective representatives in different countries is supposed to be somewhat alleviated as a result.

A one-day, internal preparatory session of the representatives is held before every EC session. Trade union representatives other than those trade unions represented in the EC can also participate at their own expense in this session. The representatives criticize that information from the management is often not passed on in a timely manner. When Bosch acquired the Mannesmann Rexroth AG (a specialist in drive technology, control and automatic control engineering with subsidiary companies in 36 countries) in 2001, the actual decision was not discussed in the EC. But according to management statements, the EC was included in the consequences of this decision for the employees. Until now, the German representatives have more influence on decisions in the supervisory board of the German parent enterprise than through the EC.

Management as well as representatives grants the Europa Committee a role as a mediation authority. According to the management, the representatives turn to the Europa Committee with local conflicts. This then endeavours towards a conflict resolution together with the corporate management.

The Europa Committee strengthens the position of the local representatives, since the latter have access to corporate management as a result. The German works council representative recognizes approaches of a European consciousness in the Europa Committee, which are said to be more strongly pronounced among the French and Spaniards than among the Germans though. The non-German representatives in the EC receive additional information which they do not obtain via other channels, and thus strengthen their prestige. The German representatives also profit from the EC, but very few German works councils take into account the Bosch sites outside of Germany in their strategies. There is also hardly any return provision of the information from the Europa Committee to the workforces in the German sites. The German corporate management sees the main advantage of the EC in the fact that it gets to know the views of representatives from other countries. It receives important informal information which will be included in forthcoming decisions.

There are connections between the representatives in Germany and those in the CEEC via the Europa Committee. But they are not very intensively characterized yet. According to the employees, there are problems with the representational structures in the CEE sites.

There has been contact with KOVO in the Czech Republic for quite some time. However, before 1 May 2004 the Jihlava works was not represented in the Europa Committee, whereas a representative from České Budějovice with guest status took part in the plenary sessions. But after that date there are two official representatives in the Bosch EC: one comes from Jihlava, the other from České Budějovice. Both representatives see the EC not only as an information body, but also at the same time as a lever for the solution of serious problems. The membership in the EC has also substantially improved the standing of both Czech representatives in their homeland enterprises.

The German corporate works council had no connection whatsoever with the Polish representatives before 1 May 2004. A Polish representative elected by the workforce from the enterprise in Mirkow participated in the EC's plenary session for the first time on 22 February 2005. But after that date quarrels came about between the Polish plant management and the EC representative (who worked as an assembly line manager), which were not founded in his representational function. This representative resigned after that. Now the plant committee is seeking a new representative, who has the trust of the trade unions and is also linguistically competent – a virtually impossible undertaking (status: June 2005).

In the opinion of the German interviewees, there is a mixture of several elements in the arrangement of industrial relations in the CEE subsidiaries. In economical/ technical terms, the company brings along its standards. Bosch transfers many principles in the corporate culture, but also adopts many local elements. The local rules are applied in the industrial relations (pay scales, provisions of the labour statute book, and so on).

The personnel policy principles (Bosch Human Resources System) apply to all subsidiaries. In the first phase of investments managers from Germany manage the subsidiary enterprises. They are successively replaced by managers from the respective host country of the investments. The corporate group management perceives a large scope for the local management if the defined performance objective is achieved. The coordination takes place at regular meetings of the division mangers with the plant managers and through monthly reports. However, the employee side thinks that the subsidiaries are led on short reins as a result of the staffing of top positions with German managers. With regard to claim the concern attempts to implement uniform guidelines, for example to quality and the environment. A document called 'principles of social responsibility at Bosch' was completed by the Europa Committee together with the International Metal Trade Union Federation in March 2004. It was worked into the 'Management System Manual for Quality, Environment and Safety'.

According to statements by the Czech trade union representatives in Jihlava, the German enterprise attempts to introduce in an authoritarian way German models of 'corporate identity'. Technical standards and management forms were rigorously transferred:

> What has functioned in Germany will be utilised here – without consideration of the Czech mentality.

In the opinion of the trade unionist, the causes for the frictions between management and representatives lie in the fact that a high number of expatriates – especially Germans – are represented in the local management. The problem was intensified through lack of communication. On the other hand, the trade union representatives emphasize the company's standing in the region, which also supports the reputation of the employees.

At Mirkow (Poland), there are three trade unions (Solidarity and OPZZ are equally strong, whereas the trade union of engineers and technicians only has 20 members), and the trade union density is about 55 per cent. All three trade unions work together in a joint trade union representatives' body. The relationship with management is split: the plant manager takes part in workforce gatherings, but discusses nothing there. He delegates the contacts with the trade unions to the line managers. In the opinion of the trade unions, the points at issue are wages that are too low, and which do not keep up with increased productivity and profits.

On account of its corporate law structure, the German corporate group management does not see the enterprise as driven by 'shareholder value' like other companies. Even with zero growth immediate personnel reduction was not a reaction. The policies vis-à-vis the employees are rather consensus-orientated. The CEE subsidiaries followed this basic alignment, but adapted to the respective national circumstances.

The German corporate works council emphasize the value of a consistent, but solution-orientated representation of interests. If necessary, actions are organized for this purpose, for example during the conflict at the German works in Leinfelden: the management demanded – under threat of relocation – an extension of working hours without pay compensation. Massive dismissals were able to be avoided through an agreement, but at the price of wage concession.

The example of the works in Jihlava in the Czech Republic illustrates the problems of establishing these kinds of representatives in the Bosch CEE sites. There were vehement disputes during the attempt by employees to hold an assembly for establishment of representatives. IG Metall and the chairman of the German corporate works council intervened locally. The establishment of a trade union organization first came about in April 2002. According to information from a German interview partner, the plant manager at Jihlava in the Czech Republic was proud that there were no trade unions in his works. The union work was compounded by the fact that the production takes place in three different workshops. Trade union rifts also occurred: after a bitter interunion dispute (the opposition accused the union management of being too compliant vis-à-vis the management), the opposition took over the ZO OS KOVO. The deposed union management subsequently initiated the formation of a new, independent trade union (UNIOS) in June 2004. Both trade unions are involved in the collective bargaining in the Czech subsidiary. The rate of unionization is weak overall: of the 4,700 members of the workforce, only 400 are organized in the ZO OS KOVO union and 30–40 in UNIOS. On top of that is the fact that in April 2005 a new union group has again split away from the ZO OS KOVO; but this union group remains in the central KOVO trade union federation and is also recognized by KOVO. The reason for this secession was the reproach of the new group to the (new) old group of not acting radical enough vis-à-vis the management. All three trade unions do not cooperate with each other, which is convenient for the management during collective bargaining, and has already had an impact in 2004 in terms of the wage level to the disadvantage of the workforce.

According to information from the Czech trade union representatives, the relations between management and trade union organization are further strained. They complain that there are no regular contacts and the information through the management is deficient. After intervention by OS KOVO in Prague and the Czech Ministry of Industry in 2003, the management promised to hold bi-monthly information meetings with the trade union representatives. But half a year later nothing has been done yet. No management representative took part in Jihlava's trade union conference in May 2004. There was a dispute between the management and the representatives regarding redistribution of the weekly working hours: instead of the previous 12 hours per day, the management wanted the workforce to work eight hours per day (maintaining the *weekly* working time). For the employees this meant working on more days per week and thus more driving time and costs.

The industrial relations at Mirkow (Poland) were also strained in 2005. The aforementioned reason is the differing views on the wage levels. The management accused older employees of applying behavioural patterns from the past (dawdling), which do not fit in a market economy. On the other hand, particularly younger employees more frequently quitted their job on account of the marginal wages and difficult promotion prospects.

These strained relations between management and trade union representatives do not have to be typical for all CEE Bosch subsidiaries. The relations between management and employees at the Bosch subsidiary in České Budějovice, the Czech Republic are obviously better (of the approximately 2,200 employees, approx. 600 are trade union members). The Czech trade union representatives attribute this to the fact that the personnel manager there is a Czech. From the very beginning the representatives were member of KOVO. But these representatives have only minimal rights, for example no guaranteed paid leave.

The trade union organization is recognized by the management at the Polish Bosch works. Many managerial employees are organized in the trade union organization (Solidarity) there. This composition obviously influences the policy of the trade union representatives in the direction of greater identification with the management.

Summary

The industrial relations in the CEE subsidiaries are considerably influenced through the concern's corporate culture. In the opinion of the corporate management it is more consensus-orientated. The company's corporate legal structure plays a role in this connection, since it permits not having to be rigidly riveted to the stock exchange quotation, but enables long-term strategies. The German works councils also set their hopes on consensual industrial relations in the CEEC, but fear that the trend is proceeding in a different direction. The company allows only the extent of codetermination in the CEE plants which is legally prescribed. The examples of the Czech establishment in Jihlava and at Mirkow in Poland demonstrate that the concern does not automatically transfer its consensus-orientated corporate culture to the industrial relations in the CEE countries. Although these were Brownfield investments at the commencement of the investment, not much was adopted from the old structures in the new enterprise (in Poland the entire plant was even relocated). That is why the works are de facto rather Greenfield investments. The union representatives in the Czech works at Jihlava suffer from its late establishment and the split into three organizations. The problems related to developing a solution and cooperation-orientated culture of industrial relations are attributed by the representatives to national mentality differences. But it is to be assumed that the management is not interested in conflict-orientated representatives, but also suffers under the rivalry between the meanwhile three unions existing within the company. From that point of view, the path towards a solution and cooperation-orientated form of industrial relations is made more difficult through the nascent trade union representatives, which have problems finding their way among conflict and cooperation. A similar situation also applies to the Polish works in Mirkow.

Bosch respects the national labour legislation. The trade union organization in the companies/sites, insofar it they exists, is a negotiation partner in the collective bargaining. But wherever a stable trade union organization is lacking there seems to be no discernible inspiration on the management side to support the build-up of a trade union organization.

If one includes the other Bosch subsidiaries, a mixture of the industrial relations between the parent enterprise and the former conditions in the CEE subsidiaries can be spoken of.

Siemens AG – Global Corporate Group with Decentralized Structure

The Enterprise

Werner von Siemens (1816–1892), together with Johann Georg Halske, laid the foundations for the subsequent worldwide Siemens Empire on 1 October 1847. Even in the incipient years the company was involved in foreign markets, first in England, and then also with extensive investments in Russia and Austria.

After the company had regained the firms in western foreign countries, which have been expropriated after the Second World War, as well as its patent and trademark rights, a stormy development of foreign business commenced after 1955. A milestone in the corporate history was the amalgamation of various Siemens firms into the Siemens AG in 1966. Currently, Siemens is represented in over 190 countries, and employed 417,000 colleagues worldwide at the end of the 2003 business year. Of those employees, 41 per cent (170,000) worked in Germany, and another 26 per cent worked in other European countries. Siemens is involved in a joint venture with Osram and other firms (BSH Bosch und Siemens Hausgeraete GmbH [household appliances], Fujitsu Siemens Computers (Holding) BV). More than half of the 74.2 billion euro turnover in the 2003 business year was achieved in Europe (of which 23 per cent was in Germany and 34 per cent in other European countries). The corporate activities are broken down into six different business sectors (information and communications, automation and control, medical, power, transportation, medical and lighting), which are respectively subjective to specific business sector managements.

Siemens is a company based on research and development and is also highly innovative. More than 50 per cent of the products are 'younger' than 3 years. Of the 417,000 employees, nearly 50,000 worked in the RTD sector in 2003. Seventy per cent of the employees have completed fully qualified vocational training, 34 per cent a university degree. The problems related to this strongly diversified and globally active concern, prompted the executive board to undertake a sweeping reorganization in the beginning of the 1990s with the objective of splitting up the large corporate units. The firm should thus be able to operate more successfully in an increasingly more complex global market. This is how the Siemens AG also retains its still currently valid *decentralized* corporate culture.

After 1990, Siemens invested to a great extent in the CEE countries. Particularly in the Czech Republic the company was able to re-establish old business contacts. In 2004, Siemens possessed a total of 25 companies here. Siemens is one of the largest employers in the country with approximately 11,000 employees (of which 10,000 are in production and 1,000 in service). According to unanimous statements from management and representatives, the interest in developing new markets and preempting competitors is predominant.

An avoidance of German codetermination did not constitute a motive for Siemens with regard to the investments in Central and Eastern Europe. Often, local firms were acquired (Brownfield investments), and the production was subsequently restructured or transferred to the newly erected factory halls. The solid level of education in the Czech Republic, Poland and parts of Slovakia played an especially important role for an RTD-based enterprise like Siemens. This expansion phase in the first half of the 1990s was followed by a period of intensified rationalization and adjustment of corporate holdings. One example is the Czech Company Osram Bruntál – a wholly-owned subsidiary of the Siemens subsidiary enterprise Osram GmbH (Munich). It produced chemical additives, among other things cobalt sulphate powder. After the acquisition through Osram in 2000 the pure chemicals production was sold to the Canadian firm MACCO in 2004. At the end of 2004, Osram Bruntál (with about 800 employees) produced – in addition to tungsten and tungsten carbide powder – coils for light bulbs, which cover 90 per cent of the requirement of the Osram enterprise as a whole.

In Slovakia Osram also acquired – with Tesla in Nové Zámky – an existing company in 1995 and subsequently expanded it (by 2003: a 630 per cent increase of turnover, 91 per cent export increase). In 2005, Osram had 1,000 employees in Nové Zámky and is the only light bulb producer in Slovakia.

Also in 2005, Siemens Polska had 10 establishments in Poland. The '*Energoserwis Lubliniec*' of special interest to us was acquired in 1995 from the firm *Monopol* and the American firm *Westinghouse Warszawa* (the latter holds the majority interest with 62.5 per cent). In turn, Siemens Polska possesses 72 per cent of Westinghouse Warszawa. Insofar as that is concerned, here we are dealing with American as well as German management influences.

In 2005, the 'Energoserwis Lubliniec' employed 530 workers, whose qualifications have to be rated as very high. The further self-confidence of the workforce is nourished by the fact that in December 1981 (that is after the imposition of martial law in Poland) the workforce protesting against the regime at that time was attacked by the Polish army. Three trade unionists and the director were arrested and sentenced to lengthy prison sentences.

In the Czech Republic and in Slovakia (less so in Poland) Siemens has – of course, within the framework of the respective national laws – an influence on the arrangement of the industrial relations through active membership in the respective national and regional employers' associations. But this does not signify the support of a dual system of employee representation.

In the technical sphere, the same norms as well as rationalization standards and environmental regulations apply in all Siemens companies worldwide.

There are also worldwide standards with regard to management and organization. The ISO Standard 9001 was also introduced in the CEE plants.

However, there can be organizational hybrids. In the realm of organization/ management, our German interview partner sees the Siemens management side as being on the path to a genuine world concern. While doing so, 'diversity' is said to be a guideline – that is the consideration of the diversity of religion, culture and gender at the sites and in the workforce. Siemens is convinced that the opportunities for creative solutions are bigger if problems are seen from different directions, even if the diversity would make the management tasks more difficult. One example is said to be the management system for occupational health and safety, the rules of which have been prepared in a project from an international team.

But in the case of the Polish Siemens subsidiary 'Energoserwis Lubliniec', 'diversity' also means that the production from 1995 to 2004 was guided by American managers, who also changed quite frequently.

Outlines of a new strategy could be recently seen to emerge in the overall concern; this was put into concrete terms in the 'Siemens Management System'. The German employee side was introduced to this strategy in March 2004 via the corporate group's economic committee in Munich. The representatives in Germany fear that its implementation could lead to a drastic personnel reduction in Germany. Siemens intends to optimize the global value added with this, that is to compile the entire range of activities as globally as possible and to place the activities as cost-effectively as possible. Not merely the production areas, but also the research and development are to be affected by this. The share of employees active in research and development (14 per cent) in Germany is still higher than in the foreign subsidiaries (9 per cent). The German works councils fear that if the new EU countries also use their cost advantage on the RTD-side and build up an excellent academic level by means of EU promotional funds, the pressure on the jobs in the research and development realm in Germany will increase enormously.

On the whole, a change of direction by the Siemens AG is discernible – even after the sale of the mobile phone division to the Taiwanese enterprise BenQ in June 2005: away from a corporate decentralization pursued until 2004 and relinquishment of consumer goods production (such as the mobile phone production) towards re-centralized, more streamlined structures. In October 2006 BenQ Germany declared bankruptcy and left the German public suspicious of Siemens' strategy.

A stronger orientation towards 'shareholder value' could already be seen to emerge in 1998 via a restructuring programme – with which, among other things, achievement bonuses were introduced for chief executives and the path towards listing on the was opened. This stronger orientation towards share value now poses considerable challenges with regard to the industrial relations in the parent concern ('erstwhile classic example for peaceful German corporate culture', *Der Spiegel*, 23/2004).

Industrial Relations

There is a complex system of employee representation in the parent enterprise: the employee side possesses half of the seats in the Siemens AG supervisory board. In addition to the works councils of the single sites, there is a Joint Works Council (JWC) (the works councils of the single Siemens AG sites are represented here), a Corporate Works Council (CWC) and a Siemens European Works Council (Siemens Europa Committee). The Joint Works Council is the most important negotiating partner for the corporate management in Germany. Its five member committee meets once a month with the personnel management board.

The Siemens Europa Committee (SEC) was established in 1996 even before the coming into effect of the EWC directive. Up until 1 May 2004 it had 36 members from 15 EU countries, plus Norway and Switzerland; since the accession of the CEE countries it comprises 39 members. Seven CEE representatives – one each from Poland, Slovakia, Slovenia, Hungary, Estonia and two from the Czech Republic – have been newly admitted. The entire SEC meets once a year, whereas the four member steering committee meets four times a year. In addition to the two German representatives, one Portuguese and one Austrian member are represented in the steering committee. In the event of major changes in the subsidiary companies, these are discussed with the respectively affected countries outside the plenary sessions. The lingua franca is German, with translations provided in Spanish, French and English. Due to the high number of employees in Germany an arrangement was reached, according to which a delegate was allocated to Germany for every accrued 20,000 employees, and one SEC member was allocated to the other countries for every accrued 6,000 employees.

All three bodies (both of the codetermination bodies in Germany and the SEC) have their own chairmen. And so there is no personal union. As a result, the independence of these bodies amongst each other is strengthened, but at the same time the need for coordination increases. To ensure the latter, there is nevertheless a personnel involvement between the chairmen of the Joint Works Council, Corporate Works Council and the Sec. The JWC chairman is at the same time a member in the SEC steering committee, the Corporate Works Council chairman is a member in the JWC steering committee as well as a member in the SEC, and the SEC chairman is at the same time a member in the JWC and CWC steering committees.

With the exception of one guest delegate from the Czech Republic, no members from the CEE countries were represented in the SEC up until 1 May 2004. The chairman of the SEC thinks that the annual separate meeting with representatives from these countries, where a representative of the corporate management gave a report, is more effective than a voluntary participation of CEE representatives in the SEC.

The weak contact with German representatives is a problem for the trade union representatives in the CEE Osram plants. The German works council also perceives this, but appraises the relations with trade union representatives in the CEEC as difficult on account of the different legal situation. That is why before 1 May 2004 there were bilateral contacts with trade unionists in Slovakia, the Czech Republic and Slovenia, but closer relations only existed with the works councils in Austria and Hungary, which have a system similar dual system of employee representation as in Germany.

The Osram subsidiary in the Czech Republic does not have a representative in the SEC. One gets by through an exchange of information with the SEC member from Osram Slovakia in Nové Zámky. The trade union chairman from Osram Slovakia anticipates improved information for the union activities in his company from the SEC, including the collective bargaining. A farer-reaching European understanding on the part of the SEC is not to be anticipated on account of the brief membership.

The workforce from the Polish Siemens subsidiary 'Energoserwis Lubliniec' (there is no union plant committee here) knows absolutely nothing about the existence of the SEC. They have no contact with the Polish representative in the SEC who comes from another site. However, the Polish trade union activists at 'Energoserwis Lubliniec' also do not know any union-friendly employees who can speak German or English and could come into question as a delegate. Insofar as that is concerned, there are no countable activities whatsoever in this direction.

In the opinion of the German CWC chairman, SEC's sphere of activity is limited. He appraises the SEC's role in the mediation between parent enterprise and CEE subsidiaries rather sceptically.

On the other hand, the German corporate management praises the SEC as a forum for a transfer of the Siemens discussion culture to other countries. The open dialogue and the contentious culture are a completely new development for some representatives from other countries.

The respective national regulations as well as the ILO standards are heeded with regard to industrial relations. According to the German management representative, the arrangement of industrial relations comes under the purview of local management. As a rule, the German headquarters does not intervene unless complaints about misconduct on the part of local management come about. But Siemens exports its dialogue-orientated discussion culture.

The representatives corroborate this statement. But wherever there are no representatives on site/company level, such as is the majority case in Poland, management also undertakes nothing to initiate such representation bodies.

Out of the 10 Polish Siemens sites, in only two sites trade union representatives are existing. But at the same time it is to be noted that these 'exceptional sites' are joint ventures with two other German enterprises (Siemens has a 50 per cent stake in '*Volkswagen Elektrosytemy*' in Gorzów Wielkopolski; Bosch has the other 50 per cent at 'Lodz Siemens'). In the subsidiary 'Energoserwis Lubliniec' which is of special interest to us (in which the interviews have also been conducted), neither the Siemens corporate management nor the Siemens national company in Poland has attended to industrial relations. This has been left up to the local Polish managers, who – under the aegis of the Americans – have restructured the plant since 1995 (from 1,250 employees to 550 in 2005), pay much higher wages than the regional average, and govern the industrial relations in a manner that does not lead to open conflicts.

About 55 per cent of the employees at 'Energoserwis Lubliniec' are trade union members, but are distributed amongst different trade unions: Solidarity, OPZZ and a technicians' trade union hardly work together. Solidarity has its base in the blue collar worker realm, whereas both of the other unions are strongly represented in the technical and commercial realm. From that point of view there are also hardly any promising approaches for the formation of collective representation of employees.

In the Czech Republic, trade union organizations exist in all Siemens subsidiaries. The organizational degree of trade unions fluctuates substantially amongst the single sites in the CEEC: in 2004, 70 per cent were unionized at the Osram sites in Slovakia, whereas only 21.5 per cent of the workforce of the Czech Osram enterprises were unionized.

In the Czech Osram enterprise the employees are represented by an independent trade union – which is a member of the Association of Independent Trade Unions (ASO). The trade union chairman at the site is not released for his union work. The weak trade union organization is not able to finance a release trade union official. Collective wage agreements are concluded on the site/company level for two years and additional negotiations concerning wages take place annually. Siemens prefers this level for collective bargaining, since collective wage agreements on the branch level in the Czech Republic are too inflexible in the opinion of the management.

Collective bargaining also take place on the site/company level in the Slovakian Osram enterprises, but are influenced through the orientation towards the sectoral collective wage agreement concluded with KOVO for the metal and electrical industry.

Insofar as the recruitment of management in the CEE Siemens subsidiaries is concerned, the top management – but at any rate the executive position – is locally staffed as much as possible. However, as an essential controlling position, the management of the commercial department is frequently held by a German or another West European manager, and a German also has a seat in the supervisory board of the respective subsidiary enterprise. Geographical and production variety necessitate a quite decentralized, 'quasi federalistic' structure. But there is an 'undulation' between decentralization and control. Globalization strengthens the trends towards stronger control; however, this is not nearly as strong as in US-managed companies (for example at General Electric). For several years there have been generally valid management guidelines, for example for staff development, treatment of national, ethnic, cultural or gender diversity in the company or regarding occupational health and safety.

The German works councils appraise the latitude of the local management vis-à-vis the headquarters as relatively marginal. The single companies and sites have been managed by agreements on targets and managerial negotiations. The corporate executive board provides the divisions with profit margins, which depending on the division amount to between 4 to 11 per cent of the turnover. Of course, Siemens (with over 300 sectors active in) may look like a Moloch from the outside, but is said to be quite precisely controllable due to the minuteness of the sectors. Uniform role models would have a major influence. The information channels on the management level are said to be optimal.

However, in contradiction to the perception of German representatives, the CEE interview partners from the Osram subsidiary enterprises think that the respective local management has considerable latitude within the strategic objectives of the parent enterprise. The Czech representatives emphasize that it is possible to discuss the predetermined objectives and to influence them in certain respects. In light of the concern's strongly diversified structure, this viewpoint corresponds more with reality than the perception that the subsidiary enterprises are led by a short rein.

The autonomy of the Polish managers at 'Energoserwis Lubliniec' vis-à-vis the parent enterprise (which in turn is dominated by Germans as well as Americans) is quite considerable in matters of human resource management, whereas the direct Siemens influence is enormous with regard to utilization of technology, and so on.

The relations between representatives and management in Germany are described as positive. Conflicts are settled openly. Plans regarding investments were announced in an early stage. During the conflict concerning the planned relocation of production from the German sites Bocholt and Kamp-Lintfort in the spring of 2004, the works council was informed in good time. After workforce actions through the intervention of IG Metall, an agreement came about under the application of a supplementary collective agreement, which secured the continuation of the production. However, the employees had to accept the reintroduction of the 40-hour week (without pay compensation) and the relinquishment of a portion of the 13th monthly income. But the works council in Germany regards the new global Siemens strategy as much more fundamental. In collaboration with IG Metall, the Corporate and Joint Works Council developed a position paper against this corporate strategy; the core points of which were presented in June 2004 by means of nationwide campaigns at the German Siemens sites. These campaigns have marred the relations with the management side. As a result of this dispute, an agreement for safeguarding and development of employment, competitivity and innovation was signed; the core points define the objective of safeguarding existing jobs at sites in Germany and creating new jobs under competitive conditions. If necessary, supplementary collective bargaining solutions are to be finalized by supra-company regional collective agreements.

In principle, the company is attempting to introduce the same standards in the CEEC with regard to personnel policy. But the national laws are said to be very different, for instance in relation to working time regulations. Siemens abides by the national laws.

In the CEE subsidiaries (with the exception of Poland), the relations between management and trade union representatives as well as in the German parent concern are described as good to very good, despite the emergent disagreements. Regular exchange of information and joint sessions take place regularly in various committees. The responsible HR manager in the Czech Osram enterprises meets once or twice with the trade union representatives. At Osram Slovakia the good relations with the social partners also extend to the middle management level. Mutual trust and long-term personal relations create the basis for effective cooperation. Slovakian management representatives emphasize that the relations with the trade unionists are very important for the system of co-management that is being introduced in the enterprise.

The industrial relations are characterized by uncertainty at 'Energoserwis Lubliniec' in Poland. Despite the offer of additional payments, the overtime demanded by the management is only reluctantly executed by the workforce. Here lies one of the largest fields of conflict between management and workforce, which is at the same time characteristic for the interest situations – less politically motivated (for example lacking representatives) and aimed more at concrete working conditions. These differences of interest are resolved by the Polish personnel management with HRM strategies – that is without *collective* representatives body, but with the declared volition of the management not to start a 'war' with the workforce.

Due to lack of knowledge, the German interviewees cannot make any statements regarding the new forms of representatives ('Works Councils') in the Czech Republic and Slovakia. Our respondent from the German management does not consider the Czech arrangement – according to which existing works councils would have to be dissolved during formation of a trade union organization – to be fortunate. In traditional industrial enterprises there would probably be more arrangements along the lines of trade union organizations. But in high-tech enterprises the management would not even promote any works council establishments whatsoever, in order not to provoke union activities as a result of their election. However, Siemens has no influence on the labour legislation. The parent company is not of the opinion that it should export its models to host countries of its investment. Separate industrial relations are said to have emerged in every country. Even the German trade unions are only able to exert a limited influence in this context.

In the Czech Republic, the perceptions of management and trade unions are diametrically opposed with regard to the works councils. The management perceptively regards the institution of works councils as more appropriate, since they would possess a greater legitimacy because of the election through the entire workforce, whereas the trade union members represent only a minority (in the case of Osram, one-fifth of the workforce). On the other hand, the Czech trade unionists regard works councils as useless, since the latter are not allowed to manage any collective bargaining. They rather perceive the works councils as a management tool.

Summary

Several path dependencies define the industrial relations in the Siemens CEE enterprises:

- They are established in their specific configuration through the respective national paths of the host countries of the investment. Siemens complies with the national regulations, and in the case of the CEEC it also plays a part in its practical implementation through collaboration in employers' organizations. A model transfer of German industrial relations is expressly rejected by the corporate management. Wherever there are not any representatives, Siemens has not attempted to establish these.
- In the Czech as well as Slovakian Osram subsidiary enterprises, traditional industrial relations have a considerable influence. There are absolutely no trade union representatives in the Polish Siemens subsidiary. Although they formally are Brownfield investments, a corresponding body is not longer existent as a result of the considerable restructurings. One of the reasons for the weak impact of external factors on the industrial relations is the lack of contacts with German representatives.

- The company's traditional, dialogue-orientated discussion culture as well as a cooperative relationship between management and representatives are transferred from the parent enterprise to the CEE subsidiaries, where representatives could remain/be established (but not in Poland). Due to the challenges of international competition and in view of the varied range of products and sites, a trend towards stronger standardization of regulations for the personnel management is recognizable in the past years. General principles and strategies have also been formulated in the realm of occupational health and safety; however, these principles and strategies are able to be implemented for every country according to the specific underlying conditions. Up to now, the specifications for uniform development of management potentials have strongly concentrated on the management and the senior salaried employee spheres.

In the case of the CEE enterprises, Europeanization of industrial relations is not discernible to date. The Siemens Europa Committee SEC had not developed any initiatives in this regard up until 1 May 2004. The German codetermination appears to be a role model for the German representatives as well as for the industrial relations in the CEE countries. The trade unionists from the two CEE Osram enterprises explicitly prefer the Rhine-Alpine model of capitalism, without this having to be put into concrete terms for the industrial relations. A dual system of industrial relations according to the German model has not been advocated previously by them.

Continental AG – A Mix of CEE and German Industrial Relations

The Enterprise

The corporate group with its headquarters in Hanover is a globally active enterprise with numerous products/brands. Including various trading companies, Continental has over 2,100 tyre and franchise enterprises in 14 countries as well as 26 plants, research centres and test tracks.

The company employed a total of 68,829 people in 2003. It is divided into the following sectors:

1. Car tyres (22,518 employees);
2. Lorry tyres (11,068 employees);
3. Continental Automotive Systems (among other things, manufacture of electronic and hydraulic brake systems, headway controls as well as air suspension and sensor systems) (19,685 employees);
4. ContiTech (drive systems and chassis bearings for the automotive industry, products for mechanical engineering and mining as well as the furniture and printing industry) (15,392 employees);
5. Remaining sectors (166 employees).

In the summer of 2004, the Continental AG acquired the Phoenix AG from Hamburg-Harburg with another approximately 10,000 employees worldwide (having produced among others auto parts as well).

Since 1994, the enterprise has aimed at building up sites in low-cost countries. In consequence the car tyre production in the German parent plant in Hanover-Stoecken will run out till the end of 2007.

In Slovakia, Continental entered into a joint venture for production of rubber profiles with the Vegum firm, and entered into a joint venture with Matador for production of lorry tyres. There are other sites in the Czech Republic (among others, in Barum) and Hungary. Both of the subsidiary enterprises in our study (Matador in Slovakia and Barum in the Czech Republic) are typical Brownfield investments. Both have a long tradition. In the case of Barum (Czech Republic), it extends back to the 1940s.

The Continental-Matador joint venture in Púchov (Slovakia) started in January 1999. The plant for production of lorry tyres has steadily expanded its production since then, from 626,000 tyres in 1999 to 1.6 million in 2003. The number of employees increased from 800–1,087 in October 2004. The parent concern invested 150 million DM (= 75 million euro) for renewal of the equipment.

Barum Continental in Otrokovice (Czech Republic) was acquired in 1993 by Continental as majority owner. Negotiations commenced already in 1991. The plant produces car tyres, lorry tyres and rubber products for industrial purposes. The production of car tyres increased from 2.31 million in 1992 to 17.1 million in 2004, the number of employees from 3,960 to 4,500.

According to the 2003 market report, every second car tyre and more than every second lorry tyre in Europe already comes from a low-cost country. It is anticipated that this proportion will increase till the end of 2006 to about 60 per cent. The company is collectively expanding the business sectors which are either among the first three in the respective market or which are emerging in the new markets in which Continental can reach a leading position relatively quickly. The company is separating itself from less viable business sectors. The growth in the new markets is particularly achieved through cooperations in the form of Brownfield investments. The production in the tyre segment is labour-intensive (labour costs amount to about 33 per cent of the overall costs). The company is following its customers with regard to the investments, above all the automotive industry. Corporate management as well as works councils in Germany emphasize that without the investments in the low-wage countries which enabled diversified calculation and corporate growth, collective dismissals would have been imminent in Germany. That is why the most important motive for the investments in the CEEC was the favourable cost structure. However, the CEE representatives perceive the danger of further relocation in an eastward direction due to the increasing wages, particularly in the Czech Republic and Slovakia.

German managers as well as representatives emphasize the high level of professional/vocational/technical qualification in the CEEC. Germany still has competitive advantages through the ability to solve complex customer problems or to rapidly develop innovations to market maturity. But this capability is also increasing in the CEEC and Asia. An 'intellectual catch-up chase' is taking place.

The company is entering into collaborations with universities and institutions of higher education for training highly qualified junior staff. According to management statements, the error (defect) rates in Central and Eastern Europe are partially lower than in Germany. The people there have a 'hunger for quality'.

Industrial Relations

Continental is subject to the respective comprehensive sector-specific collective wage agreement in Germany. A Corporate Works Council and a European Works Council (Europa Forum) do exist. Within the concern, two trade unions (IG Chemie and IG Metall) are represented in different sites in Germany.

The Europa Forum was established in 1993. The plenum meets once a year for a two to three-day session. On the first day the representatives of the single sites meet; a *joint* plenary assembly of the *employee side* is held on the second day before the meeting with the corporate management. Representatives from the personnel departments of the single works are also present. Immediately after the establishment of the Europa Forum in 1993, representatives from the CEEC were admitted as non-voting members. CEE representatives also take part in the business sector committees of the employee representation bodies.

The management perceives the role of the Europa Forum as restricted through the attempt to include codetermination and a trade union agenda and thus to dominate it. On the other hand, the Europa Forum could be useful if topics from the single sites would be treated on an equal basis.

The trade union representatives from the Czech and Slovakian subsidiary enterprises consider the membership in the Europa Forum as helpful. Most direct contacts between German and Slovakian or Czech trade unionists take place through the Europa Forum. The Slovakian trade union representative emphasizes that new information can be passed on through the Europa Forum, which opens an expanded look at the worldwide corporate strategy. Information obtained there could also be used with regard to collective bargaining with the domestic management. Further forms of Europeanization of the industrial relations are not seen by the trade union representatives to date.

The Czech trade union representatives as well as the management from Barum also appraise the expansion of the field of vision through the Europa Forum. There have already been European and global influences on the industrial relations since the acquisition through Continental.

There is a trade union organization in both of the CEE subsidiary enterprises. A company works council was established at Barum in 1993, which – beside the parent works – also represents the spun-off subsidiary enterprises. The chairman of the company works council is a member in the Europa Forum.

In the Slovakian as well as Czech subsidiary enterprises the degree the union density is 70 per cent.

Collective wage agreements are concluded on the company level in the CEE subsidiaries (in-plant/in-company agreements). The company's collective wage agreement was also influenced through sectoral agreements before the investment from Continental. This is no longer the case now.

Neither the Slovakian nor the Czech subsidiary enterprises are members in an employers' association. But Barum belongs to the Chamber of Commerce. The director of the company is the chairman of the district Chamber of Commerce.

In technical and managerial terms, the corporate group's standards are transferred to all sites worldwide; occupational health and safety as well as quality standards apply worldwide. There are also uniform management guidelines and uniform processes of management structure appraisal in the company.

The management from Continental Matador emphasizes that the corporate culture has changed considerably after the acquisition through Continental. The employees identify more with the works. The average wages have increased and lie above the national average. The working conditions have improved, especially in the sphere of occupational health and safety.

The same applies to the subsidiary enterprise in the Czech Republic. Barum Continental has clearly better working conditions than the other domestic companies in the region. First-class quality is produced, whereas the production of simpler products has been relocated eastwards. The company pays the highest wages in the region. But strong elements of the traditional working culture have also been retained. For instance, the former training system has been revived. A university graduate has to go through all workshops in the introductory phase before he assumes his scheduled position.

The key positions are staffed with people from the parent company with regard to Greenfield investments. This does not inevitably have to be someone from Germany. Subsidiary enterprises can certainly be built up by managers and experts from countries other than Germany. As many employees as possible are sought from the respective country for the first level beneath the management. At Matador in Slovakia the new managers mainly came from Germany. Now they are gradually being replaced by Slovakian managers.

With few exceptions, the management at Barum consists of locals. The local management as well as the trade unions endeavour not to have any foreign managers in the leadership of the company.

There is a bottom-up process of decision preparations and a top-down process of implementation. The financial control mechanisms of the headquarters define the framework, and 'there is no escape from that'. An exchange of personnel between the parent and subsidiary enterprise takes place only on a moderate level and excludes the highest level.

The works councils in Germany perceive the latitude of the local management as not very considerable. Continental has been managed in a very centralized manner. The company attempts to standardize the corporate structures as much as possible (for example introduction of group/teamwork).

There have been general corporate guidelines since 1989. The management assumes that this would find more recognition in the new subsidiaries than in the parent enterprise. The reason for this is that the people there placed greater emphasis on the binding link: they want to identify with the concern.

The German corporate management emphasizes that with regard to the industrial relations the valid regulations and standards of the respective country are heeded. The company advocates open and fair dealings with the representatives and includes them in the information and consultation processes within the framework of the respective national laws. The corporate management perceive cultural differences in this: on the one hand, in some of the CEE countries one encounters a certain degree of 'subservience', but on the other hand, occasionally also a certain degree of aloofness on the part of the employee representatives vis-à-vis foreign investors. The management styles of some local managers are still characterized by the communist past. There have been cases where the headquarters had to take corrective intervention measures; for instance, in one case where the representatives had to work under unacceptable office conditions.

In the two subsidiary enterprises in the Czech Republic and Slovakia, a mix of elements from local tradition and rules from the parent concern has become established with regard to the management rules. Elements of German as well as Czech and Slovakian management culture are found at Continental Matador in Slovakia. Building on the general corporate guidelines, the management from Continental Matador developed its own form of implementation. But the dependence on the parent enterprise is quite considerable. Matador is not hosting a research and development department for its own. As a rule, important decisions in the personnel policy sphere are made through the personnel department of the German headquarters and through the regional coordinator, who is also responsible for two other Slovakian subsidiary enterprises in addition to Continental Matador. The fundamental economic objectives are predetermined by the concern headquarters.

> The subsidiary enterprise is managed as independently as possible and has to take care of its own fulfilment of objectives (Slovakian trade union spokesman).

One's own tradition is emphasized in the Czech firm. The corporate identity is founded on the identification with the Barum works, not with the concern. The parent enterprise does not force a different management culture. A decentralized allocation of duties (multilayer structure) exists instead of a strict hierarchic management structure. The concern sets economic figures in advance but how the economic objectives are achieved is the business of the Barum Continental management.

The German works councils describe the relationship with the concern and sites management as basically good. Disputes are argued out objectively with certain controversial topics. Of course, there have been partially tough negotiations in the past years, but no walkouts (with the exception of the dispute concerning the closing down of car tyre production in Hanover-Stoeken in January/February 2006). The information is described as good, especially on account of the triple function of the Corporate Works Council chairman (at the same time chairman of the Europa Forum and deputy supervisory board chairman), which had led to the prevention of information losses. But this is also due to the questions posed by the representatives. If they have been precisely asked, one also receives honest answers.

The trade union representatives in the two CEE subsidiary enterprises also describe the relations with the management as good, open and fair. The management at Matador in Slovakia provides the trade union representatives with all necessary information concerning the corporate strategy and personnel matters. There is a joint committee for improvement of occupational health and safety. Other activities such as an annual joint meeting between management and trade unionists, open day, and campaigns for improvement of employee motivation and against alcohol abuse are jointly organized by management and representatives.

At Barum in the Czech Republic the trade union representatives emphasize that the local managers are not the owners, and every one of them is an employee who has to solve any problems with the *foreign* owners. The trade union chairman meets regularly with the management and obtains sufficient information about the company. The trade union chairman assumes a certain degree of joint responsibility for the company. In the event of any arising problems he immediately attempts to solve these with the management.

A local alliance between management and representatives on the site level has emerged as a result.

The development of the new institution of works councils in the Czech Republic and Slovakia is welcomed by the German corporate management as well as by the German Corporate Works Council: the management generally regards representatives – who are authorized by the *entire* workforce – as desirable. Trade unions more frequently brought interests lying outside the business enterprise into the plant.

The German works councils also appraise the new CEE works councils as positive, but does not believe that they will become rapidly established.

In view of the rather negative attitude of the CEE trade unions officers and representatives, this seems to be a realistic assessment. The Slovakian trade union representative sees a works council as a mixed 'hybrid' body, but has no personal experiences with this. The Czech trade union representative argues: since the works councils do not have the right to collective bargaining according to the present labour legislation, their introduction makes no sense. The introduction of works councils would be meaningful if there would be sectoral collective bargaining – as in the German system – which bind all enterprises.

The management in the two CEE subsidiary enterprises is of a differing opinion in this matter.

At Matador the management considers the introduction of works councils as somewhat artificial. The trade union organization works well in the company and therefore there is no need for an additional representational body. On the other hand, the Czech management thinks that works councils represent a better variation for the company's present situation, since negotiations would take place on behalf of *all* employees.

The German works councils are of the opinion that the respective national systems of industrial relations will be lasting on the site/company level. There will be a limited Europeanization on the corporate level (supervisory board, European Public Company). However, in the opinion of the German corporate management, a Europeanization of industrial relations is not perceivable. It is also questionable whether it is even desirable (in the sense of an alignment of social standards). There is a danger that the competitive advantages of the sites would be lost through an excessively rapid standardization. That is why the institution of the European Public Company – whose guideline could result in an extension of codetermination beyond Germany – is also critical.

Summary

The influences of the parent enterprise on the industrial relations in the CEE subsidiary enterprises are considerable. The concern's centralized control mechanisms (business plan, uniform safety and quality standards, uniform management guidelines, uniform corporate role model) have an effect on the industrial relations. They promote open dealings on the part of management with the representatives (improvement of communication, 'dealing more fairly' with each other). The corporate management also correctively intervenes in single cases. But the respective national laws and regulations as an institutional framework are respected while doing so. The company also partially exceeds prevailing social standards (involvement for employee families in the South Africa townships, transport service for employees in Romania). The management anticipates that the representatives in the CEEC will develop organically and gain strength. For this, the German model – the works councils elected by the entire workforce – is preferred.

Traditional elements of corporate culture and industrial relations play a substantial role in the Slovakian as well as Czech subsidiary enterprises as typical Brownfield investments – but with clear accent differences between both subsidiaries.

At Matador in Slovakia the culture of the German parent enterprise is greater and is seen by the employees more positively ('They are proud to work for Continental'). The involvement of Continental has improved the quality of the industrial relations prevailing before the German investment. In particular, the more open communication between management and employees and the observance of their rights to information and consultation has led to a greater motivation of the workforce.

In the opinion of the management as well as the representatives, the management system from Continental Matador corresponds more to the Rhine-Alpine model of capitalism – but with quite a few elements of Anglo-Saxon capitalism. Both sides prefer the Rhine-Alpine model on account of its participation possibilities and the social orientation, whereby the management also sees advantages in the other model.

Up to now, the traditional system has more strongly dominated the industrial relations at Barum in the Czech Republic; this has been enriched through new elements from the parent concern. One identifies more with Barum than with Continental. This can also be due to the fact that Barum had a much stronger market position than Matador in the former Czechoslovakia, and from that point of view the traditional corporate culture also still plays a stronger role today.

In the Barum enterprise, the management prefers the Anglo-American model, since is corresponds 'better to the wishes for flexibility and adaptability on the part of the Czechs'. The German model is seen as too rigid. On the other hand, the trade unionists welcome the fact that the German model of industrial relations is being introduced, but consider a gradual diminution of social security to be possible in the future once the standard of living has increased and stabilized.

A mixture of industrial relations from countries of origin and host countries of the investments is provided in both of the CEE subsidiary enterprises, whereby the host country's traditional cultural elements of industrial relations dominate more strongly in the Czech Republic than in Slovakia. In addition to the countable facts (higher wages, improvement of working conditions), the more open and fair communications after the takeover by Continental is also emphasized in both subsidiaries. Trade union representatives and management from both CEE subsidiary enterprises agree (with differences) in the scepticism vis-à-vis an introduction of the German dual system of industrial relations.

Aventis Pharma SA/Aventis Pharma Deutschland GmbH – A European Success Story of Limited Duration

The Enterprise

Aventis Pharma SA was a globally leading pharmaceutical enterprise up until 19 August 2004. The company's core businesses were R and D (Research and Development) as well as the production and sale of prescription products such as drugs, vaccines and blood plasma products. Among other things, the core business included Aventis Pharma' stake in the animal health business Merial and a 50:50 joint venture with Merck and Co. in 2003, Aventis Pharma achieved a turnover of 16.8 billion euro in its core business and employed about 69,000 employees worldwide.

Aventis Pharma SA was established in December 1999 through the merger of the German Hoechst AG and the French Rhône-Poulenc (SA). The concern management's registered office was Strasbourg, France – and so this new concern somewhat resembled EADS in the aerospace industry. Insofar as corporate codetermination and European Works Council are concerned, the industrial relations in the (French) parent enterprise were a mixture of the German and French model – developed after lengthy negotiations between the German and French shareholders, the involved trade unions and works councils (Vallée, 2000).

The Aventis Pharma Deutschland GmbH is the German national company with registered office in Frankfurt on the Main, and is orientated towards the German 'model' of industrial relations. It was one of the leading pharmaceutical enterprises on the German market with about 8,300 employees and a turnover of 2.9 billion euro (2003). The Aventis Pharma Deutschland GmbH encompassed the corporate functions research and development, active substance production and manufacture as well as marketing and distribution. Altogether, Aventis Pharma produced 24 different active substances in Germany, which were delivered in 40 countries and processed into medicaments. Frankfurt-Hoechst (with 6,750 employees at the end of 2003) was the largest production site of Aventis Pharma Deutschland GmbH.

In addition to sites in 11 West European countries, the Aventis Pharma SA had other sites in Poland (152 employees: pure logistics centre, union-free), in Slovakia (310 employees: 'Hoechst-Biotika' production site; a Brownfield investment transacted in 1992; subsidiary of the Aventis Pharma Deutschland GmbH, but was supported by the parent enterprise in Strasbourg; representatives), in Hungary (152 employees: field service; union-free) and in Lithuania (approx. 60 employees: field service) as CEE sites. At the same time, RTD as well as back office functions remained in Germany and France.

The Nine West European Multinationals 115

At the end of 2003 already, the Aventis Pharma SA planned restructuring measures to save about 500 million euro in the years 2004–2006. Nearly half of the approximately 50 worldwide sites were supposed to be closed.

These plans are outdated in the fact that another French pharmaceutical concern – the substantially smaller Sanofi (SA) – 'purchased' (with the help and support of the French Government) the shares in Aventis Pharma SA by means of a hostile takeover in the form of an exchange of shares. On 20 August 2004, the former Aventis Pharma SA became a subsidiary of Sanofi, which is henceforth called Sanofi-Aventis SA and has its registered office in Paris. As a result, the world's third largest pharmaceutical concern (behind the US branch leader Pfizer and the British GlaxoSmithKline) emerged with about 100,000 employees and a turnover of approximately 25 billion euro in 2004.

It remains to be seen to what extent this has repercussions on the sites in Central and Eastern Europe, whether the industrial relations in the CEE sites will now change through the dominance of the French 'model' of industrial relations in the new concern, and is thus no longer a matter of our project. At any rate, for Germany there is a guarantee of location and no dismissals until 2007 (with the exception of the pure administration/distribution location at Soden near Frankfurt/M.). At any rate, the Joint Works Council of the Aventis Deutschland GmbH aspires to the fact that, in corporate law, Sanofi Germany (with approx. 800 employees in Berlin) will be taken over by Aventis Pharma Germany (approx. 8,300 employees), and will adopt their system of industrial relations as a result.

Industrial Relations

There is a Joint Works Council for the Aventis Deutschland GmbH. There is also a works council for each of the sites in Frankfurt-Hoechst, Soden and Marburg. Two respective trade union/works council representatives from Germany and France are present in the Aventis Pharma SA supervisory board in Strasbourg.

The Aventis SA European Works Council (the formation agreement was made in 2002 and revised in 2002) has the company's chief executive as chairman, and thus follows the French model; the employee side provides the secretary and the two deputy chairman (coming from Germany and France). The EWC comprises 33 members, who up until 30 April 2004 came from Germany, France, Greece, the UK and Spain. Since the EWC contract also ran only up until this date, it was extended by five months so that it could prepare for the admission of the new members from Central and Eastern Europe. Pursuant to the EWC directive, Poland, Slovakia and Hungary would have come into question for this purpose. But major difficulties could be seen to emerge with regard to the staffing of the CEE mandates. For instance, in Slovakia there is the legal provision that an EWC member can be elected by the entire workforce and not merely by the trade union members (and thus analogous to the law on establishment of works councils). As a result, this was met with fierce resistance by the trade unions. In the Polish and Hungarian subsidiaries there were no trade union representatives on the site/company levels whatsoever (and thus not even a company/site collective agreement), and so a mandate for the EWC seemed virtually impossible here; the Lithuanian subsidiary was too small to obtain an EWC mandate. On 3 November 2004 – about three months after the acquisition of Aventis Pharma SA through Sanofi (SA), and the foreseeable end of the Aventis Pharma SA EWC – the new CEE members were admitted to the EWC during the EWC's annual meeting.

In the Aventis Pharma EWC the German representatives were most effectively organized. They provided only 12 members (and thus about 36 per cent of all EWC members), but six out of these 12 were members in the Aventis Pharma Deutschland GmbH Joint Works Council, and thus they were able to very effectively use the possibilities of German industrial relations for their work in the EWC – that is in this case, an interlocking between the European and national level was also provided in pure personnel terms.

After the merger of Hoechst AG and the Rhône-Poulenc (SA) in 1999 the EWC got a very important function with regard to diminishing the differences of industrial relations in France and Germany. Immediately after 1999 there were corresponding difficulties, but in the meantime the cooperation between management and representatives (also determined by the joint, but later on failed attempt of averting the hostile takeover through Sanofi in 2003/04) was outstanding – on the European as well as the national level of industrial relations in Germany and France.

A similar equalizing function was also ascribed to the EWC during the integration of the CEE sites. The German and French representatives were the driving forces of the 'Europeanisation' of the industrial relations with respect to national laws and traditions; the representatives from other countries only played a marginal role in this connection (also for reasons of the marginal number of mandates). But the Europeanization of industrial relations is only understood as the suppression of competitive discussions between the single European sites, under no circumstances the diminution of the importance of national law. But as the strongest expression of this Europeanization, the EWC improves the *national* underlying conditions for such representatives which *do not* have such a high level of rights as those in Germany or also in France. Insofar as the integration of CEE representatives in the EWC is concerned, this only began after the date of accession on 1 May 2004. Before that the CEE representatives still had no experience whatsoever with this committee, but – according to the new Slovakian EWC representative (who is the chairman of the Slovakian trade union committee) – placed great hopes in it.

From that point of view this may also be justified, since there were hardly any bilateral contacts between the Slovakian representatives and the representatives from the parent enterprise (Strasbourg, Frankfurt/M.). And so the only functioning contact ran via the EWC. ·

However, all of these EWC functions became obsolete after the acquisition of the Aventis Pharma SA through the Sanofi SA. Up until the autumn of 2004 there were no contacts whatsoever between the EWC at Aventis Pharma and Sanofi, and there were also no bilateral contacts between the representatives in the countries concerned (on the level of the German works council and the 'Comité d'entreprise' at Aventis Pharma and at Sanofi). The atmosphere was poisoned through the embittered takeover struggle in which the respective representatives had also taken part in alliance with the management.[1]

But back to Aventis Pharma SA: the 'model' transfer of the industrial relations from the parent enterprise to the CEE subsidiaries did not take place, or if so, only occurred on a very mediated and mixed basis.

First of all, the Aventis Pharma SA industrial relations are mixed in a French-German manner, so they can hardly be regarded as a 'national model'. In accordance with the sociological definition of Europeanization introduced above – according to which the merger of only two national systems of industrial relations is enough for the time being – one can certainly speak of Europeanisation processes here.

Secondly, our thesis on the corporate centralization of the transfer of industrial relations also applies here; however, particularly the Aventis Pharma SA is characterized by a mixture of jurisdictions which does not permit a uniform model of industrial relations. And so we have seen that the Slovakian subsidiary is assigned to the Aventis Pharma Deutschland GmbH in pure legal terms, but is de facto – also insofar as a possible transfer of industrial relations is concerned – influenced by the French parent enterprise in Strasbourg (Alsace). And thirdly, the following principle applies to the Aventis Pharma SA: the industrial relations in the single sites may be globally orientated, but are adapted to the local circumstances in the respective countries. According to the Aventis Pharma SA corporate management:

> The different national labour laws have more impact than the company-related structures.

In particular, the social standards are adapted to the local circumstances. The general Aventis Pharma principles are only reverted to if the worst comes to the worst.

And so the Slovakian management respects the increased representational structures at 'Hoechst-Biotika'. Eighty-five per cent of the workforce members are trade union members, but with a declining trend. According to their own statements, the representatives (whose chairman is not released) obtains sufficient information from the management to conduct negotiations on the site/company level; the industry-wide collective bargaining for the chemical and pharmaceutical industry are not applied at Hoechst-Biotika, since this company is not a member of the corresponding employers'

---

1   In the autumn of 2004 the representatives from the Aventis Pharma SA and the Sanofi (SA) formed a 'Special Negotiating Committee' for merger of the two EWCs. Thirty-three members from 16 countries belonged to this committee. An EWC agreement for the Sanofi-Aventis SA was signed on 24 February 2005: According to the agreement, the new EWC consists of 40 members and shall meet twice a year. In addition to representatives from the EU-25, the new EWC – which supersedes both of the old EWCs – today even includes delegates from the future EU member countries Romania and Bulgaria as well as Croatia (effective 3 October 2005 officially elevated to the status of an EU candidate country). Representatives from Turkish Sanofi-Aventis site are slated to become members of the EWC four years before Turkey's future, at the time being not determined accession to the EU. The steering committee of the new EWC consists of nine members. Furthermore, five representatives belong to the French company's supervisory board, but only with an advisory voice. They must come from at least three different countries.

association. Regular meetings between the representatives and the management have led to an atmosphere amongst the two actors which is also described as productive, and which, according to trade union statements, is substantially better than before the coming into existence of the joint venture in 1992. A new 'working culture' has actually emerged in Slovakia: more open communications between management and employees, solid and reliable documentation entity, two employee meetings per year (at which the company management then describes the development), good cooperation between the management and the representatives. In addition, the working conditions and the amount of remunerations are substantially better than in the comparable regional environment, and up to now there have not been any serious conflicts in the subsidiary.

The respect of local circumstances brought about in industrial relations is portrayed differently with regard to technical standards as well as management. Insofar as the technical standards are concerned, these have been elevated to the western level in the case of the Slovakian subsidiary (Brownfield investments). The principle with regard to the transfer of management principles is that as much self-responsibility as possible is transferred to the local management in order to adapt the general Aventis Pharma standards to the local conditions and people on the scene. This is also demonstrated in the staffing of the top management: for instance, a German initially served as the general manager of the Slovakian production site; now the manager is a Czech with domicile in Prague. In addition, there is a normal career programme for young junior staff ('high potentials'), who are sent abroad for one or two years by the parent enterprise – and thus also to the CEEC. Parallel to this, there is (for instance, in the Slovakian subsidiaries) a 'talent management programme' for promotion of local junior staff.

However, the (relative) autonomy of the CEE subsidiaries vis-à-vis the parent enterprise is subject to a much stronger restriction than that of the West European national companies (Germany, France, Spain, the UK and Italy). For Central and Eastern Europe, the parent company in Strasbourg has a direct right of intervention. For example, the personnel development is carefully pursued by the owners. Moreover, all *production* sites (no matter where they are located) are still governed by the managements of the two Aventis Pharma production divisions (chemicals and pharmaceuticals/medicaments). In principle, it is expected that the production sites are already in the black in the first year of the purchase – collective agreements and industrial relations are orientated towards these profit margins.

The difficulty of the unions within a company (if there are any whatsoever) – already described above in connection with the CEE mandates for the EWCs – to permit the election of EWC candidates through *all* members of the workforce (regardless whether a trade union member or not) is also expressed in the refusal of the Slovakian representatives to accept a works council (according to the legal provisions in Slovakia). They dread their influence. This is a persistent dispute with the German trade unions and works councils, although otherwise the relations between the Slovakian national chemicals industry trade union and the German IG BCE are very good. In the opinion of the German works council at Aventis Pharma Deutschland GmbH, a works council will come to the Slovakian production affiliates one way or another – whether with or without the approval of the trade union. As far as they are concerned, the Slovakian representatives reject a works council according to the German model because 'a works council is only useful where there are no trade union representatives'.

The dominance of the local (company) unions is also strengthened vis-à-vis their national associations through their right to enter into collective agreements.

In Slovakia there is a collective wage agreement, but not in Poland and Hungary (union-free). The problem lies not only in the fact that no unions within a company are available in most sites, but is also substantiated by the fact that the collective wage agreement on the corporate/site level dominates in almost all CEEC, and there are no collective agreements on the branch, regional and/or national level which could compensate for the lack of representatives on company/plant level as partners in collective bargaining.

Summary

The industrial relations in the Aventis Pharma SA CEE subsidiaries are characterized by various path dependencies:

- First of all, the traditional path of the host country of the investment dominates. For instance, there are representatives in the Slovakian production site, whereas there is none in the distribution sites in Poland, Hungary and Lithuania. The parent enterprise has not attempted to build up representative bodies as negotiating partners in the union-free subsidiaries. This lies not only in the fact that the parent enterprise would also like to live quite well without trade unions, but also in the fact that white-collar workers (who predominate in the Polish, Hungarian and Lithuanian subsidiaries) are more difficult to organize into a union than blue-collar workers. On top of this is the fact that – based on the experiences regarding the varying nature of the cultures of industrial relations at the German Hoechst AG and the French Rhône-Poulenc (SA) – after 1999 the management had retained a high degree of respect for the respective nationally characterized difference of industrial relations, which they also transferred to the CEE subsidiaries.
- However, the parent enterprise endeavours to implement social standards (also in the union-free sites) which lie above the level in the respective CEE region.
- In the CEE sites in which there were already representatives beforehand (such as in Slovakia), the relations between the local management and representatives are characterized by a trusting cooperation and thus by the inclusion of the workforce and its representatives; this did not exist before 1992 (the beginning of the joint venture in Slovakia).
- The latter is even more astounding, since there are hardly any bi-national relations between the representatives in the CEE subsidiaries (first and foremost in Slovakia) and those in the parent location (Strasbourg, partially also *Frankfurt/M*), and therefore no immediate pressure has been exerted by German or French representatives on the Slovakian management for better arrangement of industrial relations.

- On the whole, the culture of industrial relations at the Aventis Pharma SA is characterized by a mixture of German and French elements. If one describes – analogous to the sociological explanatory approach of Europeanization – this mixture as Europeanization (the driving forces in this connection are – based on reasons of numerical presence in the EWC – German and French representatives), the industrial relations at Aventis Pharma SA can thus be described as 'bi-national Europeanisation' (Germany and France), which the representatives from the other European sites (including those in Central and Eastern Europe) must or also want to endorse. For instance, the representatives' chairman of the Slovakian Aventis Pharma subsidiary 'Hoechst-Biotika' emphasizes that for him the Europeanization of the industrial relations in an international enterprise like Aventis Pharma become apparent through an effective cooperation between management and representatives as well as a corresponding positive social dialogue in the company/site – this also in comparison with times of the socialist planned economy. This process is strengthened even more through numerous European directives in the realm of labour and social law.

But these specific characterizations of the industrial relations in the Aventis Pharma SA CEE subsidiary enterprises are history. At the moment – in 2005/06 – it is completely open as to which direction the industrial relations will develop in the newly formed company Sanofi-Aventis SA after 20 August 2004. Due to the global alignment of this now worldwide third-largest pharmaceutical enterprise, there are fears among the representatives in Slovakia, Germany and France that future industrial relations will be more orientated towards an Anglo-American human resource management than towards the Rhine-Alpine model (which has been understood at the Aventis Pharma SA as a nucleus of Europeanization).

Henkel KGaA – a German family-owned enterprise with Austrian (clientele-bound) accent and paternalistic industrial relations

The Enterprise

The firm Henkel and Cie was established in 1876. The company quickly changed with the listing on the stock exchange in 1985. Numerous joint ventures and acquisitions were undertaken in the beginning of the 1990s (for instance, the acquisition of the cosmetics firm Hans Schwarzkopf GmbH in 1995).

The Henkel Group headquarters is located in Düsseldorf. The company is controlled by the open family-owned company Henkel, which possesses most of the capital.

Henkel is represented with its brands and technologies in over 125 countries. Of the approximately 50,000 employees (end of 2003), 77 per cent were employed outside of Germany. In 2003, the turnover declined by 2.3 per cent to 9.436 billion euro (reason: excessively strong Euro vis-à-vis the US Dollar); however, the net profit was able to increase by one-fifth in the same year (reason: sale of Wella shares).

In 2004, the turnover was able to be increased by 12.3 per cent to 10.6 billion euro on account of the margin-strong US market; but at the same time a savings programme (until 2006) was announced with the cut back of 3,000 jobs (at a total of 51,000 at the end of 2004) worldwide. Five hundred jobs are affected in Germany (one of two detergent works in Düsseldorf as well as the glue works in Hanover will be partially closed).

The strategic business segments of the Henkel Group are divided into four globally active divisions (status end of 2003):

- Detergent/cleaning agents (33 per cent share of group turnover),
- Cosmetics/personal hygiene (22 per cent share of group turnover),
- Adhesive agents for consumers and craftsmen (14 per cent share of group turnover), as well as
- Henkel Technologies: Adhesive agents and surface technology-system solutions for industrial applications (28 per cent share of group turnover).

The remaining 3 per cent of the group turnover in 2003 were attributed to holding company activities.

The Henkel Austria Group was emerged in 1994 as an umbrella organization for the Henkel companies in Central and Eastern Europe (renamed Henkel Central and Eastern Europe after 1998). In addition, there was also the Persil company (established in 1927 in Vienna; after 1982 as the Henkel Austria GmbH), which was active in the product areas detergent and cleaning agents, cosmetics and personal hygiene, adhesive agents and surface treatment.

The amalgamation of the production site Vienna (Henkel Austria) with the company responsible for Central and Eastern Europe ('Henkel CEE') took place in 2003. The new group is henceforth called Henkel Central and Eastern Europe, or briefly: 'Henkel CEE'.

In the 2003 annual average, 'Henkel CEE' employed 7,939 workers in 13 national companies and 15 production sites, and had a turnover of 1.109 billion euro in 2003 (= 12 per cent of group turnover). From Austria it controls – in addition to Austrian sites – activities in Poland (in 2003: 25.1 per cent of the total 'Henkel CEE' turnover), Hungary (15.01 per cent), Czech Republic (11.1 per cent), Slovakia (3.6 per cent), Slovenia (6.1 per cent), Romania (5.2 per cent), Croatia (3.5 per cent), Bulgaria, Serbia and Montenegro, Estonia, Latvia, Lithuania (the Baltic states are consolidated in a 'Baltics' national company), Russia and in the Ukraine.

Alone in Poland 'Henkel CEE' has four plants with a total of more than 1,000 employees. The factory in Raciborz (which is of particular interest to us) was purchased as a Brownfield investment in 1991 and produces (2004 status: approx. 300 employees) detergents, soaps, and so on for the national market, but also for export – particularly to other CEE countries. In 1991, 17 million DM (approximately 8.5 million euro) were paid for the purchase, and an additional 50 million DM (25 million euro) were invested up to 2004 – that is Raciborz is a Brownfield *and* Greenfield investment at the same time.

Primary reasons for the Henkel involvement in the CEEC are the opening up of new markets – (labour) cost reasons play only a subordinate role with an average of 10 per cent of labour costs in all production costs (in which case, however, the labour cost share amounts to about 25 per cent at Raciborz in Poland); moreover, 'the salaries for good personnel are meanwhile just as high in Warsaw as in Vienna'. From that point of view, there is also no discussion in the Henkel Group about relocations of entire locations from West to East; whereas, however, product lines are shifted amongst the single sites for reasons of capacity and demand. The Henkel Group's strategy in Central and Eastern Europe was the purchase of factories (Brownfield investments) and further production of traditional products/brands. The Brownfield investments generate the cash flow, from which the subsequent (much more expensive) Greenfield/expansion investments are paid. The Henkel premium brands are also marketed there on a parallel basis to production in the CEEC.

Industrial Relations

In Germany there is no Joint Works Council for the Henkel Group. All of the approximately 20 companies in Germany have their own works council. The works council chairman at the Henkel headquarters in Düsseldorf-Holthausen (at the same time member of the Henkel KgaA supervisory board and chairman of the European Works Council 'European Employee Committee') informally coordinates all German works councils, which meet twice a year.

The relationship between the works councils and management in Germany is described by both sides as good and problem-free.

Since 1995 there has been an EWC (Henkel 'European Employee Committee'), which had a total of 28 members in the autumn of 2004. The EWC representatives come from almost all countries/sites in Europe (Germany provides most of the members, but under-proportionately to the number of employees). Since 1 May 2004 there have also been two representatives from Poland, and one each from Hungary, Czech Republic, Slovakia and Slovenia. The first joint session of this new expanded committee was held on 27 May 2004. Before the date of accession the CEE sites had no rights of representation whatsoever in the EWC – and no observer status.

There had been severe difficulties with the nomination of the CEE candidates for the EWC on account of the questionable legitimacy of the unions within a company to speak for the entire workforce. In Poland these difficulties were intensified even more through the lack of representatives. The management in Raciborz, guided by the 'Henkel CEE' in Vienna, had now called on the entire workforce to elect the representative for the EWC. With 60 per cent of the votes a woman was elected, who worked in the plant since 1992 and as a local was well-known to everyone. She was also selected by the management on account of her good command of English. The second Polish EWC representative also has a good command of English (and German), and works as a production manager at the Henkel factory in Starporkow. Except for the Hungarian and Slovenian site (which each have a legally prescribed works council that can speak for the entire workforce), the nomination process proceeded according to the 'English Henkel model': in the UK one had searched for the trade union representative ('trustee') in the pension funds and then appointed this person as the representative from the UK in the Henkel EWC. In the CEE countries the respective personnel managers of the national companies were called together and asked who possessed the greatest amount of trust in the concerned workforces. If the sought after individuals agreed, they were sent to the EWC as representatives.

The Henkel Group pays for the English language courses (because, like everywhere, deficient knowledge of languages represents the greatest structural obstacle for the EWC work) and provides every EWC member with email access directly at his/her workplace.

From the viewpoint of the German members, the EWC does not play any significant role in the *mediation* between East and West. There are three essential reasons for this:

- First of all, representatives from the CEE sites have only been members in the EWC since 1 May 2004. Previously, there were no contacts whatsoever on this level. As far as that goes, the EWC (expanded by the CEE sites) first had to find its new role.
- Secondly, an EWC can only be as 'good' in the mediation between East and West as it had already been before in the mediation between the single (west) European sites. The EWC has never grown into this intermediary role at Henkel: because the individual members in the EWC see themselves first of all as representatives of their sites and less as members in an (equalizing) European committee. There are considerable apprehensions and fears among the representatives that their respective sites are generally subject to internal Henkel competition. Nevertheless, the EWC manages to have an equalizing effect in certain areas. Two examples are mentioned for this purpose: in France there was an internal locational quarrel. The president of the EWC visited the location and brought the management and representatives together – thus the problem was solved. In Belgium, Henkel decided on the complete closure of a plant in 2002 due to the declining sales figures of a product. The Belgian residual production was allocated to other sites. The EWC made sure that the employees were paid high redundancy payoffs (far above the legal norm). Both examples illustrate that the EWC fulfils equalizing functions *within* national companies, but not on the supranational (European) level.
- Thirdly, despite a numerical majority of German representatives in the EWC, their organized influence is not large enough to be able to eliminate the national competition within the EWC (as this is frequently to be observed amongst other EWCs in other enterprises). This is also due to the organization of the German representatives (no Joint Works Council), which in addition hardly have any independent – bilateral – contacts with representatives in the CEE sites. There are no connections on the part of the works councils in Germany and Austria with the subsidiaries in Poland, surely also due to the fact that there are no trade union representatives in the respective companies/sites in the last-named country. If there are any contacts between the representatives, they proceed indirectly via the responsible (supra-company) trade unions in Germany and the respective CEE countries.

However, from the viewpoint of the Central and Eastern Europe EWC representatives, the EWC *should* play an important role in the mediation between East and West.

Many hopes rest upon this contingency. This could certainly lead to conflicts between western and eastern EWC representatives in the future.

The Central and Eastern Europe sites are controlled by the 'Henkel CEE' in Vienna, which sets relatively precisely defined goals and objectives for the single sites. There is a business plan with ongoing coordination measures (top-down), the specifications of which are binding. And so even in the first year of the investment in Central and Eastern Europe, no red figures are anticipated – which also never led to problems previously.

The top managers in the CEE subsidiaries are in many cases Austrians and Germans, with the exception of Slovakia (where a Czech manages the business). In addition, between 105 and 155 Germans/Austrians constantly work in the CEE subsidiaries with the objective of gathering foreign experience (one to two years) as a prerequisite for climbing up the career ladder later. The level beneath the business management consists of local personnel.

The corporate culture – also with regard to its effects on the industrial relations (identification of the employees with Henkel) – is being rearranged at the moment in the Henkel Group. Whereas the (premium) brands were first and foremost the essential thing for the corporate culture before 2002, a common bond with every product in the Henkel Group has been referred to since 2002 with the slogan 'A Brand like a Friend'. Moreover, the corporate culture is also characterized through the dominance of the Henkel family with its paternalistic – but also aimed at cooperative willingness – notions of industrial relations. Ceremonies at every company 'founding birthday', giving away commemorative medallions, and so on are the visible expression of this. On the other hand, the corporate group management also demands a high degree of individual loyalty from the employees in Central and Eastern Europe.

Of course, Henkel has also not been able to elude the pressure of globalization, but they nevertheless also attempted to maintain certain standards in the non-German subsidiaries. However, in the CEE Brownfield investments this could only be accomplished on a limited basis due to structural reasons: here the workforces were accustomed to 'all-around care' from the times of the planned economy, which is not affordable in a market economy. Henkel was able to introduce good working conditions and pay higher wages – as well as offer considerable social benefits (holiday pay, company pension, and so on) – in comparison with the average in the East, but some other customary conditions from the planned economy (such as lifelong employment guarantee, holiday camp, and so on) had to be done away with – much to the initial disappointment of the employees there. Since the workforce has been reduced from 500 to a current level of 300, and another portion has been exchanged on account of the substantially higher qualification requirements (one has to bear in mind the high level of investments after 1991), the present-day employees in Raciborz (Poland) really appreciate the working conditions (which also include the high level of occupational health and safety).

The control of the CEE subsidiaries through the Austrian 'Henkel CEE' also influences the industrial relations in Central and Eastern Europe. The CEE subsidiaries have a certain degree of Habsburgian thinking in common with the Austrian sub-parent enterprise (naturally also mixed with the mentality of the Germans). As far as they are concerned, the Germans suspect the Austrians of encouraging a

'Balkanization' of the CEE sites with their policy. Of course, the Henkel Group organizational models are also being introduced to the CEE sites (and to that extent the 'Henkel CEE' is very similar to the parent enterprise in Düsseldorf), but the Austrians attempt to implement these principles by persuasion and not via more stringent directive – with occasionally somewhat spotted results. Nevertheless, the result also seems satisfactory for the group headquarters in Düsseldorf, particularly since the Austrians have already been doing business in the CEEC for approximately 20 years, and have built up a correspondingly trusting relationship.

These fine differences between German and Austrian approaches are not so evident for the employees at Raciborz in Poland. The (Polish) manager responsible for HRM was previously active in Polish subsidiaries of American companies. Together with his other Polish colleagues beneath the executive board level he organized the industrial relations very strictly and rigidly. But the trade unions were still ousted from the plant (see below). The high wages, the secure jobs, an expanded social system and a high level of unemployment in the region engender a certain degree of loyalty vis-à-vis the employer. The (Polish) management is of the opinion that they employ the best workers and offers them substantial developmental opportunities by means of (internationally aligned) further qualification measures. The management's autonomy in the Polish site for the development of industrial relations is tolerated by the parent enterprise in Vienna as long as the Henkel Group's reputation as a socially responsible, law-abiding enterprise obligated to the region is not damaged as a result.

As aforementioned, there are no union representatives at Raciborz in Poland, although there had been one there up until the acquisition by Henkel in 1991. Due to the inability of the trade union at that time to develop its own visions for privatization and restructuring (which led to disappointment on the part of the employees and trade union members), and on account of a 'gentle' management endeavour to govern the industrial relations without trade unions, the trade unions gradually vanished from the plant. Wage increases and working conditions in accordance with Polish law were announced to the employees. Wage determinations are made according to individual qualification and ability.

Problems such as weekend work are unilaterally resolved or ordered by the management – but sweetened through high bonuses. According to statements by the managers, human resource management adequately replaces the regulations otherwise to be negotiated with the unions within a company. There is an 'open door policy', that is every employee has the right to ask their direct superiors questions. If this employee is afraid of sanctions, he or she can also ask these questions by bypassing the hierarchy to the next higher level. Workforce meetings are organized four times a year on the departmental level. In the opinion of the management, a well-functioning 'cascade system' of providing information to the employees has been installed as a result.

This system naturally prevents any anonymity – every step beyond loyalty is registered by the management. From that point of view, paternalism can certainly be spoken of here.

Despite the lack of unions within a company, there are two types of representatives in the Polish subsidiaries of the Henkel Group: First of all, the already aforementioned two EWC representatives, and secondly, the 'shop stewards'.

In Raciborz there are four 'shop stewards', who have been elected by the entire workforce and co-administer the site's social welfare regime (one of the four is a member of Solidarity, the other is a foreman and the remaining two are machinery operators). This committee can absolutely be described as a workforce body for social matters. It also happens that these representatives are also contacted by the workforce in other difficult matters. This social welfare committee meets regularly with the management. These forms of representation are absolutely to be appraised as attempts to a works council system that protects the anonymity of the individual workforce member and permits general – not just single – regulations of industrial relations.

Summary

The Henkel Group does not stand alone with regard to the transfer of responsibility for the CEE sites to their Austrian subsidiary. At the end of October 2004, over 1,000 international companies had their Central and Eastern Europe headquarters in Austria (Welt am Sonntag No. 45, 7 November 2004, 33). Not merely geographical conditions are decisive for this – after all, Berlin lies only 1.5 degrees of longitude further west than Vienna. More important are – in addition to the lasting effect of the traditionally better relations between Austria and the former East Bloc states after 1945 and the conquest of the CEE Financial markets *immediately after* the fall of the Berlin Wall (especially through Austrian banks) – the 'soft skills' of the Austrian negotiating mentality, which is also orientated towards results, but does not intend to implement these results directly and within the shortest time (as actually corresponds more to the German mentality).

The 'model transfer' of industrial relations is to be described as a mixed situation: on the one hand, this entails a solution and cooperation orientation on the part of the German and (on account of clientele commitment) even more the Austrian industrial relations, and conflict-shy paternalistic orientations on account of the ownership conditions and traditions (family-owned sub-enterprise) – this also corresponds quite well to the Austrian mentality. And so one could speak of a unilateral path dependency of industrial relations (one jointly considers Germany and Austria, which emphasizes the more traditional elements of the German model).

On the other hand, the human resource policy and the arrangement of the industrial relations in the Henkel Group CEE subsidiaries are orientated towards the global requirements, and above all the legal-historical circumstances in the respective CEE countries. And for the Polish Henkel plants that means a mixture of an exclusion (also jointly brought about by the trade unions) of the traditional union representatives from the regulation of the industrial relations (typical for SMEs in Central and Eastern Europe), and at the same time the careful build-up of works council structures.

On the whole, the industrial relations in the CEE Henkel plants are characterized by a mixture of conditions in the country of origin and host country of the investments. Europeanization stakes as third-state influences do not play a role (yet) in the arrangement of industrial relations.

RWE AG – a Provincial Rhine-Westphalian Enterprise on the Global Passing Lane

The Enterprise

The over 100 year-old RWE AG (Rheinisch-Westfaelisches Elektrizitaetswerk 'Rhine-Westphalian Electricity Works') has changed at a rapid pace since 1998: a typical German, indeed Rhine-Westphalian enterprise with interests not only in the energy sector, but also in the printing machinery, construction and telecommunications industry has become at least a major European player if not even a global player in the realm of integrated energy and water supply. RWE is the second-largest German energy concern after 'E. on'.

The generation and distribution of energy, water and environmental services in the target markets Germany, Austria, the Netherlands, the UK, Central and Eastern Europe and North America are the core businesses of the RWE AG. The holding company with registered office in Essen concentrates as a group centre on corporate-controlling tasks.

While doing so, the group is structurally arranged in the following seven business segments/companies:

- *RWE Energy*: this company (approx. 42,000 employees in 2004) represents the core area of the RWE AG. Integrated product offers are bundled here. This company encompasses all sales activities, transport and distribution networks for supply of electricity, gas and water as well as services in continental Europe. Six regionally integrated energy companies in Germany and another six in the rest of the European markets (Austria, the Netherlands, Poland, Czech Republic, Slovakia and Hungary) operate under the umbrella of this enterprise.
- *RWE Power*: the extraction of raw materials for energy and electricity generation through nuclear energy, hard coal, gas and oil (RWE DEA) and through regenerative energies such as water, wind and biomass (Harpen) takes place here.
- *RWE Innogy* Is responsible for the group's energy business in the UK.
- *RWE Trading* is the interface to energy wholesale markets and the group-wide hub for global commodities.
- *RWE Thames Water* develops and controls – as the third-largest enterprise in the industry – the group's worldwide water business (sold by RWE in October 2006).
- *RWE Umwelt* [environment]: as Germany's largest environmental services provider, RWE Umwelt controls the core business with waste and recycling activities (was sold over the course of 2005).

- *RWE Systems* is responsible as provider for comprehensive group-wide services. The tasks range from information technology via central procurement to real estate management.

In addition, there is also the Group Business Committee (comprised of the RWE AG executive board, the chairmen of the aforementioned seven companies, RWE DEA and the group development manager), which is essentially responsible for portfolio management, projects, strategy and planning.

The implementation of the so-called 'multi-utility strategy' – that is the compilation of power, gas and water activities on a regional basis – is the main focus of the restructuring and cost-reduction measures which have been quite intensively expedited since 2003. The objectives are efficiency increases and improved customer orientation. But this might be counteracted by national protectionism (including Spain and France) and by big cross-border energy conglomerates, which will create an oligopoly with hidden price agreements (status March 2006).

This restructuring process, which has been estimated at five years (2003–2007), is being expedited through the mandatorily prescribed fulfilment of the EU's 'unbundling provisions' for the energy market (the entry into force of the single provisions is occurring on a graduated basis from 1 July 2004 up until 1 July 2007). This distribution network provision shall create discrimination-free competition for energy in Europe. The European energy market is actually supposed to be liberalized as a result.

In the 2003 business year (status 31 December), the RWE Group (with 127,028 employees) generated a turnover of 43.875 billion euro. A double digit corporate profit surplus is anticipated for 2004 (2003: 953 million euro). Over 50 per cent of the employees work in the RWE companies outside of Germany, and about 50 per cent of the turnover is also made in these companies.

In 2005, the process of concentration on the RWE AG's core business was decisively expedited with the sale of RWE Umwelt (10,408 employees) and other peripheral segments. As of 30 June 2005, the group employed a total of 86,540 employees, of which about half continue to be employed abroad.

As the parent company of the CEE subsidiary enterprises, RWE Energy has exclusively transacted Brownfield investments.

Czech Republic
Transgas is the monopoly gas provider in the Czech Republic (100 per cent owned by RWE). On top of this there are majority holdings in six and minority holdings in two regional distribution enterprises (GDC – Gas Distribution Companies). The latter are controlled in southern Bohemia by the Upper Austrian Ferngas company and the German firm E. on and in Prague by the City of Prague.

RWE has been active in the Czech Republic since 2002; about 6,000 employees worked for RWE in mid-2004.

Slovakia
The eastern region of Slovakia is the distribution area of the VSE RWE Group in Kosice. RWE acquired 49 per cent of the stakes in VSE in 2003 (51 per cent remains

in the hands of the Slovakian state). Since the power supply area borders directly on that of Hungary's ÉMÁSZ (the RWE AG also has a majority stake in this enterprise), both companies work closely together. At the end of September 2004, 1,827 people were employed by VSE – the target size in 2007 is 1,400 employees.

Poland
In December 2002, RWE acquired 85 per cent of the stakes of STOEN (monopoly provider for electricity in metropolitan Warsaw). The firm has been responsible for the distribution of electricity, gas and water in Poland since 2003. STOEN employed 1,476 employees at the end of 2004. Altogether, 1,980 employees worked for the RWE AG in Poland on the same cut-off date.

The incomes of the employees in all three of the surveyed CEE RWE investments and affiliated companies lie slightly above the average in the regions in which the enterprises are located (comparatively high income was also already acquired in this sector before the acquisition through RWE). RWE always orientates itself towards the regional average; for instance, in the Czech Republic this means that varying wages are paid on a regional-specific basis for the same work. The prevailing working conditions at RWE, including occupational health and safety, are also pegged on a high level.

Therefore, RWE has also been able to afford the continued payment of these high incomes since the CEE investments yielded profits from the very first year: in this industrial sector, investments are de facto 'licenses to print money', since monopoly positions are usually secured. This will only change at the time of the complete European-wide liberalization of the energy market in 2007. Until then RWE aims at the completion of the necessary restructuring measures and the development of new business segments in Central and Eastern Europe.

Industrial Relations

The RWE AG with its six management companies (status: June 2005) and their respective corporate headquarters in North-Rhine Westphalia (excluded here are RWE Innogy and RWE Thames Water), as well as a vast number of subsidiary companies, is a prime example for the German system of industrial relations (Works Constitution Act and codetermination laws). And as far as that goes, RWE is a clear example for the German model of Rhine-Alpine capitalism – strengthened even more for decades through the provider's monopoly positions in the energy sector and the subsequently related amalgamation of local/regional energy companies and city/district administrations.

There is a works council for every single RWE enterprise within Germany. There are joint works councils in three of the six companies (excluded are the companies responsible for the UK or settled there). RWE Trading has 'only' one works council, whereas RWE Energy has something like a Corporate Works Council with 'ARGE Energy'. Underneath the 'ARGE "working group" Energy' there are also an additional seven joint works councils and naturally the vast number of works councils.

On the RWE AG's holding company level there is also an extra works council for the holding company employees as well as an 'ARGE Concern' – a sort of super

Corporate Works Council that encompasses *all* of the group's works council bodies. However, the Joint Works Councils of the single companies are the decisive bodies.

The corporate codetermination (parity of shareholders and employees on the supervisory board and codetermination with regard to the appointment of the personnel (labour) director) applies not only to the holding company (RWE AG), but also to the companies which meet the criteria of the German codetermination in the mining, coal and steel industry and the German Codetermination Law of 1976 – whereby the RWE AG's CEO (who who came between 2002 and 2007 from the Netherlands) expressly welcomes the German industrial relations scheme and the codetermination regulations on the corporate level as the form of industrial relations adequate for *Germany*.

In view of this highly developed (and very complex and difficult to comprehend from outside) structure of participation/codetermination on the corporate/site level, it is all the more astonishing that until the end of 2004 there had been no European Works Council – despite nearly three years of preparation to date.

Three forums have been or shall be set up for preparation of an EWC:

- Energy forum: includes six countries (without the UK)
- Water forum: includes seven countries (including the UK)
- Power Forum: is in planning.

This persistent planning process for establishing an EWC contracted the fact that the Special Negotiating Committee (as the EWC's founding committee) had already positioned itself at the end of 2004 with highly-political topics: two resolutions were passed at the second international conference of this committee on 24 November 2004 in Bochum, Germany: a declaration on the regulation of electricity and gas markets, the second regarding separation of the value added chain (in this regard, see the 'unbundling' provisions above). The EWC agreement for RWE Energy was finally signed on 1 March 2005. The new EWC includes delegates from Germany, Austria, the Netherlands, Poland, Czech Republic, Slovakia and Hungary. Two sessions/year are planned, which as a rule will be held in Essen or Dortmund (Northrine-Westphalia). A training entitlement of three days per EWC member has been agreed upon for the four-year term of office. The EWC's steering committee includes seven members from all seven countries involved.

The Slovakian company VSE is still an RWE minority stake, and to that extent its representatives will only have a guest status in the new EWC. Nevertheless, there had already been a preparatory committee for the Slovakian RWE company, which had already elected the chairman of the representatives as an observer for the EWC before the establishment of the EWC in March 2005. All representatives in the RWE investments in Poland, Czech Republic and Slovakia expect a better source of information from the newly established EWC than what they previously had, especially insofar as the income situation in the other respective RWE enterprises is concerned: because the CEE representatives certainly negotiate the collective agreements with the local management (in-house agreements, see below) and regard their operative negotiating position as strengthened through the EWC as well as through an improved information position.

Until the end of 2004 there were no bilateral relations worth mentioning between German representatives and representatives in the CEEC. For instance, the representatives from the Slovakian company VSE have only met with German RWE works councils just before the privatization/sale to RWE – but no more than that. There has been a similar contact between the representatives at STOEN in Poland and the German trade unions represented in the European Region Viadrina, which advised the Poles to approve the sale to RWE.

The persistent lack of an EWC and the rather sporadic bilateral contacts are due to several reasons, of which only two are to be mentioned here:

- The complexity of the corporate structure with the relatively independent companies and subsidiary companies and the subsequently conditioned complexity of the structure of workforce representation in Germany lack clear spheres of responsibility.
- The rapid pace of the RWE Group's corporate restructuring in Germany – particularly since 2003 – hardly allowed the German representatives any time to sufficiently deal with European/international topics. In legal and political terms, they were and are first of all forced to deal with the *internal* consequences of this reorganization.

There the management is already a bit further. The RWE Group's management principles, labour organization, communications regulations, and so on have been implemented as a standard in the CEE investments (the technology is similar in the West and East). And so the planned economy model and the Anglo-Saxon model of the solely responsible chief executive have for the most part been eliminated, and instead the principle of departmental (board) responsibility commensurate with German corporate law has been introduced. Also entirely new for the Central and Eastern Europeans was the introduction of the principle that *every* management level bears its *own* responsibility. As a result, the local managerial personnel (wherever there are any) still have substantial difficulties. The RWE AG has rapidly implemented radical changes in the management system (expedited through the preferential treatment given to young, English-speaking junior management personnel) at a pace that was partially too fast for the employees (with the exception of the Slovakian involvement in Kosice). For instance, alone 60 per cent of the second management level at STOEN in Poland (with the exception of technical management personnel) and altogether 40 per cent of all levels below the executive board have been replaced with newly hired (predominantly local) managers. This also transpired with the objective of reducing the number of hierarchy levels and the introduction of a 'flat' management structure.

Contingent upon this pace of changes, there has not been any clear communication of the objectives of these changes vis-à-vis the employees in the CEE RWE investments. On account of the experiences with the RWE investments in the Czech Republic, Slovakia and Hungary, the STOEN executive board now publishes 'letters to the employees' and has organized 28 working groups, which accompanied the various aspects of the upheaval and supported the integration into the RWE Group. This radical upheaval of structures was accompanied by a strong orientation towards human resource management (*direct* relations between management and employees without intermediaries, a system that was heretofore alien to the Central and Eastern Europeans), through which the errors of the management and problems/desires of the employees can be denominated – for instance, with the means of systematic superior-employee discussions and (anonymous) written employee surveys.

In the first phase of the investments (which still continued in 2005), the executive boards of the CEE national companies and managing directors of the regional companies are almost exclusively German – also for the reason of breaking the power of the old 'top management functionaries'. However, the medium-term objective is to at least staff the business managements of the regional companies in the CEEC with locals. Also in the Czech national company a qualification/career programme with the name 'Perspectives' has been announced for qualifying local management trainees. Similar programmes have also been announced for the Polish and Slovakian investments.

The latitude of the single investments vis-à-vis the parent company RWE Energy is relatively large within RWE's general framework and budgeting measures, particularly since the energy market is always a regional market and to that extent also has to be transacted flexibly. An essential control instrument of the RWE Group is the 'Balanced Scorecard', which with the help of a code number system operationalizes the strategy of the respective company to scalable control dimensions and additionally takes into account financial as well as non-financial perspectives. Qualitative instruments such as agreements on site-specific targets have been applied on a parallel basis.

The basic principle is a 'result-oriented control' of the single national companies and the regional companies on the level below: Financial latitudes are defined via the medium-term planning and budgeting and controlled via the aforementioned Balanced Scorecard Programme in a complex planning process. This gives rise to decision-making latitudes, which also ultimately influence the collective bargaining. There is a so-called 'Higher Collective Agreement' in the Czech energy industry. This collective agreement (as a skeleton agreement) – similar to the German overall collective agreement – formulates minimum conditions: from the wage group via allowances to working hours. It is negotiated on the association level. In turn, the single DDCs (sites) organize their own collective bargaining from the association agreement.

A similar procedure takes place in Slovakia and Poland: in Slovakia there is a company collective agreement and an additional industrial-sector overall collective agreement for minimum standards; in Poland there are also two collective agreements – one is directly for the STOEN enterprise (in-company agreement), and the other is an industrial-sector collective agreement with specific framework conditions and minimum standards.

RWE will also not diverge from this decentralized principle (that means in-house agreements) to avoid levelling the quite different regional wage levels upwardly. But of course all those structures are standardized which are able to be standardized. Examples for this are: equal wage groups, equal variable scales and equal allowance structure. The objective is the more efficient and more cost-effective arrangement of processes.

The local RWE management and the respective trade union representatives are doing the collective bargaining (company/site-related) in all three CEE countries.

A second control instrument could be a joint corporate culture, which could signify a help for management and workforces/representatives in the definition of industrial relations outside of the legal provisions. But RWE's rapid transformation process from a typical German (Rhine-Ruhr characterized) enterprise into an at least European enterprise has not previously allowed the emergence of such a corporate culture in the German parent enterprise – the perseverance of the employees in the Rhine-Westphalian environment is still too strong. Furthermore, the introduction of a general RWE corporate culture also conflicts with mentality-conditioned obstacles: for instance, in the Czech and Slovakian RWE enterprises there is a peculiar contradiction between a considerable improvizational ability of the employees on the one hand and a partially insane bureaucratic gullibility on the other hand. On top of this is the fact that there is still a deficiency in the rule of law and a high degree of willingness to engage in corruption, which co-determines the actions of the individual RWE employees. RWE is attempting to counteract this with the introduction of role models. This is underlined with a rigorous corporate policy which results in an immediate firing of the involved employee in the event of proven corruption.

Insofar as the RWE Group's self-understanding with regard to the arrangement of industrial relations in its CEE enterprises is now concerned, the German managers in the CEE companies as ex-patriates were also forced to reorientate themselves in an initial phase: because none of the customary company's/site's contact partners (à la works council) from Germany were found. Instead, there were union representatives, which were additionally fragmented in many areas: with STOEN in Poland there are three unions (which together constitute the union works committee and have a total of 42 per cent of all employees as members); in some Czech regional companies there are partially between 10 and 12 unions, whereby the latter have already started to work together and there is an umbrella organization – UNIOS – on the Czech national level; only in Slovakia there is merely one trade union with 75 per cent membership on the part of all employees. Modernizations of the industrial relations were implemented relatively rapidly on the basis of the 'old' structures (representatives): firstly, through the up to now principle of solution and cooperation orientation (previously unaccustomed in Central and Eastern Europe), and secondly, through an open information and communication structure. Before RWE's entry in the CEE energy companies the representatives were often the 'fifth wheel on the wagon'. Now a closer and more open cooperation is organized, naturally also with responsibilities for the representatives. As a result, it was also possible to carry out the dismissals – that were necessary after privatization and acquisition – without considerable frictional losses.

However, the industrial relations in the three CEE countries are quite different. For the management of the Polish STOEN, all three represented trade unions (as the largest Solidarity, thereafter OPZZ, and the smallest is the shift worker trade union) are very difficult partners with regard to the arrangement of social dialogue on the company level. The trade unions frequently change their opinion, and it costs the management quite a bit of time and arranging the industrial relations also calls for great caution. At STOEN, the trade union organization also always has a political component which was rather unusual for the German managers due to their experiences in Germany. Nevertheless, attempts are made to govern conflicts through an in-house mediator system and not to allow any open conflict to come about. As far as they are concerned, the representatives consider the managers as 'nouveaux riches', who have no 'technical' competence and as far as that goes only a deficient legitimacy for fulfilment of management tasks in a 'power company'. One also has to know that through the restructuring of STOEN into a market-orientated company (and away from a purely technically-orientated planned economy enterprise) the technology realm has lost a considerable degree of importance in the overall business enterprise. And most trade union representatives particularly come from this technology realm. Nevertheless, one cannot describe the industrial relations at STOEN as conflictive per se; in the case study period (end of 2004) it is more of a trial of strength between the two actors in the company.

On the other hand, the situation in Slovakia and in the Czech Republic looks quite different (despite the union fragmentation): the industrial relations are developed from information, communication, regular meetings between management and the representatives and the subsequently increasing trust between both actors in stringent observance of prevailing laws. The management in the single works as well that of the Czech and Slovakian national company is willing to discuss lasting proposals on the part of the trade unions regarding arrangement of working conditions, and takes the representatives seriously as partners in this business. According to statements by the representatives in the Czech Republic and Slovakia, these representatives have been able to develop a much broader understanding of the common objectives (despite all differences, particularly with regard to collective bargaining). Starting from the Czech and Slovakian national companies, joint working groups were established by management and representatives in 2004, which also incorporate the management representatives of the RWE investments in Poland and the parent company in Germany.

As a result, the current RWE management in the CEE subsidiaries/joint ventures differs quite positively from those business managements as they existed before the acquisition in 2002/03.

But nothing was considered about the introduction of (equal) codetermination à la German parent enterprise (this would then take place on a voluntary basis). A (minority) involvement of the employees in the supervisory board is legally prescribed in Poland, the Czech Republic and Slovakia. For instance, Slovakian and Czech representatives have three seats on the supervisory board of the Slovakian/ Czech national company. These representatives in the CEE RWE enterprises are now always invited to preliminary discussions with the supervisory board chairman before the actual supervisory board meeting – a novelty for CEE relationships.

In summary, it can be said that the German – or better, the RWE model – has not been transferred, but some of its basic principles with the most essential elements of solution orientation and cooperative willingness. But this does not include the 'German works council' with its far-reaching rights of codetermination, participation and information. The business managements and human resource managers definitely distance themselves from this one-to-one transfer of the German 'model' with the argument that the legal and informal conditions of the industrial relations in Poland, the Czech Republic and Slovakia are much more flexible. According to statements from the management, in the three CEEC only two years were necessary (from 2002 to 2004) for what would have taken 10 years in Germany for implementation of far-reaching reforms.

Insofar as that is concerned, it is also only logical that the (German) executive board chairmen and managing directors in the CEE RWE companies take a very sceptical view of the existing legal regulation pertaining to the introduction of 'works councils' in the Czech Republic and Slovakia – for them the system with the (partially competing) trade unions within one company/site is much better and more clearly arranged (also according to the 'divide and conquer' principle) than the dual system with the two different contact partners on the employee side. A second coordinating committee would be provided on the employee side through the erection of a second pillar. Up to now, it is by no means clear as to which areas the 'works council' is responsible for and which areas the trade union representatives might responsible for (differently than in Germany with the deep-rooted division of labour between works council and supra-company industrial trade union).

This rejection does not even refer to the dual system in Germany, but rather to the mixed RWE experiences with regard to the 1992 introduction of the works council in Hungary (which in terms of its rights is much weaker vested than the works council in Germany). The management is supported by the CEE trade union representatives in this rejection – even if the latter do so for somewhat different reasons (fear of new competition and apprehensions that works councils could mutate into employer-friendly institutions – 'yellow unions'). But both actors – the management and the trade union representatives in the CEE RWE subsidiaries – are also always concerned with the retention of their respective positions of power.

Summary

Until the end of the last century the RWE AG was a typical German – indeed, Rhine-Westphalian – enterprise. Since then, it has been restructured by a 'rapid passage' into a global, but at the very least European player. The top management is very internationally staffed (the current executive board chairman is a Dutchman). However, the group's employees in Germany as well as in the CEE investments do not (yet) get along well with this internationalism. But the RWE 'history' in Poland, the Czech Republic and Slovakia only began in 2002, and as far as that goes there has only been a short period for acclimatization up to now. The employees feel themselves to a great extent regionally anchored, which is also partially rooted in the business itself (regional nature of energy production and distribution). This is also reflected in the industrial relations in Germany: the handed-down (often locally/regionally anchored in the Rhine-Ruhr region) industrial relations respectively the works council do not (yet) think and act in European or even global dimensions. This rapid internationalization of the RWE Group signifies a structural overburdening for the workforces and their representatives in Germany. For the RWE Group Management this signifies a split between the necessary identification (also to be borne by the employees) with RWE as a multinational company and the slower proceeding 'human resource' learning and adaptation processes.

But particularly between 2003 and 2005 important influences on the arrangement of industrial relations in the CEE RWE companies would have been possible through the German works councils, perhaps even the installation of a dual system – at least à la Hungary. There was not even an EWC as a possible influence and bridge function until the end of 2004 – it was first established in 2005. As a result, the management alone was left with the configuration of industrial relations in Central and Eastern Europe, which rests on the prevailing legal provisions there (but which reject the establishment of works councils) and which is based on the structures found in the Brownfield investments.

But the strict observance of the legal provisions does not signify their restrictive interpretation – on the contrary: the RWE management in Poland, the Czech Republic and Slovakia – for the most part supported by the CEE trade union representatives already existing before the RWE investments (the Polish representatives on the site/ company level constitute a certain exception; their competing trade unions are to a great extent still politically and ideologically aligned) – has created an open culture of solution orientation and cooperative willingness (not necessarily to be confused with the strong codetermination rights of the representatives). Also associated with this is the recognition of the trade union representatives as negotiating partners taken seriously by the management, the subsequently resulting promotion of the professionalization of the representatives, improved qualification/career opportunities for the employees and a higher demand for willingness to perform (assessed by the workforce as positive). As a result, the newly arranged industrial relations fundamentally differ from that type as it had existed there before 2002/03 – not to mention the relationships during the communist time.

Nestlé SA – a Global Player with Dialogue-Orientated Industrial Relations

The Enterprise

The concern was founded in 1867 by the German Heinrich Nestlé in Vevey/ Switzerland. In Germany, the company became established in 1874.

The Nestlé SA is the world's largest food concern with about 8,000 produced brands. In 2003, the turnover was nearly 88 billion Swiss francs – with a net profit of at least 6 billion Swiss francs. In the same year the company employed about 250,000 workers in 508 factories in 85 countries. As a result of the high productivity growth on the one hand and the stagnating demand situation on the other hand, there are high overcapacities: for instance, the capacity utilization in the ice cream industry amounts to only 21 per cent; in many other sectors it varies between 40 and 50 per cent.

In addition to the increased wages in Central and Eastern Europe (among other things), this resulted in the fact that – without spectacular plant relocations (strongly noticed by the public) having to come about – it was smaller, 'quieter' relocations of production lines, which led to 'adaptations' – such as in 2003 from Hungary to Poland. Moreover, for reasons of cost and market development, more and more factories are relocated or newly established further eastwards. For instance, in 2004 a chocolate factory was relocated from the Czech Republic to Bulgaria; in the Russian region Krasnodar – also in 2004 – the construction of a 120 million US dollar factory (processing green coffee into instant coffee) was started; and in Kuban – also in Russia – a factory was opened in August 2005, which produces the Nestlé brand Nescafé Classic (with an annual capacity of 18,000 tonnes).

Insofar as that is concerned, the sites in the CEEC also came under a similar pressure as the West European factories some years before, since this entailed the exploitation of the CEE markets. The company's measuring instrument for examining productivity and profitability of the single sites is the High Performance Factory system (HPF). With this, cost objectives are agreed upon within a certain product category – called 'class' in-house (for example ice cream or chocolate). The benchmarking is made on this basis that is the comparison of factories (which produce this product) amongst each other. In addition to cost reduction, the second objective of the HPF system is the best possible capacity utilization within a 'class'. Any factory can become 'best in class'. Then, according to this sequence, the production lines are redistributed to the single sites. However, these streamlining and consolidation programmes on the part of the Nestlé SA ('Target, 2004' and 'Target, 2004 +') were not so dramatic in their consequences for the employees as with, for example, the rival Unilever firm.

The Nestlé SA is divided into three geographic groups/zones: Europe; North and South America; Asia, Oceania and Africa zone. These zones essentially define the respective national companies, which on their part direct the factories in the respective countries. The Nestlé Waters business segment is situated crosswise to this. The wages in the CEE Nestlé subsidiaries are partially about one-third higher than in the regional average; the working conditions and the qualification possibilities for the employees are also better. Nestlé employs a high percentage of seasonal personnel (for example in the chocolate production for Easter and Christmas, which are provided in the factory via an agency (temporary employment firm). The job satisfaction is high; according to an independent study in the Polish Nestlé factory in Winiary, 80 per cent of the employees are satisfied with the working conditions and income.

In 2004, there were nine sites in Poland, three in the Czech Republic and one in Slovakia; in comparison with this, there were 24 sites/plants in Germany. About 400 million USD were invested by the Nestlé SA in the Polish sites up until 2004, and about 4,300 employees worked here in 2004. The site of special interest to us is located in Winiary (580 permanent employees and 40 seasonal workers in 2004). It is a Brownfield investment with a considerable product range of food processing, the names (brands) of which the Polish consumers have already partially known and appreciated for 40 years.

In Slovakia, 740 employees work for Nestlé (everything in relation to the year 2004). Most of the employees were concentrated at the Prievidza factory (590 employees, of which 400 are permanent employees and 190 are seasonal workers). In addition to well-introduced domestic products, the works (taken over in 1992) also produces Maggi products, of which about two-thirds are re-exported – mainly to other CEE countries.

In the Czech Republic, Nestlé employed 2,122 people in 2004, of which 491 were at the headquarters in Prague (which is responsible for the Czech Republic as well as for Slovakia). The main production sites in the Czech Republic are (also all Brownfield investments) ZORA in Olomuoc, Sfinx in Holesov and Orion. The main products are chocolate and other sweets. The traditional product names/brands have been retained.

Industrial Relations

The decisions concerning investments and the fundamental principles for arrangement of industrial relations are made at the Swiss group headquarters. Nevertheless, the Nestlé Deutschland AG has indirect influence on the arrangement of the industrial relations in the CEE sites. This is manifested via the body 'NECIC – Nestlé European Council for Information and Consultation' – the European Works Council. Due to a strong influence on the part of the German representatives in this body, the German 'infrastructure' of workforce representation and codetermination bodies (corporate codetermination on the supervisory board) also gains a certain degree of importance for the EWC at Nestlé. The (coming from Germany) co-chairman of the EWC (the other co-chairman comes from the management) active in this position since 1993 is at the same time a member of the Joint Works Council and in the Nestlé AG Deutschland Corporate Works Council (which is organized as a voluntary working group), and has been an external employee representative on the Nestlé Deutschland AG supervisory board since 1989. At the same time, since 1988 he has been the person in charge of the German trade union NGG (food processing and restaurants) for the Nestlé Deutschland AG, and – via the international food trade union IUF – also coordinator for the Nestlé SA EWC.

The EWC was established in 1990 on a voluntary basis and without a *written* contract between the International Union of Food, Agricultural, Hotel, Restaurant, Catering, Tobacco and Allied Workers'Associations IUF and the Nestlé SA. A contract within the framework of the corresponding EU directive exists since 1996. In 2003, a new contract was concluded, which streamlines (reduces in numbers) the EWC and has granted more space for the representatives coming from the sites: in the old EWC there were 51 members (of which 34 were representatives companies/ sites and 17 were from the supra-company's trade unions). In the new EWC there are between 35 and 38 members (the number fluctuates a bit due to the rapid purchase and sale of factories), of which only three or four are external members. In the opinion of the representatives, this has made the discussions much more open, 'since now things are discussed without (union-political) ideology': Trade union representatives from the countries in which there was no unified trade union – but several rival trade unions within one industrial sector – competed very strong with one another and now carried out their national conflicts on the European level.

However, the German representatives in the EWC find themselves in a much stronger position than their colleagues from the other EU countries: unity trade union, good information situation through the German industrial relations scheme and corporate codetermination. In the UK, there is no such infrastructure, the same in France and Spain. This is why Nestlé UK has voluntarily established a representation scheme on the site level; this is also encouraged by the British Nestlé management.

In accordance with the provisions of the new EWC contract concluded in 2003, there is now only one session a year instead of two sessions. In addition, the EWC's steering committee meets twice a year, together with the management. In the event of certain problems there is a third level – the ad hoc committee.

Before 1 May 2004 (EU accession date of the eight CEE countries) there were also representatives from Hungary, Poland and the Czech Republic in the EWC, but only as observers. The CEE representatives found this status to be inadequate and discriminating. Although the CEE representatives were treated as full EWC members, they nevertheless felt like second-class representatives.

This has changed on a merely formal basis since 1 May 2004.

Two EWC members come from Poland, two from the Czech Republic, and one member (each) comes from Slovakia and Hungary. The EU accession (Romania, Bulgaria), candidate (Croatia, Turkey) and pre-candidate countries (like Serbia, Montenegro, and so on) are not – also not as observers – represented in the EWC.

Of the two Polish EWC representatives, one is a Solidarity representative from Winiary, and the other representative was nominated by OPZZ and works in the factory at Poznań. The Polish EWC representatives are torn between the solidarity with the already concluded (and affected by shrinkage processes) Nestlé sites and the understanding of the necessity that these closures/shrinkages could entail a recovery of the entire Polish location. In their opinion, the EWC is merely an information body, but not a decision-making institution.

The Slovakian EWC representative has been nominated by the responsible site representatives. His expectations of the EWC are similarly restrained like those of his Polish colleagues. Perhaps later the EWC could become something like a bridge between East and West.

Of the two Czech EWC representatives, one is the human resource manager and the other is the chairman of representatives. In the opinion of the last-named representative, the EWC can certainly play an intermediary role between the single subsidiaries and the parent company. The local representatives hope to obtain information through the EWC that it cannot otherwise receive from the local management.

In perspective terms, the EWC could also play an important role in the mediation between Central and Eastern Europe and Western Europe. But this is also up to the individuals and their individual commitment/ability.

Furthermore, this 'mediatory perspective' is clouded by the fact that – in the opinion of the EWC's union co-chairman – the employee side is not well-organized in this body. The representatives had to demand much more information from the management of their respective national companies, that is on the national level (as the German representatives already demand from their German management on account of the different tradition of codetermination). The upshot of the German co-chairman regarding the EWC:

Only if the national level is well-organised can the EWC also work effectively.

Moreover, there is hardly any bilateral understanding between representatives in the CEE subsidiaries on the one hand and, on the other hand, those in the parent company or also in the Nestlé Deutschland AG (as in comparison with other countries the best-organized network of representatives).

There are several comprehensive supra-company collective wage agreements for the Nestlé Deutschland AG (because Nestlé is active in several sectors), whereas the CEE subsidiary enterprises are subject to an in-company wage agreement. This can be quite a problem in countries with several trade unions in the site. For instance, Solidarity and OPZZ in Poland argue about who is allowed to negotiate this contract with the management and sign it afterwards.

Both CEE Nestlé national companies (Poland and Czech Republic/Slovakia) have a wage/income budget allocated by the parent enterprise, which is then broken down to the single sites. The collective bargaining partners (local management and representatives) are now able to exhaust this framework through collective bargaining – in compliance with legal provisions (like the minimum wage negotiated for the Slovakian food processing industry on the whole). In Poland, Nestlé abolished the old collective agreements without the resistance of the two unions during the acquisition of the factory in Winiary. The latter remained passive, since they could hardly hope for the support of the workforces in the event of a possible protest. And so the local management could more or less totally 'dictate' their visions.

The Nestlé SA corporate employee representatives have been 'tinkering around' with a World Works Council since 1990. There have been regular meetings amongst representatives from all Nestlé national companies since 1994. Now, since 2004, there is a new project through which the three Nestlé world regions/zones are supported by coordinators of the IUF international trade union. However, the regional secretaries on the scene fear having to share their power with this new body. Even the Nestlé management tolerates these activities and appears (in the entity of the personnel manager) more often at this world meeting. In 1999, these world meetings of the Nestlé representatives developed a 'Manila Protocol' for protection of minimum standards; but until the beginning of 2005 this had not been worked into the general 'business principles' by the Nestlé corporate management – despite a promise to the contrary. It remains unclear as to what extent the CEE industrial relations will be influenced by these minimum standards.

The parent concern Nestlé SA is attempting to implement a uniform global management system. The latitude of the single subsidiaries vis-à-vis the headquarters is very marginal as a result of the constant comparison amongst each other and the specifications through the headquarters are quite rigid; for instance, the Europe zone has to transfer 15 per cent of the net turnover to the headquarters. Through the project 'GLOBE' all figures and code numbers of the Nestlé enterprises are globally standardized and thus also made comparable. The single national countries cannot produce country-specific products quickly and on their own initiative without the consent of the Swiss parent. The self-responsibility and self-initiative of the manager according to the motto 'there is always a superior who decides' is also severely restricted through the principle of centralization.

Of course, the CEE Management is not prescribed *how* it has to achieve its objectives, but there are constant controls of the single sites through the Swiss headquarters. This centralization is confronted with local decentralization: the single plants are not only allowed (on their own authority) to input their own data in the corporate files, but are also allowed to look at quite a bit of general corporate data which goes beyond the respective plant. Furthermore, the strength of the local management vis-à-vis the headquarters also stems from the relative value of the products manufactured in the respective subsidiary in the Nestlé SA's general production association.

The recruitment of management for the subsidiaries is determined by four principles: First of all, managers are recruited on a company-specific basis. Secondly, it applies that top managers shall not build up any excessively strong bonds with the respective site (managers are replaced every two to three years, at a maximum of five years). Thirdly, young managerial personnel from the West are specifically sent abroad (also to CEE countries) as an important contribution towards their further career. Fourthly, in the initial phase of the acquisition the top management of the CEE plants came from the western countries, to break the old networks in the CEE subsidiaries. Nearly all Nestlé investments are Brownfield investments with subsequent restructurings. Overall the recruitment of managers – also for the CEE Nestlé plants takes place more through in-house selection and less through national origin – Nestlé really is a global player: differently than in other companies with West European origin, the staffing of the top positions at the Nestlé AG does not occur according to the criterion that the nationality of the works managers must coincide with the parent enterprise's country of origin.

Moreover, expatriates are usually dispatched only on an ad hoc basis: for instance, foreign (and not just Swiss) managers in the Polish sites only stay on if an acute problem crops up (for example the formation of a project group or the implementation of strategic decisions). After completion of this assignment these managers turn their back on Poland.

Trade union representatives (and not the new works councils possible under the law in the Czech Republic and Slovakia) exist in all of the sites in Poland, the Czech Republic and Slovakia – they were Brownfield investments. However, the relations between the representatives and the local management are quite differently characterized: in Slovakia, only very few conflicts are reported in the Carpathian sites with a trade union membership of about 50 per cent of the employees. In the Czech Republic, conflicts did not previously have to come to any supra-company conciliation, although the management there does not have to pass on more information than is legally prescribed. In comparison, the situation is Poland is more difficult with a much higher proportion of union membership: Solidarity and OPZZ represent the employees here – a third existing trade union is insignificant. The Solidarity representatives[2] complain about very selective information policy of the local management: despite monthly meetings with all trade unions in the plant, none of the plant's economic figures are announced, but merely general figures from the Nestlé national company in Poland, and thus the work of the trade unions in the respective plant is substantially curtailed. The management – particularly in

---

2   There is a union of the Solidarity representations from all Polish works in an 'Intercollegiate Coordination Commission of Trade Unions Nestlé' – a type of Corporate Works Council according to German model, but without any negotiating mandate whatsoever.

Winiary – considers Solidarity as ideological, revolutionary and hardly capable of cooperation. The management would rather work together with the (weaker) OPZZ, and thereby strengthens the split that exists between the two unions anyway. The employees themselves suspect the management of bribery and corruption, and are hesitant in the compliance with the ideas of the business management. They are strengthened even more in this belief through Solidarity.[3]

One reason for the different quality of industrial relations in the three CEE countries could lie in the union fragmentation in Poland and the subsequently resulting intensified legitimating compulsion of the represented trade unions. Whereas in the Czech Republic and Slovakia there are strong, formalized in-house regulations of the industrial relations, which allow little leeway for different interpretations of the conflict settlement mechanisms.

This all means that the industrial relations in the CEE Nestlé plants are thoroughly fragmented: for one thing, Nestlé advocates the principle that the underlying legal conditions are applied in the respective countries – nothing less, but also nothing more. For instance, the demand from Portuguese representatives to increase the rights of representatives in the Portuguese sites to the level of the EU-15 was rejected.

In addition, on account of the high workforce fluctuation the trusting relations between management and representatives must be repeatedly re-established so that the legal framework can be at all effective.

The build-up of these personnel relations is made even more difficult through two factors:

- First of all, as seen above, in-corporate/in-site collective agreements are valid in the CEE subsidiaries. That is to say that – at least on the management side – the negotiating partner changes every two to three years (up to a maximum of five years) and does not necessarily come from the host country of the investments (keywords: international management).
- Secondly, a corporate culture is being built up at the Nestlé SA; but this does not appear exculpatory (at least not at the moment) in relation to the foundation of identity and thus the establishment of a fundamentally trusting relationship between the plant management and representatives could be promoted independently of the actors acting at the moment: because the principles of corporate culture are very generally formulated and refer too much to abstract ILO standards – among other things, to be able to engender an identity. On the other hand, the traditional corporate culture of the sites with their local brands produced there (for example at the Czech works in Orion and Zora) has an identity-providing effect, but this does not relate to Nestlé on the whole.

The management in the CEE subsidiaries often does not acknowledge the representatives there as full discussion partners, especially not if the latter are only weakly represented (such as in the Prague headquarters responsible for the Czech Republic and Slovakia). This is also due to reasons which are even to be found on

---

3   Besides, all trade unions in the CEE countries are lacking junior staff: New employees, especially young people, hardly ever join the trade union.

the part of the representatives. For instance, in one CEE Nestlé site there are often several – competing – trade unions (such as in Poland) which reciprocally block each other. On top of this is the partially lacking trustworthiness of the trade unions there, which have not yet fully completed their own transformation process from former instruments of the communist party into free trade unions.

Insofar as a legally possible establishment of works councils in Slovakia and in the Czech Republic is concerned, the Nestlé CEE management and the representatives fundamentally welcome such an establishment in Slovakia, but up to now have not contributed anything to the application of this desire. In the Czech Republic, where according to the law there may not be any coexistence of trade union representatives and works council, the trade union representatives are more strongly interested in the establishment of works councils (in the form of a stable dualism) than the management – but even here nothing has happened up top now.

Summary

The self-image of the Nestlé SA is that of a multinational and global player whose headquarters – according to the core principle of this corporate culture – rather coincidentally is located in Switzerland. This means that the arrangement of the industrial relations in the CEE Nestlé subsidiaries partially emanates from the principle of the 'footloose' enterprise – that is from a path independency. But this path independency entails four supplements.

First of all, the legal provisions (the observance of which Nestlé strictly heeds) in the host countries of the investments are to be mentioned. Secondly, there is a cooperative willingness (exceeding the legal provisions) on the part of the management, which is much stronger than in the American and/or East Asian dominated sites. Thirdly, the change in ownership with regard to the Brownfield investments (there were no Greenfield investments) at the beginning of the 1990s entailed – in comparison with the previous management – a complete change of labour relations (relative openness, flat hierarchies, better wage-performance relationship, and increased qualification and career opportunities for the employees). And fourthly (less official), the strong influence of the German representatives (trade unions and works councils) in the Nestlé EWC is to be mentioned; they informally managed to include their experiences and traditions of the arrangement of industrial relations into this body. However, the Nestlé EWC's commitment to the representatives in the CEE subsidiaries is partially quite weak, and so only a very indirect and coincidental influence of German industrial relations on those relations in the CEE plants can be spoken of.

Dr. August Oetker KG – a Patriarchal-Led International Enterprise

The Enterprise

The basis of the company's business success was the discovery of 'Backin' baking powder by the Bielefeld pharmacist Dr. August Oetker in 1891. Right after the First World War the company expanded to Eastern Europe – Poland and Hungary. After the Second World War the CEE subsidiaries were expropriated and repurchased by Oetker after 1990.

The Oetker Group is still a family-owned enterprise with headquarters in Westphalian Bielefeld. The corporate group is active in various business segments under the umbrella of the Dr. August Oetker KG. The 2003 group financial statement encompassed five consolidated business segments with a total of 17,664 employees on 31 December 2003:

- food processing (7,462 employees);
- beer and alcohol-free beverages (2,643);
- sparkling wine, wine and spirits (1,879);
- shipping (2,692);
- remaining business segments (2,988).

A total of 324 firms were recorded, of which 199 have their registered office in Germany and 125 abroad. After shipping, the food processing sector was the second most important performer (2003 turnover about 1.5 billion euro).

The business activities are becoming increasingly more internationally-orientated. The Oetker International GmbH constitutes the umbrella organization of numerous Oetker production and distribution companies. Foreign Holdings are also gaining importance in growth.

In contrast to 2002 (45.1 per cent), the share of domestic turnover in the total turnover declined in 2003 to 41.6 per cent. According to statements by a group spokesperson, a large-scale relocation of production to low-wage countries is not planned. The allocation of nearly 80 per cent of the investments transacted at German sites (53 million euro out of a total of 67 million euro) in 2003 seems to indicate this.

Oetker has subsidiaries in all three of the CEEC examined by us, as well as in Romania, Hungary and Russia. The CEEC are among the core countries for the concern's foreign investment activity. Management and representatives emphasize that the German market is saturated ('a contested predatory market'). The new EU countries are good options as expanding markets, in which old traditions can be continued. One example of this is the acquisition of the food processing factory at Gdańsk-Oliva in Poland, which belonged to Oetker before the Second World War. In 1991, the trade unions and workforce in Poland voted in favour of the acquisition through Oetker. The Gdańsk nutriment factory, a 100 per cent subsidiary of the Oetker Group, employs about 200 workers. Of those workers, 100 are active in production; and most of them are women between 30 and 40 years old with a relatively low level of qualification. The white-collar workers also take care of the marketing for the two other Oetker factories (yoghurt factory in Maków Mazowiecki, pizza/ sandwich factory in Leba), and are often bilingual. The Gdańsk investment in 1991 was a pioneering feat for the region and at the same time symbolic for the improving German-Polish relations. The employment has remained stable until today (2005), and the fluctuation rates among the employees are relatively marginal.

But the lower labour costs also play an important role for investments. Old sites from Germany have partially been relocated. These sites can still be operated profitably with lower labour costs in the CEEC, whereas more modern sites have been constructed in Germany. According to management statements, the avoidance of German industrial relations has not played any role as an investment motive.

The company is constantly expanding its market position through acquisitions. In Slovakia, the main competitor in the baking sector, Kavoviny Sered, was acquired in November 2003. In the spring of 2004 Oetker purchased the Onken GmbH in Moers, Germany with a total of 500 employees, which on its part operates works in *Russia and Poland.*

In 2003, the Radeberger Group (which belongs to Oetker) implemented a restructuring on the hotly contested market for beer, during the course of which the Polish brewery Białystok was repurchased. The number of employees in this sector fell from 2,960 to 2,643. In the Czech Republic, the historic Krusovice brewery – which looks back on an over 400-year-old history – belongs to Oetker. After the investment by Oetker, the brewery was extensively modernized in 1993. In 1997, Oetker increased its stake to 98 per cent. Today Krusovice belongs to the Radeberger Group (in which the Oetker brewery activities are consolidated), and is ranked fifth among the Czech breweries. In 2004, exports (among other things, to Germany) came up to 22.3 per cent of overall production.

Oetker has Brownfield as well as Greenfield acquisitions in the CEEC. The management side emphasizes the advantages of Greenfield investments, in which the flow of material can be optimized from the very beginning.

Industrial Relations

In Germany, Oetker is subject to a supra-company collective wage agreement (sectoral, regional) concluded with the NGG trade union. The works council in Bielefeld is responsible for the German production plants in Bielefeld, Brackwede and Oerlinghausen (all located in Westphalia). In addition, there are further production plants with other companies with different legal forms and their own works councils. There is no Joint Works Council. Instead, the various works councils are consolidated in a working group which meets three to four times per year. In addition, a conference is held once a year. The international networking on the employee side is correspondingly less formalized too. Instead of a European Works Council there is a 'Europa Forum'. It only meets every two years. Not only the works councils/trade union representatives, but also the management of the different sites meet from different countries in this connection. Some managers from the sites serve as interpreters. This makes informal contacts between the representatives from different countries more difficult.

The Europa Forum is known in Gdańsk-Oliva in Poland, but until 2005 there was no representative from this works in the forum. A former Solidarity trade union official – trained in EWC matters – regards such a forum as very useful for the exchange with the German representatives – because at the moment there are no bilateral contacts (on the employee side) between the two countries.

The management does not perceive the Europa Forum as a modification of a European Works Council:

Up to now, there is no European umbrella [organization] in our company.

The works councils in Germany are doubtful whether the Europa Forum can play the role of a bridge to the CEE representatives, since there have been no autonomous discussions among the representatives in this body.

According to management information, no works councils exist in the CEE subsidiaries, but exclusively trade union representatives. The (trade union) representatives partially take part in regular meetings with the management. In Hungary, one production worker sits on the supervisory board; a trade union representative is on the supervisory board in Poland. Oetker pays well and the jobs are relatively secure. This is why the identification with the company is high. According to a management representative, 'everybody is proud to work at Oetker'.

At Krusovice in the Czech Republic there is a trade union organization which belongs to the 'Independent Trade Union of Workers in the Food processing industry of Bohemia and Moravia' (NOS PPP). It is a member of the umbrella organization of trade unions (MKOS). Only about 10 per cent of the approximately 300 employees are organized in the trade union.

There is only one trade union (Solidarity) with 50 members (about one-fourth of the workforce is unionized) at Gdańsk-Oliva in Poland. The local management pursues the corporate culture from Oetker and defines it as family-characterized. Social welfare regime, and so on has been arranged and administered by the management alone. The local top management (German ex-patriates) discusses problems with the employees and trade unions. In matters relating to wage level the management is contrary to the demands of the workforce. In the past 15 years the wage increases have merely corresponded to the inflation rate. In 2004, an informal plant representatives body (consisting of three individuals, this representatives group was supposed to advice the plant management in matters relating to the employees) was elected in 'heave-ho' procedure during a workforce meeting at the suggestion of the management. This was adopted by the trade union with a feeling of unease, although Solidarity did not appear openly against it. Nevertheless, it must be said that even in the opinion of the trade union representatives the (German) top management in Gdańsk-Oliva is very loyal vis-à-vis the Polish location and – despite partially differing opinions – discusses the pending problems with the trade union, but even also solves the problems very flexibly in its own way.

With regard to the management rules, the framework is set by the corporate headquarters. According to group management statements, the managers – also the top managers – for the CEE subsidiaries are recruited locally, with a few exceptions (see Poland). The reason for this is that the headquarters does not perceive itself as being able to accurately assess the local behaviour, mentalities and the consumer habits in the single countries. However, a central control is performed through defined goals and objectives, the compliance of which is controlled through monthly reports from the site managers, meetings – at least three times a year – and through visits to the subsidiary enterprises by the corporate management. Plans from site managers, investments and introduction of new products must be submitted to the headquarters and coordinated with HQ personnel. The brand constitution plays an important role in the corporate role model. Quality management, the outward appearance, and the cooperative management style are elements which are transferred to all (even CEE) subsidiaries. For example, the works management at Gdańsk-Oliva in Poland still enjoys a relative degree of autonomy. The local top management – here two Germans – initiated the investments in the yoghurt and pizza/sandwich factory.

With regard to industrial relations, the management side is of the opinion that there is a good working climate in the CEE subsidiary enterprises. There are no problems with the local trade unions, whilst the previous growth of the company was met with low-conflict cooperation. The high flexibility of the CEE personnel is to be particularly emphasized. For instance, rules pertaining to holidays are made in-house.

The representatives in Germany and in the Czech Republic as well as Poland perceive the relationship with the management more critically, and refer to a conflict (in their opinion) due to the company's deficient information policy.

However, the German representatives believe that new management structures could evolve in the CEEC. In Germany, the company has somewhat more rigid management structures with many hierarchy levels.

According to the perception of the German group headquarters, there is brisk contact between the works councils in Germany and the CEE subsidiaries.

According to information from the representatives, this does not correspond to reality. There are no connections and no contact with the representatives there; in turn, this has been confirmed. The 'Lotus Notes' electronic information and schedule coordination programme has been introduced in all sites. Therefore, contact is theoretically conceivable, but the works councils in Germany do not have any CEE contact partners known by name. This statement is confirmed through the works council at Radeberger (the brewery belonging to the Oetker Group), which also has no contact with the beer producing subsidiary in the Czech Republic. A few years ago German works council representatives visited the Czech Krusovice brewery. But at that time they were only received by the brewery management. In 2004, due to the acquisition of the 'Brau und Brunnen' (Brew and Well) through Radeberger the German works council also lacked the time to establish connections with the Czech Republic. There is merely a loose contact with the works councils of the other Oetker companies in Germany. A rather informal meeting of the German works councils is held once a year, at which the single sites are reported on. One general problem for the representatives of the non-listed parent enterprise seems to be that information is very hard to obtain – even for the works councils in Germany – in the Oetker sites.

Summary

Oetker represents the typical case of a patriarchal-led multinational company. Even if the technology in the CEE subsidiaries is not up everywhere to the same standard as in Germany, the influence of the parent enterprise in other areas is substantial. The parent enterprise determines the management system, marketing and guidelines of the Oetker establishment, which is very strongly orientated towards the brand image. The management trainees from the CEEC are committed through training sessions in Germany to the fundamental guidelines of the Oetker group. The respective rules of the host country are accepted with regard to industrial relations.

There are no discernible initiatives whatsoever to influence the industrial relations in the direction of German models. What does play an important role for this is the fact that the German representatives have not undertaken – or were not able to undertake – any previous efforts to establish lasting connections with representatives in the CEEC. As a family-owned enterprise, Oetker is traditionally characterized by rather patriarchal industrial relations. The works councils in Germany appreciate the quite good relationship with the owner family, but for quite some time perceive this relationship as under pressure since the current chairman has returned after a lengthy stay in the USA and more American visions have been introduced to the company. The new challenges – resulting from a modification of patriarchal-characterized industrial relations as well as through the internationalization – pose substantial problems for the works council in Germany. It seems as if the works council has not been able to find any conclusive responses up to now. The contact amongst the works councils within the group is even loose in Germany – a continuous cooperation is missing. There are virtually no relations with the representatives in the CEEC. In the case of the Radeberger Group (breweries), this restriction to Germany is also supported through the group corporate identity, which (under the slogan, 'Protector of German Beer Culture') strongly differs from the Czech sister companies, although both – Germans and Czechs – internalize similar values (industry characterized by traditional handicrafts). A direct influence on the industrial relations in the CEE subsidiaries is therefore not given.

However, it lies within the tradition of the house that the 'shareholder value' is not perceived as a guiding maxim. As is emphasized by the management side, the long-term build-up of markets with regard to the investments abroad plays the main role. In CEE industrial relations, the management correspondingly anticipates a resulting mixture of elements from German and respective CEE industrial relations. The German representatives cannot make any statements on these international perspectives – in the 'food processing' group as well as at Radeberger they are still considerable fixated on the enterprise in Germany. Due to lack of contacts, the representatives in Central and Eastern Europe do not know the German system of industrial relations.

Chapter 6

Conclusions

Differing Path Dependencies of CEE Industrial Relations

The following typology of the nine corporate case studies occurs under the restriction that these types are never to be found in pure culture, that in addition to the mentioned main features there are still numerous other – but less dominant – influences, and overlaps between these types are often perceivable. But nevertheless, this form of typification has its purpose wherever sharp-edged contours become visible.

For this, we refer to the above, already theoretically substantiated categories regarding the various possibilities of 'cross-border model transfer' from multinational companies (Doerrenbaecher, 2003; Almond et al., 2005),[1] whereby we add an additional Type 3:

- Type 1: predominant characterization through the industrial relations in the parent enterprise/country of origin of the investments – unilateral path dependency;
- Type 2: predominant characterization through the industrial relations in the host country of the investments/handed-down industrial relations with Brownfield investments and laws/visions of the CEE trade unions and employers – unilateral path dependency;
- Type 3: characterization through conditions in the country of origin *and* the host country of the investments – mixed industrial relations;
- Type 4: substantial influences through third countries/organization as external agents – Europeanization;
- Type 5: the rootless enterprise – 'footloose' company.

The trend is clear. The mixture of industrial relations from the country of origin and the host country of the direct investments predominates (Type 3). Type 1 industrial relations (unilateral path dependency/country of origin), Type 2 (unilateral path dependency/host country), Type 4 (third-country influences/Europeanization) and Type 5 (footloose companies) constitute the exceptions.

The VW AG on the one hand (Type 1: dominance of the country of origin in the arrangement of CEE industrial relations), the Dr. August Oetker KG (dominance of the host country as Type 2), the French-German Aventis Pharma SA as a 'prototype' for third-country influences (here: EU / Type 4) and the Nestlé SA as representative of Type 5 (bound neither to the country of origin nor the host country nor a third

---

1   In the application of the conceptualities of the path dependencies we relate primarily to the real conditions of the respective parent enterprises and their CEE subsidiaries, which are naturally embedded in the respective national 'models' of industrial relations.

Table 6.1   Division of the companies into the five types

	Unilateral path dependency/ country of origin investment	Unilateral path dependency/ host country investment	Mixture of industrial relations in the host country and country of origin	Third-country influences/ EU	Footloose Companies
Volkswagen AG	X				
Robert Bosch GmbH			X		
Siemens AG			X		
RWE AG			X		
Nestlé SA					X
Dr. August Oetker KG		X			
Continental AG			X		
Aventis Pharma SA (Sanofi Aventis SA after 20 August 2004)				X	
Henkel KgaA			X		

country) represent the minorities. One can describe them as the 'mavericks' in the 'normal distribution' of companies with regard to the influence on the industrial relations in their CEE subsidiary enterprises/sites.[2]

In the aggregate, the hybridization thesis[3] is thereby also corroborated through the study encompassing the three CEE countries (Poland, Czech Republic and Slovakia) at issue.

At the same time, this 'hybridisation of industrial relations' – as a mainstream type of influence from West European/German parent enterprises on the industrial relations of their CEE subsidiaries in their *not precisely* determinable borders, contours and contents – also presents substantial definition and arrangement possibilities for actors taking action.[4]

In the subsequent cornerstones, it will also have to be summarily addressed as to what extent this arrangement latitude resulting from the hybridization of industrial relations is also actually utilized.

---

2   However, what is conspicuous – even if not able to be generalized on account of the negligible number of cases – is that among the 'mavericks', the non-German companies (Aventis Pharma SA and Nestlé SA) are assigned to the types with international or non nationally-determined path dependencies, whereas German companies attempt to transfer either the industrial relations from their country of origin – or more or less attempt to entirely adapt the conditions in the host country of the investments.

3   Doerrenbaecher (2000, 2003) tested this thesis in only one CEE country (Hungary), though on a broader branch dispersion.

4   Marginson (2006) are drawing similar cnclusions from their research of inward-investments by German and US Multinationals in Poland, Hungary and Slovenia.

Solution Orientation and Cooperative Willingness, Corporate Centralization and 'Hybridisation' of Industrial Relations – Theses for Development in the CEE Subsidiary Enterprises

The corporate case studies and the typology shall be subsequently confronted with our incipient hypotheses. While doing so, we also refer to the theoretical reference points of the study and the findings of the supra-company expert interviews.

This summary in the form of theses is a mixture of 'classical' summaries from scientific research findings and the demonstration of action possibilities as they are preferred by practitioners in the form of 'executive summaries'. From that point of view, the findings are presented in a form which merely represents a selection of – even if essential – findings from our study. They do not supersede the detailed information in this study, but facilitate orientation.

We point out that – due to the specific subject matter – the following theses and the underlying study can only represent a partial depiction of the development of industrial relations in Central and Eastern Europe.

Thesis 1: Solution-Orientated Cooperative Willingness of the Social Actors in Companies/Sites as a Basic Model of Industrial Relations in Central and Eastern Europe

First of all, it has to be maintained that despite all differences among the 'types', one characteristic feature is common to all types: the *solution-orientated cooperative willingness* of the actors on the corporate/site level. As a result, these industrial relations differ in one essential feature from those relations which have prevailed in many cases during the period *before* the foreign direct investments in these companies – to say nothing of the industrial relations throughout the communist era.

And so the direction of this process (Scandinavian, German, Romance model, and so on) is not indicated yet. This basic understanding encompasses a considerable spectrum of characterizations: from the codetermined model with collective representatives bodies to management human resource strategies, which favour direct negotiations between corporate managements and employees without intermediaries (such as works councils and trade union representatives).

But despite all of the different characterizations, this solution-orientated cooperative willingness fundamentally expresses a certain degree of democratic understanding. As a result, there is a common denominator in Europe, which features quite substantial differences to the American or even East Asian basic understandings with regard to the arrangement of industrial relations.

Thesis 2: No Transfer of German Industrial Relations – Path Dependencies

Of course, technology, labour and process organization and partially also management concepts are not always transferred one-to-one, but are surely transferred to a great extent from the German parent enterprises to their CEE subsidiaries.

This looks different in the industrial relations on the corporate/site level. Based on a culture of negotiation solutions as the main path towards regulation of industrial relations (see Thesis 1), our study corroborates the findings of other studies regarding a 'selective transfer'. German companies also make their accumulated positive experiences with the cooperative management model of codetermination an element of a cross-border regulation of industrial relations – but only on a limited basis.

In particular, German companies avoid a *legally stipulated* agreement on regulation of 'cooperative willingness' in their transfer of industrial relations.

This 'restrained' involvement of German companies regarding the general transfer of their German experiences (with industrial relations) to the CEE subsidiary enterprises is also expressed in the fact that, as a rule, no efforts are undertaken to establish a system of representatives (legally protected) in the Greenfield investments – despite difficulties related to this for the management through the lack of a corresponding collective bargaining partner on the side of the employees.

However, the German 'model' of dualistic system of representatives has also changed considerably; it is faced with considerable challenges (undermining trends with regard to regional/branch collective bargaining – hardship case regulations, initiatives for more works council competencies during company's deviations from supra-company's collective agreements, and so on).

And so the 'German production model' is not transferred in its entirety, but the basic assumptions of this model (negotiation and cooperation on various levels with different radii of action) are also reflected – even if with many variations – in the industrial relations of the CEE subsidiary enterprises.

As a result, a mixture of various 'models' of industrial relations emerges in the CEE subsidiaries of West European and especially German parent enterprises.

Thesis 3: The Corporate-Centred Characterizations of Industrial Relations – Decentralization in the Context of Global Modernity

There is no general model by which specific strategies from German parent enterprises in the manufacturing industry for arrangement of industrial relations in their CEE subsidiaries would be identifiable. Naturally, there are nuances between the branches of the single companies (for instance, between the chemicals, energy, automotive and food processing sector).

Furthermore, the size of the parent enterprise plays a role: as a rule, medium-sized and large companies in Germany have a works council (which theoretically could exert influence – see the following Thesis 4 concerning this), whereas this is often not the case in small companies.

However, the different company sizes do not signify different models of the transfer of industrial relations from the parent enterprise to the CEE subsidiaries. Insofar as that is concerned, our case studies (which encompass large parent enterprises and partially small CEE subsidiaries) contradict the assessment from Bluhm, who has observed a 'country-of-origin' effect in large companies, and by contrast, a model exchange of the industrial relations with smaller companies in Central and Eastern Europe (Bluhm, 2000, 2003). Even with the large parent enterprises this 'country-of-origin' effect does not exist per se, nor is there anything to speak of with our typology: Type 1.

The corporate reasons for investment (market development or cost reasons) also have no dominant influence on the arrangement of industrial relations.

Of course, the type of investments – Greenfield or Brownfield – also plays a certain role (whether union-free or not), but not to the extent that we have initially assumed through our initial hypothesis No. 1 – particularly since the difference between both types of investments starts to become blurred. For instance, investments which were Brownfield investments under corporate law correspond to real Greenfield investments, since immediately after the acquisition the workforces were to some extent completely replaced, new sites were installed and the old union works committees were partially abolished. Conversely, as of 2007 there will also be a corresponding organization in Greenfield investments due to the EU directive on formation of informing and consulting employees in the EU level from March 2002 (see Thesis 6).

In the aggregate, all of these independent variables do not construe any general explanatory models in the sense implied above. For instance, the existence of a works council in the German parent enterprise does not signify per se the possibility, the intention or even the attempt to establish representatives in CEE subsidiary enterprises with Greenfield investments. Another example is the very different attitude of German works councils regarding integration of CEE representatives in the European Works Council (if available) before 1 May 2004 (accession of the eight CEE countries into the EU).

As the host countries of the investments, the (quite different) CEE countries also offer no explanatory model for the German parent enterprise's different country strategies with regard to the arrangement of industrial relations in their subsidiary enterprises, even if – on account of their scarce resources – the local trade unions in Central and Eastern Europe favour the *larger* subsidiaries of foreign investors in their support efforts. Furthermore, it can be generally ascertained that the investing companies obey the respective laws, which are naturally different from country to country. But apart from this general assessment there is no indication that historical, social, political and economical differences in the CEE countries lead to a different, country-specific strategy on the part of the parent enterprise in the configuration of the industrial relations for their subsidiaries.

This all indicates that it especially depends on the strategies of the *individual* parent enterprises (including the works council's position and policy) – irrespective of branch affiliation, share of labour costs in the overall costs of the product, company size, and so on. We call this a corporate-centred approach for explanation of the corporate policy with regard to the arrangement of the industrial relations in their CEE subsidiary enterprises, which also entails the history of the company, the corporate culture, the size and the subjective behavioural patterns of the corporate actors, and so on.

If one also asks whether the direction of the development of industrial relations in Central and Eastern Europe with regard to this thesis, it must be assumed that the instrument of *corporate* collective bargaining (socalled in-house agreements) currently prevailing in Central and Eastern Europe is in the interest of the German parent enterprises. The parent enterprises depart from the principle of collective bargaining between the industrial unions and the employers' associations on the branch/regional level that are customary in Germany and thus also support the current forms of monism/hybrid dualism in Poland, the Czech Republic and Slovakia (primacy of trade union representatives on the site/company level). They think that one could thereby react faster and more flexibly to the decentralization trends in the context of globalization.

On the other hand, this corporate-centred approach also opens up considerable creative latitudes for the representatives on the corporate/site level as well as on the supra-company level. In the next thesis it will be clarified as to whether the representatives/trade unions actually take advantage of this action scope.

Thesis 4: Marginal Influence of the Parent Enterprise's Representatives on the Arrangement of Industrial Relations in the CEE Subsidiaries

In principle, the position and situation of the works councils in the German system of industrial relations allow an influence in the co-arrangement of industrial relations in the CEE subsidiary enterprises. Despite uniform legal fundamentals there are considerable differences with regard to the position and power of the works councils in the single German parent enterprises. As a rule, works councils with relatively marginal influence in the parent concern do not have the additional power, to support the build-up and expansion of CEE representatives. But even in parent companies with a strong works council ('co-management') there is no guarantee per se that greater influences are to be expected here. Apart from a few exceptions, the role of the works councils in this field is relatively marginal.[5] In general, it is more restricted to passive-reacting behaviour (such as gathering and passing on information) than to active-acting utilization of the existing structures and possibilities of German corporate codetermination (Works Constitution Act, codetermination on the supervisory board).

In turn, there are certain reasons for this, of which several shall be mentioned here:

- So the theoretical concept of negotiation as a structural feature of industrial relations (see our theoretical 'building blocks') offers a necessary, but insufficient explanation of works council action as a socio-political process. Because in this context it must be pointed out that the structure of capitalism produces an unequal balance of power, that is bargaining between corporate management and works council are never negotiations amongst equals.
- In the course of Europeanization and globalization there are certain fields in which *pure* national regulations and corresponding influences of *national* interest representation bodies are insufficient. For example, this is the case with regard to cross-border relocations and restructurings of companies. Here the European Works Council should have the right to make binding agreements. But till 2006 the revision of the EWC directive was blocked by UNICE.

5　　As a result, our findings explicitly contradict those from Rehder (2005, p. 72), that the supra-sites bodies of representatives (joint works councils, corporate works councils) existing in large companies enable and support the establishment of collective representatives bodies at the new CEE sites.

- The works councils in Germany are partially included in investment decisions of their corporate executive boards and frequently form 'social pacts' with them (see also Rehder, 2005, p. 68/European Fondation for the Improvement of Living and Working Conditions, 2006, p. 1, 15–17). But nevertheless these alliances (such as in the form of locational safeguarding agreements) are restricted to factors which play a large role in the internal corporate benchmarking competition between a company's single sites (working hours, wages, productivity, labour organization, and so on). Soft factors such as the industrial relations at one's own site and – beyond that – even the quality of the industrial relations in other (in our case, CEE) sites hardly play a role. Incidentally, such a restriction to one's own location is also prescribed by the Works Constitution Act. An expansion of the policy of the works councils of the German parent enterprises to the co-arrangement of the industrial relations in the CEE subsidiaries would thus be an act of voluntary nature and solidarity – and consequently a purely political decision, which would also have to be made plausible to one's own workforces (here German). An improved role on the part of the EWC would then be effective here.
- Never to be underestimated, but hard to measure is the subjective factor, that is the individual willingness of, for instance, works council members and the works council body in the German parent enterprise on the whole to recognize the given action scope, to take advantage of it accordingly, and perhaps also to exceed the scope occasionally – consequently, to push the limits further.

So that no misunderstandings crop up here: action scopes and creative latitudes are not merely restricted to works councils of the *German* parent enterprises: in the aggregate, all involved corporate actors bear an enormous responsibility that is also at the same time creative latitude – trade unions and employers' associations, corporate management and workforce/unions representatives on the corporate/site level. In the wake of the direct investments in the CEE countries, the aforementioned actors from the West European countries of origin could intervene creatively, but the actors in the CEE host countries of these direct investments would also contribute quite a bit to the fact that not merely the requirements of the economy are taken into account, but also those of a 'social Europe' with a basic orientation towards democracy and participation by employees – without which a united Europe cannot function.

Thesis 5: Autonomy of the CEE Subsidiaries, Learning Management and Industrial Relations

The autonomy of the CEE subsidiaries vis-à-vis the western parent enterprises is increasing step-by-step – even with some differences, which result from the objectives of the investment (market or cost reasons), the type of product, the subsequently resulting diversity of the corporate cultures, the size of the parent enterprise as well as of the subsidiary, and so on.

This was accompanied by an augmented recruitment of local managers ('in-patriats'). Local personnel have been/are quite frequently taken on particularly as personnel managers, since they are more familiar with the local circumstances, the national industrial law, language, mentality, and so on. The personnel sector in a company is rooted deeper in the local context than any other sector. Under this aspect, this position in management forms the bridge to the representatives (if existent) in the subsidiary. Both roles are thus staffed with local personnel and have an overriding importance as intermediaries. However, this increasing replacement of western/German managerial personnel ('ex-patriats') through locals does not necessarily signify an improvement of solution-orientated cooperative willingness, since partially old (cadres still accustomed to the communist era) and/or young junior staff have been recruited, who – in exaggerated demarcation to communist times – seek their role models in the 'radicalism' of certain market concepts.

On the other hand, western/German management generally behaved respectfully in the CEE subsidiaries, which is not only attributable to a longstanding, proven dialogue culture with the inclusion of collective bodies of representatives in the western/German parent enterprises, but can also be substantiated through the respect vis-à-vis the existing technical and engineering competencies of the Central and Eastern Europeans, as well as consideration – particularly on the part of the German managers – arising from the war history. These reasons had an effect to the extent that an authoritarian manner on the part of western/German management could be relegated to the closets in the CEE subsidiaries.

Considerable differences between the management styles of various western countries are described at the same time. Although not a main object of our case studies, it can be deduced from the literature and our expert interviews on the supra-company level that Asian companies/managers most easily and consistently pursue a model transfer of corporate culture and (authoritarian) management style, and French managers in Central and Eastern Europe behave in a much more authoritarian manner ('le patron') than Germans, who perceive themselves as more committed to a cooperative corporate culture and industrial relations.

The company's image, especially with regard to brand name producers, additionally plays a very important role in the arrangement of industrial relations through the managers. *Independent* of the respective company size, these western/German companies are very interested in a positive image – first of all in the region of the subsidiary, and moreover in the country on the whole – which is also depicted through the workforces, their representatives and through the media, and so on. Thus, not only the products, not only the quantifiable working conditions (such as wages, working hours, and so on) play a role, but also the quality of the industrial relations. As soon as this image is damaged through an excessively authoritarian attitude on the part of the local management or also through mere politically-motivated action from representatives and any subsequently related disputes in the public realm, the foreign headquarters intervenes. Here lies a major difference in contrast to the domestic-owned companies in Central and Eastern Europe.

Large as well as small companies from the EU-15 (and first and foremost here from Germany) not only brought their technology and organization with them, but they also attempted to assert the visions of the parent enterprise in matters of industrial relations and corporate culture in an initial phase of investment. But in a second phase they gradually adapted to the conditions of the host country and the respective region. They also continued to expand these aspects in accordance with their own visions:

company collective agreements (and not the supra-company collective bargaining still dominating in Germany), human resource management (that is direct relations between plant management and workforces without intermediaries) as an additional pillar of industrial relations, and 'works councils' without union involvement are all elements of the CEE industrial relations which did not have to be forced on the western/German management, but were certainly also enthusiastically adopted.

Thesis 6: Hybrid Dualism of Industrial Relations in Central and Eastern Europe? The New 'Works Councils' in the Czech Republic, Slovakia and Poland

The legal provisions in Slovakia, in the Czech Republic and (since April 2006) in Poland for the introduction of 'works councils' – expedited through the EU directive regarding information and consultation on the corporate/site level from March 2002 – obtain an additional importance through the corporate centralization of industrial relations: in Central and Eastern Europe, the corporate/site level plays a much more important role in the arrangement of industrial relations than in Germany, for instance. The current legal construction of the new 'works councils' (dualism in Slovakia, but without the right for collective bargaining; in the Czech Republic and in Poland an 'ad hoc' works council, which then has to give way if a union works committee is established) had a form that was not based on the same division of labour 'works council-trade union' as, for example, in Germany. To that extent these new provisions appear as a 'hybrid' dualism from a western point of view.

Now there are advantages and disadvantages with regard to this new pillar of representatives on the site/company levels, which are quite differently evaluated from the view of the actors in the three CEE countries on the one hand and in Germany on the other hand.

The justification of the CEE trade unions against the introduction of a second representational level – that a rival institution would be created with the works councils – appears from their point of view and current weakness, which hardly allows room for the integration of works councils in the union organizations, quite plausible on the one hand. On top of this is the fact that a legitimation deficit of the handed-down trade union representatives becomes obvious through the new workforce representatives (so-called works councils) (which are to be elected by *all* employees, irrespective of trade union membership); this could lead to a splitting of the CEE industrial relations. Moreover, it seems that the employers who partially welcome these new 'works councils' do not want to encourage their union embedment at all.

On the other hand, hardly any trade union representatives are to be found in the Greenfield investments, that is they are 'union and representative-free' – which is in other respects is also partially lamented by the employers. Here there would be the opportunity for the CEE trade unions to substantially expand their area of influence through the 'unionisation of works council entities', and thus also to decisively extend their social standing via the current 'pseudo-strength' of tripartism. There would also be a subsequently conditioned compulsion for the fragmented trade unions in Central and Eastern Europe to work more strongly together than previously, at least on the corporate/site level.

Furthermore, with the more or less open rejection of this new form through the CEE trade unions, the production model of the respective company (to which the industrial relations essentially belong) will also be internationally weakened, since a comparative competitive advantage of this internationally active West European/ German parent enterprise vis-à-vis their most important competitors could be lost as a result.

The partially contrary views of the CEE and the German trade unions regarding the organization of new 'works councils' can also certainly lead to difficulties of cooperation on other political fields between CEE and German trade unions on a long-term basis.

Because it is to be asked as to what extent a monistic representative system can endure the classical conflict between the interest in wage increases (as *the* strategic instrument of union action) on the one hand, and on the other hand the interest in retention of the company's comparative competitive advantage. In Germany, a division of labour between industrial unions (collective agreement partners on supra-company level) and the works councils (within the companies/sites) and a mechanism for conflict disaggregation has been installed through the dual system.

Thesis 7: Europeanization of Industrial Relations – European Works Councils are Not (Yet) Intermediaries between East and West Europe

The European Works Councils as the hitherto strongest expression of a Europeanization process (not to be understood as standardization) of industrial relations are often misused in the academic as well as political discussion as the 'last rescue anchor' when other institutions of cooperation do not function on the European level. And so it is in the case of cooperation between the European sites of internationally active companies when they feature an EWC. Here the EWC is intended to have an intermediary role between East and West, which it – at least at the moment – cannot (yet) fulfil:

- An EWC with CEE representatives (obligatory since 1 May 2004) can only be as 'good' as it was beforehand on the basis of the EU-15. And there our empirical studies as well as the findings of other studies depict a realistic picture of an EWC that is to be settled between information and consultation, and is partially seen by the actors themselves as not necessarily a European body, but rather as a collection of national representatives on the European level. Only a minority of West European EWCs have managed to develop functioning networks of the representative systems in different countries and 'European' thinking in the approach. But if even the EWCs in West Europe are still in an early stage of development, then how can the *increased* requirements (through the EU enlargement) of the EWC with regard to its intercultural competence and capability for integration of other traditions and industrial relations be fulfilled?
- The differential between West and East Europe with regard to wages and other working conditions is currently still so great that substantial – concealed – conflicts of interest can come about between the trade unions in the East

and West, from which even the EWC does not remain unaffected. Western – and in particular the German – representatives hope for a levelling of wages between East and West that is as rapid as possible to more favourably create certain competitive conditions for their sites. On the other hand, CEE trade union representatives (which often conclude the collective agreements with the management) are particularly interested in a retention of this (for them) favourable competitive factor that is a long as possible. The classical conflict between wage increases on the one hand and retention of comparative competitive advantage on the other hand also come to bear here.

• The ambiguity pertaining to the selection of CEE EWC representatives (partially determined by the management on account of lacking representatives in CEE sites) complicate clear definitions of interests and role attributions within the EWC body.

• The EWC's potential is rated by the CEE trade unions and EWC members more quite considerable (differently than this is the case with the legal establishments of 'works councils' in Poland, the Czech Republic and Slovakia), but on a quite low level of expectation. Whereas the CEE representatives were previously more or less cut off from the information regarding the situation of the overall enterprise, the EWC body now offers them an undreamt-of wealth of information for more effective arrangement of company-related collective bargaining – though Europeanization is less obvious here. But the German representatives in the EWC particularly obtain this wealth of information (and probably also more) not through this body, but via the institutions of German codetermination (Works Constitution Act, codetermination laws). As far as that is concerned, a dissimilarity of interests in the East and West is also determinable in this field.

Such a dissimilarity of experiences, traditions and role attributions must be taken into account before one overloads the EWC with objectives such as the intermediary function between East and West.

In accordance with our findings, there are three developmental stages of an EWC encompassing East and West European sites:

1. EWC as an information body. For the CEE representatives, this is the place to obtain information about the overall enterprise and thus to develop an economical-political competence. For West European/German EWC representatives, the EWC is the institutional body for obtaining information about the industrial relations in the company's CEE sites and thus to develop an intercultural competence.

2. EWC as an integration body. In a second step – building on the EWC as an information body – the EWC can be the place of the integration of the CEE representatives in this body as not merely formal, but also politically equal members.

3. EWC as an intermediary body between East and West. In this stage, the (still) serious differences with regard to wages, working conditions, and so on in East and West can be reconditioned to such an extent that these undeniable

differences are not only discussed in the form of national location rivalries, but at least also show the beginnings in the form of European solutions.

At the moment, most EWCs are still between stage one and stage two in their development.

Such a developmental process can be promoted through:

- a revision of the EWC directive (blocked by UNICE), which had to take into account the fact that there are certain processes (such as corporate relocations and mergers on the European level) which can no longer be (solely) accompanied by trade unions and representatives within their national boundaries, but urgently require the EWC as an actor in the company;
- The subjective-individual attitudes of the respective actors regarding the formation of European elements of industrial relations. Many EWC members currently do not even take advantage of the framework that is given through the currently valid EWC directive (see also Knudsen, 2004; Kotthoff, Kruse, 2002).

Open Questions

Any empirically-based study can only evaluate and systematize the practice *one bit* further. Open questions, which require further research, also always remain, such as those questions pertaining to:

- the interests of the employees in these subsidiary enterprises themselves; which forms of representatives are preferred, how could the strained relations between the workforce and institutionalized representatives be arranged more productively, and so on;
- the differences of foreign investments with regard to the regional origin of the parent enterprise (Asia, North America, various regions in Western Europe) and the influence on the industrial relations of the respective CEE subsidiaries;
- the spill-over effects of the industrial relations practiced in the CEE subsidiary enterprises on the regions and societies in which these sites are geographically located;
- the repercussions of the industrial relations practiced in Central and Eastern Europe on the industrial relations of the parent enterprise in Western Europe/ Germany.

The End of Transformation Process Uniqueness: The Commencement of Consolidation Processes Regarding Industrial Relations in Central and Eastern Europe

Now there are attempts to classify the industrial relations in the new EU member states either as a special model, different from the previously known West European model, or otherwise as a procedural evolution into a different, already existing model of industrial relations.

For instance, Steger (2002) refers to three main models (liberal market model in the USA and the UK; model of social market economy in Germany and Sweden; and conflict model in Italy and Spain), and describes the current status and the future development of industrial relations in Poland, the Czech Republic, Hungary and Slovenia as typical for the liberal market model.

Kohl and Platzer (2003a, pp. 40, 50 and 47) attribute – on the basis of the differentiation from Ebbinghaus et al. (1997) between the North European corporatism, the Continental European model of social partnership, the Anglo-American pluralism and the polarization model in the Romance countries of Europe – a special model to the industrial relations in the CEEC that strongly depends on the support of the governments to reduce the deficits in the economic and social realm.

However, we do not act on the assumption of a separate CEE model.

Particularly during the period of EU enlargement (officially started on 1 May 2004), only 17 years after the start of dramatic upheavals in the former East Bloc states – which we consider in this form as historically singular, not even recurrent events in the foreseeable future – the industrial relations were also subject to a dramatic change. This change currently marks the *starting conditions* for a new beginning as members of the EU and at the same time shows initial, landmark contours. That is to say that up to now *prerequisites* for a 'consolidated' development of industrial relations in the CEEC as EU members – but at the same time also initial, fundamental contours – have been created through the rapid catch-up process in the CEEC.

If we concentrate on 'our' three CEE countries, we assume that Slovakia approximates a German model of industrial relations on the corporate/site level (dualism of workforce representatives on the corporate/site level, comparably stronger orientation of the collective bargaining on the branch and national level than in Poland and the Czech Republic), whereas the Polish and Czech industrial relations on the corporate/site level rather correspond to a mixture of French (weak 'works councils') and British 'model' (collective bargaining on the corporate level). This implies that the process of transformation in Central and Eastern Europe has reached its end and no independent East European path of industrial relations is evolving, but a 'consolidation process' has started.

However, the reference point of solution orientation and cooperative willingness of the companies' actors (management and representatives) with regard to the arrangement of industrial relations as a basic model is common among all developments in these CEE countries; and not merely as a uniform model for all countries, but on the basis of a common self-image of the recognition of the interests of the respective counterparts and the dialogue-orientated negotiation of differences and under consideration of national-state, branch and corporate-related differences – that is truly European.

References

Almond, P., Edwards, T., Colling, T., Ferner, A., Gunnigle, P., Mueller-Camen, M., Quintanilla, J. and Waechter, H. (2005), 'Unraveling Home and Host Country Effects: An Investigation of the HR Policies of an American Multinational in Four European Countries', *Industrial Relations*, **44**(2), 276–304.

Altmeyer, W. (2003), 'The Clock is Ticking', *Mitbestimmung*, **8**(2003), 14–17.

Altvater, E. and Mahnkopf, B. (1996), *Grenzen der Globalisierung. Oekonomie, Oekologie und Politik in der Weltgesellschaft* (Muenster, Westfaelisches Dampfboot).

Apeldoorn, B. van (2000), The European Round Table of Industrialists: Still a Unique Player? Paper presented at the EuroConference 'The Effectiveness of EU Business Administrations', Brussels, September, 18–22.

Artus, I. (2003), 'Die Kooperation Zwischen Betriebsraeten und Gewerkschaften als neuralgischer Punkt des Tarifsystems Eine exemplarische Analyse am Beispiel Ostdeutschlands', *Industrielle Beziehungen*, Zeitschrift für Arbeit, Organisation und Management, **2**(2003), 250-272.

Baccaro, Lucio (2003), 'What is Alive and What is Dead in the Theory of Corporatism', *British Journal of Industrial Relations*, **41**(4), 683–706.

Bank for Reconstruction (2000), Transition Report (2000) (London).

Baumann, Z. (1997), *Postmodernity and its Discontents* (New York: New York University).

Berger, C. and Langewiesche, R. (2001), EU – Osterweiterung und Interregionale Gewerkschaftsraete', *WSI – Mitteilungen*, **1**(2001), 57–58.

Bispinck, R. and Schulten, T. (2003), 'Decentralisation of German Collective Bargaining? Current Trends from a Works and Staff Council Perspective', *WSI - Mitteilungen* (**2003**, Special Issue), 24–33.

Bluhm, K. (2000), 'East-West Integration and the Changing German Production Regime: A Firm-Centred Approach, Program on Central and Eastern Europe', Working Paper Series 53, Jena, December 2000.

Bluhm, K. (2003), 'Flucht aus dem Deutschen Modell? Arbeitsbeziehungen Deutscher Tochtergesellschaften in Polen und Tschechien', in *Entstaatlichung und soziale Sicherheit. Verhandlungen des 31. Kongresses der Deutschen Gesellschaft fuer Soziologie in Leipzig. Teil 1*, Allmendinger, J (ed.) (Opladen: Leske und Budrich).

Boehlert, B. (2004), 'A Meeting Between German and Hungarian Works Council Members. Getting on With One Another is Not Enough', *Mitbestimmung*, **8**(2004), 64–67.

Bontrup, Heinz, J. (2004), 'Zu Hohe Loehne und Lohnnebenkosten – Eine Oekonomische Maer', *WSI – Mitteilungen*, **6**(2004), 313–318.

Borbély, D. and Meier, C.-P. (2003), 'Zum Konjunkturverbund zwischen der EU und den Beitrittslaendern', *EU – Osterweiterung*, **4**, 492–509.

Brandl, B. and Traxler, F. (2005), 'Industrial Relations, Social Pacts and Welfare Expenditures: A Cross-National Comparison', *British Journal of Industrial Relations*, **43**(4), 635–658.

Braun, S., Eberwein, W. and Tholen, J. (1992), *Belegschaften und Unternehmer. Zur Geschichte und Soziologie der Deutschen Betriebsverfassung und Belegschaftsmitbestimmung* (Frankfurt/M., New York: Campus-Verlag).

Brigl-Matthiass, K. (1926), *Das Betriebsraeteproblem* (Berlin and Leipzig: Walter de Gruyter and Co.).

Bruecker, H. (2003), 'Die Arbeitsmarkteffekte der Ost-West-Migration: Theoretische Überlegungen, Simulationen und Empirische Befunde', *EU – Osterweiterung*, **4**, 579–593.

Buch, C.M. and Toubal, F. (2003), 'Economic Integration and FDI in Transition Economies: What Can We Learn from German Data?' *EU – Osterweiterung*, **4**, 594-610.

Bundesvereinigung der Deutschen Ernaehrungsindustrie (2003), *Jahresbericht 2002/3*, Bonn.

Campos, N.F. and Coricelli, F. (2002), 'Growth in Transition: What We Know, What We Don't and What We Should Know', CEPR Discussion Paper No.3246 (London: CEPR).

Carley, Mark (2002), *'Industrial Relations In The EU Member States And Candidate Countries', European Foundation for the Improvement of Living and Working Conditions* (Luxembourg)

Carroll, W.K. (2004), *Corporate Power in a Globalizing World* (Toronto: Oxford University Press).

CCOO de Catalunya u.a., Projekt unterstuetzt von DG for Employment and Social Affairs (o.J.) (2001), *European Works Councils – Cases of Good Practice*, http://www.conc.es/internacional/comites.htm.

Czíria, L. (2003), Law on Employee Participation Amended, European Industrial Relations Observatory on-line (eiroline), www.eiro.Eurofound.eu.int/2003/08/feature/sk0308102f.html.

Dehley, J. (2005), 'Das Abenteuer der Europaeisierung. Ueberlegungen zu einem *Soziologischen Begriff Europaeischer Integration und zur Stellung der Soziologie zu den Integration Studies', Soziologie*, Deutschen Gesellschaft fuer Soziologie (Leske und Buderich, Opladen),. **34**/1, 7–27.

Deiss, M. (2003), 'Ausgewaehlte Ergebnisse Aus Der Empirie Und Zwischenfazit Des Projektes "Risiken Und Chancen Der EU – Osterweiterung Für Die Arbeitnehmerinnen Am Beispiel Der Ostbayerisch/Tschechischen Grenzregion"', in *ISF Muenchen: Forschungsprojekt 'Risiken und Chancen der EU – Osterweiterung fuer die Arbeitnehmer am Beispiel der ostbayerisch/tschechischen Grenzregion': Dokumentation zum 2 Arbeitsgespraech (April 2–3, 2003) in Regensburg*, www.isf-muenchen.de/pdf/284_dokumentation2_030624.pdf.

Deppe, R. and Schroeder, W. (2002), 'Doppelte Transformation und Gewerkschaften in Polen, Ungarn und Ostdeutschland', *WSI – Mitteilungen*, **11**(2002), 663–669.

Deutsche Bank Research (2003a), *Deutsches Wachstumspotenzial: Vor Demografischer Herausforderung*, 14 July, 2003, (Frankfurt/M), www.dbresearch. de.

Deutsche Bank Research (2003b), 'Internationale Migration: Wer, Wohin und Warum', 8 May, 2003,(Frankfurt/M), www.dbrsearch.de.

Deutsche Bundesbank (2002), 'Kapitalverflechtung mit dem Ausland 2000', *Statistische Sonderveroeffentlichung* (10, May, Frankfurt/M).

Deutsche Bundesbank (2003), 'Kapitalverflechtung mit dem Ausland 2001', *Statistische Sonderveroeffentlichung* (10 June, Frankfurt/M).

Deutsche Bundesbank (2004), 'Kapitalverflechtung mit dem Ausland 2002', *Statistische Sonderveroeffentlichung* (10 May, Frankfurt/M).

Deutsche Bundesbank (2005), 'Kapitalverflechtung mit dem Ausland 2003', *Statistische Sonderveroeffentlichung* (10 April, Frankfurt/M).

Deutsche Bundesbank (2006), 'Kapitalverflechtung mit dem Ausland 2003', *Statistische Sonderveroeffentlichung* (10 April, Frankfurt/M).

Deutsche Welle (2004), *Interview mit Ludwig Georg Braun*, (21 March 2004, Cologne), (www.dw-world.de/dwelle/cda/detail/dwelle.cda.detail.artikel).

Deutscher Industrie und Handelskammertag (2003), 'Produktionsverlagerung als Element der Globalisierungsstrategie von Unternehmen', (26 May, 2003), www. dihk.de/inhalt/informationen/news/meinungen/.

Dietz, B., Protsenko, A. and Vincentz, V. (2001), 'Direktinvestitionen in Osteuropa und ihre Auswirkungen auf den Arbeitsmarkt in Deutschland', in Osteuropa-Institut, Munich, Working Papers, No. 229.

DIHK/German Chamber for Economy and Trade (2005), *FuE-Verlagerung: Innovationsstandort Deutschland auf dem Pruefstand*, DIHK– Studie auf Basis einer Unternehmensbefragung durch die Industrie – und Handelskammern, (Berlin).

DIW (2000), Deutsches Institut für Wirtschaftsforschung, *Wochenbericht* **21**, 2000.

DIW (2003), Deutsches Institut für Wirtschaftsforschung, *Wochenbericht* **43**, 2003.

DIW (2004a), Deutsches Institut für Wirtschaftsforschung, *Wochenbericht* **14**, 2004.

Doerr, G. and Kessel, T. (1999),'Restructuring Via Internationalization The Auto Industry's Direct Investment Project in Eastern Central Europe', in *Schriftenreihe der Abteilung Regulierung von Arbeit, Forschungsschwerpunkt Technik – Arbeit – Umwelt am Wissenschaftszentrum* (Berlin: Social Science Research Centre).

Doerre, K. (1995),'Postfordismus und Industrielle Beziehungen – Die Gewerkschaften zwischen Standortkonkurrenz und Oekologisch-Sozialer Reformpolitik', in *Jenseits von Öko-Steuern*, Bulmahn, E., Oertzen P. v and Schuster J. (eds.) (Dortmund: Sozialforschungsstelle Dortmund, from 2007 University of Dortmund), 145–172.

Doerre, K. (1997),'Globalisierung – Eine Strategische Option. Internationalisierung von Unternehmen und Industrielle Beziehungen in der Bundesrepublik', *Industrielle Beziehungen*, **4**(4), 265–290.

Doerre, K., Elk-Anders, R. and Speidel, F. (1997),'Globalisierung als Option Internationalisierungspfade von Unternehmen, Standortpolitik und industrielle Beziehungen', *SOFI Mitteilungen*, **25**, 43–70.

166   *Labour Relations in Central Europe*

Doerrenbaecher, C. (2003), 'Grenzueberschreitende Modelltransfer in Multinationalen Unternehmen. Heimat – Gast – und Drittlandeffekte Am Beispiel Deutscher Investitionen in Ungarn', in *Modelltransfer in multinationalen Unternehmen. Strategien und Probleme Grenzueberschreitender Konzernintegration*, Doerrenbaecher, C (ed.) (Berlin: Sigma), 151–171.

Doerrenbaecher, C. (2004), 'Interview zu Verlagerungen Deutscher Unternehmen nach Mittel – und Osteuropa', *Mitbestimmung*, 3/2004, 16–17.

Doerrenbaecher, C., Fichter, M., Neumann, L., Toth, A. and Wortmann, M. (2000), 'Transformation and Foreign Direct Investment: Observations on Path Dependency, Hybridisation and Model Transfer at the Enterprise Level', *Transfer*, 2(2000), 434–449.

Domanski, B. (2001), 'Poland: Labour and the Relocation of Manufacturing from the EU' in *CEE Countries in the EU Companies' Strategies of Industrial Restructuring and Relocation*, Gradev, G. (ed.) (Brussels: ETUI), 21–50.

Ebbinghaus, B. and Visser, J. (1997), 'Der Wandel der Arbeitsbeziehungen im Westeuropaeischen Vergleich' in Hradil, S. and Immerfall, S. (eds.), *Die Westeuropaeischen Gesellschaften im Vergleich* (Opladen: Leske and Budrich), 333–376.

Eberwein, W. and Tholen, J. (1990), *Managermentalitaet. Industrielle Unternehmensleitung als Beruf und Politik.* (Frankfurt/M.: Frankfurter Allgemeine Zeitung-Verlagsbereich Wirtschaftsbuecher).

Eberwein, W. and Tholen, J. (1993), *Euro Managers or Splendid Isolation? International Management – An Anglo-German Comparison* (Berlin/New York: De Gruyter).

Eberwein, W. and Tholen, J. (1994), *Zwischen Markt und Mafia. Russische Manager auf dem Schwierigen Weg in eine Offene Gesellschaft* (Frankfurt/M.: Frankfurter Allgemeine Zeitung-Verlagsbereich Wirtschaftsbuecher).

Eberwein, W. and Tholen, J. (1997), *Market or Mafia. Russian Managers on the Difficult Road towards an Open Society* (Aldershot: Ashgate).

Eberwein, W., Tholen, J. and Schuster, J. (2000), *Die Europaeisierung der Arbeitsbeziehungen als politisch-sozialer Prozess. Zum Zusammenhang von nationaler und Europaeischer Ebene am Beispiel von Deutschland, Frankreich, Großbritannien und Italien* (Munich and Mering: Rainer Hampp Verlag).

Eberwein, W., Tholen, J. and Schuster, J. (2002), *The Europeanisation of Industrial Relations. National and European Processes in Germany, UK, Italy and France* (Aldershot: Ashgate).

Edwards, V. (2003), 'Organisational Leadership In Transforming Economies: Leadership Management And National Culture In Selected Countries Of Central And Eastern Europe', *Journal for East European Management Studies*, 8(4), 415–429.

EIRO (2004), European Industrial Relations Observatory on-line, published by the European Foundation for the Improvement of Living and Working Conditions, Dublin; country reports on Poland. www.eiro.eurofound.eu/int/2004/09/pl0409102f.html, Czech Republic (www.eiro.eurofound.eu.int/2004/09/feature/cz0409102f.html) and Slovakia (www.eiro.eurofound.eu.int/2004/09/feature/sk04009102f.html).

Elger, T. and Smith, C. (1998a), 'New Town, New Capital, New Workplace? the Employment Relations of Japanese Inward Investors in a West Midlands New Town', *Economy and Societye*, **27**, 578–608.

Elster, J., Offe, C. and Preuss, U.K. (1998), *Institutional Design in Postcommunist Societies, Rebuilding the Ship at Sea* (Cambridge, UK: Cambridge University Press).

EMF (2003), *Arbeitsmethoden des EMB: Das 'Ulysses-Projekt'*, Prague, 12 June 2003 (Brussels: EMF).

Ernst&Young (2004), 'Kennzeichen D: Standort – Analyse 2004. Attraktivitaet Deutschlands als Investitionsstandort. *Internationale: emfrnehmen bewerten Deutschland'*, *EY Niederlassung Ruhrgebiet* (Dusseldorf: Ernst and Young).

ERT (1999), 'The East-West Win-Win Business Experience' (Brussels: ERT).

ERT (2001), 'Opening up the business opportunities of EU enlargement' (Brussels: ERT).

EU – Directive (2002), Directive 2002/14/EC of the European Parliament and of the Council of 11 March 2002, establishing a general framework for informing and consulting employees in the European Community (Brussels: EU).

Eurochambres (2000), 'The Road to EU' (Brussels: Eurochambres).

Eurochambres (2001), 'CAPE – Corporate Readiness for Enlargement in Central Europe', Summary Report (Brussels: Eurochambres).

Eurochambres (2002), 'CAPE – Corporate Readiness for Enlargement in Central Europe. Summary Report' (Brussels: Eurochambres).

Eurochambres (2002b), 'The Road to EU' (Brussels: Eurochambres).

European Bank for Reconstruction (2000), *Transition Report 2000* (London: European Bank for Reconstruction).

European Commission (1999a), *Guidelines for PHARE Programme Implementation in Candidate Countries for the Period, 2000–2006* (Brussels: European Commission).

European Commission (2002a), *Industrial Relations in Europe 2002* (Brussels: European Commission).

European Commission (2003), *The PHARE Programme Annual Report 2001* (Brussels: European Commission).

European Commission (2003a), *Comprehensive Monitoring Report on Poland's, Slovakia's and Czech Republic's Preparations For Membership*, 5 November 2003 (Brussels: European Commission).

European Commission (2003b), *European Competitiveness Report 2003,* Commission Staff Working Paper, 12 November 2003 (Brussels: European Commission).

European Commission (2004), *European Competitiveness Report 2004,* Commission Staff Working Paper, 8 November 2003 (Brussels: European Commission).

European Commission, DG for Economic and Financial Affairs (2003), '2003 – Pre-Accession Economic Programmes Of Acceding And Other Candidate Countries, Overview and Assessment, European Economy', Enlargement Paper No. 20, November, http://Europa.eu/int/comm/economy_finance.

European Council for Economic and Social Affairs (2003), 'Stellungnahme zum Thema "Konkrete Anwendung der Richtlinie 94/45/EG ueber Europaeische Betriebsraete

und eventuell ueberpruefungsbeduerftige Aspekte"', ttp://eescopinions.esc.eu.int/
    EESCopinio...oc/soc/39/es1164-2003_ac.doc&language=DE.
European Foundation for the Improvement of Living and Working Conditions (2002),
    'Challenges and Opportunities for Social Dialogue and Tripartism' (Dublin:
    European Foundation for the Improvement of Living and Working Conditions)
European Foundation for the Improvement of Living and Working Conditions
    (2003), 'Arbeitsbeziehungen in der Automobilindustrie', (Dublin: European
    Foundation for the Improvement of Living and Working Conditions). http://www.
    eiro.Eurofound:ie/2003/12/study/tn0312102s.html.
European Foundation for the Improvement of Living and Working Conditions
    (2004), 'European Works Councils in Practice' (Dublin: European Foundation for
    the Improvement of Living and Working Conditions).
European Foundation for the Improvement of Living and Working Conditions
    (2006), 'Relocation of Production and Industrial Relations' (Dublin: European
    Foundation for the Improvement of Living and Working Conditions). www.eiro.
    eurofound.eu.int/comparativestudies.html.
European Trade Union Institute (2003), The Community Social Acquis in Labour
    Law in the CEEs and beyond, (Brussels: European Trade Union Institute).
European Trade Union Institute (2004), *European Works Councils Database 2004*
    (Brussels: European Trade Union Institute).
European Trade Union Institute (2004), *European Works Councils Facts and Figures
    2006* (Brussels: European Trade Union Institute).
Financial Times (2004b), 'Budapest, the Next Bangalore? New EU Members Join
    the Outsourcing Race', 21 September 2004 (London), 13.
Fraunhofer, I. (2003) 'Inlaendische und Auslaendische Standorte Richtig Bewerten,
    Karlsruhe', in *Erfolgsfaktor Standortplanung*. Kinkel S. (ed.) (Heidelberg:
    Springer Verlag).
Friedrich Ebert Stiftung, Budapest (2003), 'Gewerkschaftsprojekt,
    Gewerkschaftsnachrichten aus Ungarn', No. 3, 4, 5 and 6.
Friedrich Ebert Stiftung, Warschaw (2003), 'Projekt "*Regionale
    Gewerkschaftskooperation*", Aktuelle Informationen aus den EU –
    Beitrittslaendern', (Warsaw: Friedrich Ebert Foundation).
Friedrich Ebert Stiftung (2004), 'Konferenz: Der Sozialdialog in Polen Zwischen
    Heute und Morgen', 15 December 2004.
Galgóczi, B. (2003), 'Passing from Low-Road to High Road Competition Strategies
    in CEE Countries with a View to Working Relations' *Prospettive Delle Condizioni
    Sociali E Ruolo Lavoro Nella Società Italiana ed Europa*. (Bologna, Italy: *IPL
    (Istituto per il Lavoro)*).
Galgóczi, B. (2004), 'Deutsche Direktinvestitionen und die Prozesse der
    Standortentwicklung und industriellen Beziehungen in den neuen EU –
    Mitgliedslaendern', in *Gewerkschaftsnachrichten aus Ungarn*. Friedrich Ebert
    Stiftung (ed.), **1**(2004).
Galgóczi, B. and Kluge, N. (2003),'Pragamatic Multinationals', *Mitbestimmung*, **8**,
    41–43.

Gerstenberger, W. and Schmalholz. H (2002),'Standortbedingungen in Polen, Tschechien und Ungarn und die Position Sachsens im Standortwettbewerb', *ifo dresden Studien* 33.

Giddens, A. (1990), *The Consequences of Modernity* (Cambridge, UK: Polity Press).

Gordon, M.E. and Turner, L., (eds.) (2000), *Transnational Coopeation Among Labour Unions* (Ithaca, NY: ILR Press).

Gradev, G. (2001),'EU Companies in Eastern Europe: Strategic Choices and Labour Effects' in *CEE Countries in the EU Companies' Strategies of Industrial Restructuring and Relocation*, Gradev, G. (ed.) (Brussels: ETUI), 1–20.

Green Cowles, M. (1998),'The Changing Architecture of Big Business' in *Collective Action in the European Union*, Greenwood, J. and Aspinwall, M. (eds.) (London: Routledge), 108–126.

Grzesiuk, A. (2001), 'Market Orientation of German Companies on the Polish Market, Research Project', *NATO Advanced Fellowship Programme, Final Report*, September,(Szczecin).

Habermans, J. (1981), *Theorie des kommunikativen Handelns*, (2 Volumes) (Frankfurt/M.: Suhrkamp Verlag).

Hall, P.A. and Soskice, D., (eds.) (2001), *Varieties of Capitalism, The Institutional Foundations of Comparative Advantage* (Oxford: Oxford University Press)

Heery, E. and Wood, S. (2003), 'Employment Relations and Corporate Governance', *British Journal of Industrial Relations*, **41**(3), 477–479.

Helpman, E. and Krugman, P. (1985), *Market Structure and Foreign Trade* (Cambridge: MIT).

Helpman, E., Melitz, M.J. and Yeaple, S. (2004), *Export v FDI with Heterogenous Firms'*, *American Economic Review*, **94**, 300–316.

Hickel, R. (2004),'Deutschland – keine Basaroekonomie', *Blaetter für Deutsche und internationale Politik*, **12**.

High Level Group on Industrial Relations and Change In the European Union (January 2002), Final Report (Brussels) (grey paper).

Hirsch-Kreiensen, H. and Schulz, A. (2004), 'Tolpersteine der Auslandsverlagerung', *Mitbestimmung*, **3**(2004), 30–33.

Hodson, R. (2005), 'Management Behaviour as Social Capital: A Systematic Analysis of Organizational Ethnographies', *British Journal of Industrial Relations*, **43**(1), 41–65.

Hoenekopp, E. (2001), 'Labour Markets and the Free Movement of Labour' in *The Unity of Europe. Political, Economic and Social Dimensions of EU Enlargement*, Langewiesche, R. and Tóth, A. (eds.) (Brussels: European Trade Union Institute (ETUI)), 141–161.

Hoffmann, J., Hoffmann, R., Kirton-Darling, J. and Rampeltshammer, L (eds.) (2002), 'The Europeanization Of Industrial Relations In A Global Perspective: A Literature Review' (European Foundation for the Improvement of Living and Working Conditions, Dublin)

Hoffmann, R. (2001), 'Europaeische Gewerkschaftsstrukturen und die Perspektiven Europaeischer Arbeitsbeziehungen', in *Zwischen Kontinuitaet und Modernisierung:*

Gewerkschaftliche Herausforderungen in Europa. Waddington, J. and Hoffmann, R (eds.) (Münster: Verlag Westfaelisches Dampfboot), 437–455.

Hofstede, G. (1980), *Culture's Consequences: International Work-Related Values* (London: Sage).

Hofstede, G. (1991), *Cultures and Organisations: Software of the Mind* (London: McGraw-Hill).

Horn, G. and Behncke, S. (2004), 'Deutschland ist Keine Basaroekonomie' *DIW Wochenbericht,* **40**(2004), 583-589.

Hummel, T. and Zander, E. (2005), 'Interkulturelles Management' in *Schriften zum Internationalen Management,* Hummel, T. (ed.), **10**.

Hunya, G. (2004), 'Manufacturing FDI in New EU Member States – Foreign Penetration and Location Shifts Between 1998 and 2002', The Vienna Institute for International Economic Studies, wiiw Research Report 311 (Vienna).

Hyman, R. (2000), 'Editorial', *European Journal of Industrial Relations,***1**, 5–7.

IAB (2003), 'Institut für Arbeitsmarkt – und Berufsforschung der Bundesagentur für Arbeit', *Entwicklung der Flaechentarifbindung* (Nuremberg).

IAB (2004), 'Institut für Arbeitsmarkt – und Berufsforschung der Bundesagentur für Arbeit' *Betriebspanel 2004* (Nuremberg).

IG Metall/Industriegewerkschaft Metall (2002–1), 'Gewerkschaften und Betriebliche Interessenvertretung in den Neuen EU – Laendern' (Polen, Frankfurt/M).

IG Metall/Industriegewerkschaft Metall (2002–2), 'Gewerkschaften und Betriebliche Interessenvertretung in den Neuen EU – Laendern'(Slowakische Republik, Frankfurt/M).

IG Metall/Industriegewerkschaft Metall (2002–03), 'Gewerkschaften und betriebliche Interessenvertretung in den neuen EU – Laendern' (Tschechische Republik, Frankfurt/M).

IG Metall/Industriegewerkschaft Metall (2003), 'EBRs go East, Anleitung zur EBR – Erweiterung' (Frankfurt/M).

IG Metall/Industriegewerkschaft Metall (2004), EU – Osterweiterung, (Frankfurt/M).

IG Metall/Industriegewerkschaft Metall (2004a), *EBR – News,* (Frankfurt/M), http://www.Euro-betriebsrat.de.

IG Metall/Industriegewerkschaft Metall Bayern (1999), Memorandum Interregionale Tarifpolitik (Vienna).

Industrie – und Handelskammer Dresden (2003), 'Die EU – Erweiterung aus Sicht der Wirtschaft im Kammerbezirk Dresden', in *Nordboehmen (Tschechien) und Niederschlesien (Polen). Ergebnisse einer Unternehmensbefragung im Fruehjahr* (Dresden : ifo-Dresden studien).

Institut der deutschen Wirtschaft (2003), *Neue Sterne Am Himmel,* Die Osterweiterung der Europaeischen Union (Cologne: Deutscher Instituts-Verlag).

Ishikawa A.(Hg), Krause, D., Kuczi, T., Mako, C., Stastny, Z. and Tobera, P. (2003), 'Small and Medium-sized Enterprises in Central Europe: An Overview', in *Voices from the World* (Tokyo).

Jachtenfuchs, M. and Kohler-Koch, B. (1996),'Einleitung: Regieren im dynamischen Mehr – Ebenensystem' in *Europaeische Integration,* Jachtenfuchs, M. and Kohler-Koch, B. (eds.)(Opladen: Leske und Budrich).

Javorcik, B.S. (2004), 'Does Foreign Direct Investment Increase the Productivity of Foreign Firms? In Search of Spillovers through Backward Linkages', *American Economic Review*, **93**, 605–627.

Jungnickel, R. and Keller, D. (2003), 'Deutsche Direktinvestitionen im Europaeischen Integrationsprozess', *Wirtschaftsdienst*, **10** (Hamburg: the HWWA (Hamburger WeltwirtschaftsArchiv), Hamburg .

Kaedtler, J. (2004), 'Vom Fordismus zur Globalisierung – Schluesselprobleme der Deutschen Industriellen Bezeihungen', *SOFI – Mitteilungen*, **32**, 63–78.

Kaelble, H. and Schmid, G. (2004), 'Einleitung zu: Das europaeische Sozialmodell' 'Auf dem Weg zum transnationalen Sozialstaat' in *Jahrbuch 2004 des Wissenschaftszentrums*, Kaelble, H. and Schmid, G. (eds.) (Berlin), 11–28.

Kaufmann, F. and Menke, A. (1997), *Standortverlagerungen Mittelstaendischer Unternehmen nach Mittel – und Osteuropa: eine empirische Untersuchung Am Beispiel der vier Visegrad-Staaten, Schriften zur Mittelstandsforschung, Neue Folge, 7* (Stuttgart: Schaeffer-Poeschel).

Keane, M.P. and Feinberg, S.E. (2005), 'Intra-firm Trade of US MNCs: Findings for Models and Policies. Towards Trade and Investment' in *Does Foreign Direct Investment Promote Development?*, Moran, T., Graham, E. and Blomstrom, M. (eds.) (Washington, DC: Institute for International Economics), 245–271.

Kerkhofs, P. (2002), *'European Works Councils. Facts and Figures'* (Brussels: European Trade Union Institute).

Kluge, N. and Voss, E. (2003), 'Managementstile und Arbeitnehmerbeteiligung bei auslaendischen Unternehmen in Polen, Tschechien und Ungarn', *WSI – Mitteilungen*, **1**/2003, 66–74.

Knogler, M. (2001), 'Die Arbeitsmaerkte der Beitrittskandidaten vor dem Hintergrund der EU – Osterweiterung', *Working Papers, No. 228* (Munich Osteuropa-Institut).

Knudsen, H. (2004), 'European Works Councils – Potentials and Obstacles on the Road to Employee Influence in Multinational Companies', *Industrielle Beziehungen*, **11**(3), 203–220.

Kohl, H. (2002), 'Arbeitsbeziehungen in Mittel – und Osteuropa: Betriebsraete als neue Form der Interessenvertretung?' *WSI – Mitteilungen*, **7**/2002, 410–415.

Kohl, H., Lecher, W. and Platzer, H.-W. (2000b), 'Arbeitsbeziehungen in Ost/ Mittel Europa Zwischen Transformation und EU – Beitritt, Politikinformation Osteuropa', *Schriftenreihe der Friedrich-Ebert-Stiftung*, **85** (July 2000) (Bonn) (short version).

Kohl, H. and Platzer, H.-W. (2003), 'Arbeitsbeziehungen in Mittel/Osteuropa, Transformation und Integration. Die acht EU – Beitrittslaender im Vergleic' (Baden-Baden: Nomos Verlagsgesellschaft).

Kohl, H. and Platzer, H.-W. (2003a), 'Arbeitsbeziehungen in Mittel/Osteuropa und das "Europaeische Sozialmodell"', *WSI – Mitteilungen*, **1**/2003, 40–50.

Kotthof, H. and Kruse, W. (2002), 'Alltaegliche Europaeisierung Deutscher Interessenvertretungen', in *Forschungsantrag an die Hans Boeckler-Stiftung*, (Dortmund: Sozialforschungsstelle Dortmund, now: Universityof Dortmund).

Kozek, W., *Federowicz, M. and Morawski, W.* (1995), 'Poland' in *Labour Relations and Political Change in Eastern Europe*, Thirkell, J., Scase, R. and Vickerstaff, S. (eds.) (New York: ILR Press), 109–135.

Lecher, W., Nagel, B. and Platzer, H.-W. (1998), '*Die Konstituierung Europaeischer Betriebsraete – Vom Informationsforum zum Akteur?*' (Baden-Baden: Nomos Verlagsgesellschaft).

Lecher, W., Platzer, H.-W., Rueb, S. and Weiner, H-P. (2000), 'Verhandelte Europaeisierung in Europaeische Betriebsraete: *Ihre Einrichtung nach Art. 6 der EBR – Richtlinie und der Gesamtprozess; Bilanz und Perspektiven*' (Baden-Baden: Nomos Verlagsgesellschaft).

LO (Daenischer Gewerkschaftsbund), u.a., Unterstuetzt von der Europaeischen Kommission (2002), 'Towards more influence, Bericht von der Konferenz in Aarhus', November 25–26 (Aarhus/Denmark).

Luhmann, N. (1964), *Funktionen und Folgen formaler Organisation* (Berlin: Duncker & Humblot).

Lyotard, J-F (1984), *The Postmodern Condition* (Manchester: Manchester University Press).

Madeuf, B. (1995), 'Foreign Direct Investment, Trade and Employment Delocalisation', in *OECD: Foreign Direct Investment, Trade and Employment (Paris: Trade and Employment)*, 41–65.

Mailand, M. and Due, J. (2004), 'Social Dialogue in Central and Eastern Europe: Present State and Future Development', *European Journal of Industrial Relations*, **9**(2), 161–178.

Mako, C. and Ellingstad, M. (2000), 'Globalisation, FDI and Modernising Management Practising', *Journal for East European Management Studies JEEMS*, **4**(2000), 341–360.

Marginson, P. (2000), The Euro Company and Euro Industrial Relations', *European Journal of Industrial Relations*, **6**(1), 9–34.

Marginson, P. and Meardi, G. (2006), 'European Union Enlargement and the Foreign Direct Investment Channel of Industrial Relations Transfer', *International Relations Journal*, **37**(2), 92–110.

Marginson, P. and Sisson, K. (2006), *European Integration and Industrial Relations. Multi-Level Governance in the Making* (Basingstoke: Palgrave/Macmillan).

Marginson, P., Sisson, K. and Arrowsmith, J. (2003), 'Between Decentralisation and Euroeanization: Sectoral Bargaining in Four Countries and Two Sectors', *European Journal of Industrial Relations*, **9**(2), 163–187.

Martin, B. (2005), 'Managers after the Era of Organizational Restructuring: Towards a Second Managerial Revolution?', *Work, Employment and Society*, **19**(4), 747–760.

Marx, K.(1974), *Grundrisse der Kritik der Politischen Ökonomie*, (2nd ed.) (Berlin: Dietz Verlag).

Meardi, G. (2003), 'Foreign Direct Investment in Central/Eastern Europe and Industrial Relations: Lessons from the European Works Councils in Poland', *Paper Presented to the 13th IIRA World Congress*, 8–11 September (Berlin).

Meardi, G. (2004), 'Short Circuits in Multinational Companies: The Extension of European Works Councils to Poland', *European Journal of Industrial Relations*, **10**(2), 161–178.

Merkel, W. (1999), *Systemtransformation. Eine Einfuehrung in die Theorie und Empirie der Transformationsforschung* (Opladen: Leske und Budrich).

Moran, T., Graham, E. and Blomstrom, M., (eds.) (2005), *Does Foreign Direct Investment Promote Development?* (Washington, DC: Institute for International Economics).

Mueller-Jentsch, W. (1995), 'Auf dem Pruefstand: Das deutsche Modell der Industriellen Beziehungen', *Industrielle Beziehungen*, **2**(1), 11–24.

Mueller-Jentsch, W. (1996), 'Theorien industrieller Beziehungen', *Industrielle Beziehungen*, **3**(1), 36–64.

Mueller-Jentsch, W. (2001), Mitbestimmung und Arbeitnehmerpartizipation auf dem Pruefstand, *Industrielle Beziehungen*, (4), 359–363.

Mueller-Jentsch, W. (2003), 'Re-Assessing Co-Determination' in *The Changing Contours of German Industrial Relations*. Mueller-Jentsch, W and Weitbrecht, H (Rainer Hampp Verlag: Munich and Mering), 39–56.

OECD (2001), '*International Direct Investment Statistics Yearbook*', 1980–2000, Paris.

Otto Brenner Stiftung, in Kooperation with Friedrich Ebert Stiftung, Hans Boeckler Stiftung and Europaeisches Gewerkschaftsinstitut (2003), 'Tagung "Freizuegigkeit in Europa-Chancen und Risiken der EU-Erweiterung"' (Berlin: Otto Brenner Stiftung).

Parsons, T. (1949) 'The Professions and Social Structure', in *Essays on Sociological Theory, Pure and Applied*, Parsons, T. (Glencoe: Illinois, USA), 185–199.

Platzer, H.-W. (1999), 'Die EU – Sozial – und Beschaeftigungspolitik nach Amsterdam: Koordinierte und verhandelte Europaeisierung', *Integration*, **3**(99), 176–198.

Podkaminer, L., Havlik, P. and Landesmann, M. (2004), 'Transition Countries on the Eve of EU Enlargement', The Vienna Institute for International Economic Studies, wiiw, Research Report 303, February (Vienna).

Polany, K. (1978), *The Great Transformation* (Frankfurt/M.: Suhrkamp Verlag).

Polish Council of Ministers (2001), 'Investment Increase Strategy', March, www. mg.gov.pl/engllish/dai_neu/inv_strat/karnisz.htm.

Protsenko, A. and Vincentz, V. (1999), 'Direktinvestitionen und Andere Kapitalstroeme Nach Osteuropa', Working Papers, No. 222 (Munich: Osteuropa-Institut), December.

Quaisser, W. (2001), 'Kosten und Nutzen der Osterweiterung Unter Besonderer Beruecksichtigung Verteilungspolitischer Probleme', *Working Papers No. 230 (Gutachten im Auftrag des Bundesministeriums für Finanzen)* (Munich: Osteuropa-Institut), February.

Quaisser, W. (2003), 'Ökonomische Indikatoren zur Beitrittsfaehigkeit der MOE – Laender – Eine vergleichende Bewertung', Working Papers No. 245 (Munich: Osteuropa-Institut).

Rainnie, A., Smith, A. and Swain, A. (eds.) (2002), *Work, Employment and Transition: Restructuring Livelihoods in Post-Communism* (London and New York: Routledge).

Rehder, B. (2005), 'Mitbestimmung im Investitionswettbewerb', *WeltTrends*, **47**(13), 64–76.

RELACEE Project (2003), *Implementation of the EWC Directive in the Future Member States*, June.

Riedel, J., Untiedt, G., Alecke, B. and Pintarits, S. (2001), *EU – Osterweiterung und deutsche Grenzregionen*, IFO – Dresden Studien 28/I und 28/II (Dresden).

Rondinelli, D.A. and Black, S.S. (2000), 'Multinational Strategic Alliances and Acquisitions in Central and Eastern Europe: Partnerships in Privatisation' in *Academy of Management Executives*, **14**(4), 85–98.

RWI/Rheinisch – Westfaelisches Institut für Wirtschaftsforschung (1996), 'Deutsche Direktinvestitionen im Ausland: Export von Beschaeftigung', RWI Konjunkturbrief No. 3, Essen.

Sachs, J. (1993), *Poland's Jump to the Market Economy* (Massachusetts: Cambridge University Press).

Sachsen Metall (2002), *Wirtschaftsatlas Sachsen – Tschechien – Niederschlesien*, Heft 3 (Dresden).

Scharr, F., Aumüller, A., Barczyik, R., Riedel, J. and Untiedt, G. (2001), *Grenzueberschreitende Unternehmensaktivitaeten in der saechsisch-polnischen Grenzregion* (Dresden: it ifo – Dresden Studien 29).

Schintke, J. and Weiß, J-P. (2004), 'Zunehmende Arbeitsteilung daempft Wertschoepfungsentwicklung im verarbeitenden Gewerbe', *DIW Wochenbericht*, **4** and 7(2004) (Berlin), 715–722.

Schlecht, O. (1994), 'Soziale Marktwirtschaft für das Ganze Europa', in *Marktwirtschaft als Aufgabe,* Hermann-Pillath, C., Schlecht, O. und Wuensche, H.F. (eds.) (Stuttgart: Ludwig Erhard Stiftung, Fischer Verlag), 789–803.

Schuettpelz, A. (2003), 'Die Arbeitsmaerkte in den EU – Beitrittslaendern', *WSI – Mitteilungen*, **1** (Düsseldorf), 33–39.

Schumpeter, J. (1942–50), *Capitalism, Socialism and Democracy* (3rd edn) (New York: Harper and Brothers).

Srubar, I. (ed.) (2003), *Problems and Changes of the East Enlargement of the EU: Integration and the Eastward Enlargement of the European Union* (Hamburg: Kraemer-Verlag).

Stadtmann, G., Hermann, H. and Weigand, J. (2003), 'Markterschliessung und Expansion in den EU – Beitrittslaendern Mittel – und Osteuropas'. *Teil 1, Wettbewerbsfaehigkeit Der Beitrittskandidaten, Osteuropastudie, Manager Magazin*, **43**(2003), Hamburg, 43–46.

Stark, D. (1994), 'Path Dependency and Privatization Strategies in East Central Europe', *East European Politics and Societies*, **8**(1).

Stark, D. and Bruszt, L. (1998), *Postsocialist Pathways, Transforming Politics and Property in East Central Europe* (Cambridge: Cambridge University Press).

Statistische Bundesamt (2003), 'Deutschlands Handelspartner in Mittel – und Osteuropa, *Ein Beitrag der deutschen Außenhandelsstatistik*', *Sonderheft* 2003 (Wiesbaden).

Steger, T. (2002), On the Way to Neo-Liberalism? Trends of Industrial Relations in Central and Eastern Europe, Working Paper, TU Chemnitz.

Stirling, J. and Tully, B. (2004), Power, Process, and Practice: Communications in European Works Councils', *European Journal of Industrial Relations*, **10**(1), 73–89.

Streeck, W. (1995), 'German Capitalism: Does it Exist? Can it Survive?', *Discussion Paper 5/95* (Cologne: Max-Planck-Institut für Gesellschaftsforschung).

Streeck, W. (1997), 'Neither European nor Works Councils: A Reply to Paul Knudsen', *Economic and Industrial Democracy*, **2**, 325–337.

Stumpf-Fekete, M. (2001), 'Mitbestimmung bei Investitionsentscheidungen. Fallstudien in Deutschen multinationalen Konzernen', *Industrielle Beziehungen*, **8**(4), 430–445.

Szélenyi and Istvan (1989), 'Sozialistische Unternehmer, Verbuergerlichung im laendlichen', Ungarn (Hamburg: Junius-Verlag).

Thirkell, J., Petkov, K. and Vickerstaff, S. (1998), *The Transformation of Labour Relations, Restructuring and Privatization in Eastern Europe and Russia* (Oxford, UK: Oxford University Press).

Tholen, J., Czíria, L., Hemmer, E., Mansfeldová, Z. and Sharman, E. (2003), 'EU Enlargement and Labour Relations. New Trends in Poland, Czech and Slowak Republic', IAW – Working Paper 3/2003 (University of Bremen).

Tholen, J. and Hemmer, E. (2005), *Die Auswirkungen von Direktinvestitionen Deutscher Unternehmen in Central & Eastern Europe – Groeßenordnung, Motive, Strategien, A./The Effects of Direct Investments by German Companies in Central & Eastern Europe – Scope, Motives, Strategies, Jobs*, I.A.W. Forschungsbericht/ Research Report 8/2005, University of Bremen.

Tóth, A. and Ghellab, Y. (2003), 'The Challenge of Representation at the Workplace in EU Accession Countries: Does the Creation of Works Councils Offer a Solution Alongside Trade Unions?', *Paper to the Tripartite Conference in Warsaw*, 12–13 December, 2003 (Budapest: ILO, Sub-Regional Office for Central and Eastern Europe).

Traxler, F. (1995), 'Entwicklungstendenzen in den Arbeitsbeziehungen Westeuropas', in *Sozialpartnerschaft und Arbeitsbeziehung in Europa*. Mesch, M. (ed.) (Vienna: Manz-Verlag), 161–214.

Traxler, F., Blaschke, S. and Kittel, B. (2002), *National Labour Relations in International Markets: A Comparative Study of Institutions, Changes and Performance* (Oxford, UK: Oxford University Press).

UEAPME (2002a), *UEAPME Supports Positive Report on Enlargement but Asks Commission to Closely Monitor New Entrants*, Press Release (Brussels: UEAPME).

UEAPME (2002b), *Social Dialogue Summit: UEAPME Also Underlines Improvements to be Made on Convention and Enlargement*, Press Release (Brussels: UEAPME).

UNCTAD (2002), World Investment Report (2001); Promoting Linkages (Geneva: UNCTAD).

UNCTAD (2003), World Investment Report (2002); Transnational Corporations and Export Competitiveness (Geneva: UNCTAD).

UNCTAD (2004), World Investment Report (2003); FDI Policies for Development (Geneva: UNCTAD).

UNCTAD (2005a), World Investment Report (2004); The Shift Towards Services (Geneva: UNCTAD).

UNCTAD (2005b), World Investment Report (2005); Transnational Corporations and The Internationalization Of R and D (Geneva: UNCTAD).

UNICE (2000), UNICE Position Paper on Enlargement (Brussels: UNICE).

UNICE (2001), *Enlargement: Free Movement of Workers and Social Policy* (Brussels: UNICE Position Paper).

UNICE (2002), *Ensuring EU Enlargement is a Success* (Brussels: UNICE Position Paper).

Vallée, P. (2000), 'Die strategische Bedeutung der Europaeischen Betriebsraete in Frankreich und das Beispiel Aventis Pharma' in Eberwein, W., Tholen, J. and Schuster, J. (eds.) *Die Europaeisierung der Arbeitsbeziehungen* (University of Bremen, Kooperation Universität – Arbeitnehmerkammer).

Vatta, A. (2003), 'The EU Support to the Development of Employers' Organizations in Central and Eastern Europe', Paper for the 6th Conference of the European Sociological Association (Murcia, Spain).

Vaughan-Whitehead, D. (2000), 'Social Dialogue in EU Enlargement: Acquis and Responsibilities', *Transfer*, ETUI (ed.), **3**, 387–398.

Verband der Automobilindustrie (VDA) (2002), Jahresbericht (2002) (Frankfurt/M).

Vincentz, V. and Knogler, M. (2003), 'Szenarien der mittelfristigen Konvergenz der EU – Beitrittslaender Polen, Slowakische Republik und Ungarn', in Osteuropa-Institut, Munich, Working Papers No. 244, March 2003.

Waddington, J. (2003), 'What Do Representatives Think of the Practice of European Works Councils? Views from Six Countries', *European Journal of Industrial Relations*, **9**(3), 303–325.

Waddington, J. (2006), 'The Views of European Works Council Representatives', Paper Presented to the 7th International Conference of the Otto Brenner Foundation, Bratislava, 30 May–1 June.

Weber, M. (1905-1979), 'Die protestantische Ethik und der Geist des Kapitalismus', in *Eine Aufsatzsammlung Die protestantische Ethik I*. Weber, M. (Winckelmann, J., ed.) (5th ed.) (Guetersloh, Germany: Gütersloher Verlagshaus Mohn), 27–114.

Weber, M. (1915–1972), *Wirtschaft und Gesellschaft, Grundriss der verstehenden Soziologie* (5th ed.) (Tuebingen, Germany: J.C.B. Mohr (Paul Siebeck)).

Weinstein, M. (2000), 'Solidarity's Abandonment of Workers Councils: Redefining Employees' Stakeholder Rights in Post-Socialist Poland', *British Journal of Industrial Relations*, **38**(1), 49–73.

Weiss, M. (2002), 'How EC Directives Are Producing Changes', *Mitbestimmung*, **8**, 37–38.

Weitbrecht, H.J. (2001), 'Der Theoretische Blick Auf Die Sich Veraendernde Wirklichkeit Der Industriellen Beziehungen – Der Theorieansatz Walther Mueller-Jentschs Und Seine Erweiterung', in *Pespektiven Nationaler und Internationaler*

Arbeitsbeziehungen, Abel, J., and Sperling, H. J. (eds.) (Rainer Hampp-Verlag, R., Munich and Mering), 15–30.

Welz, C. and Kauppinen, T. (2005), 'Industrial Action and Conflict Resolution in the New Member States', *European Journal of Industrial Relations*, **11**(1), 91–105.

Wills, J. (2000), Three Years in a life of a European Works Council, *European Journal of Industrial Relations* (Sage: London), **6**(1), 85–107.

Wirtschaftswoche (2003), 'Management Trends "Wirtschaft Positive Impulse", Befragung von Europaeischen Managern ueber die Bedeutung der EU – Erweiterung für ihr Unternehmen'. www.wiwo.de.

Wirtschaftswoche (2004), 'Managerbefragung 2004', www.wiwo.de.

Zemplerinova, A. (2001), 'Czech Republic: FDI in Manufacturing, 1993-1999' in *CEE Countries in the EU Companies' Strategies of Industrial Restructuring and Relocation*, Gradev, G. (ed.) (Brussels: ETUI), 51–52.

Ziltener, P. (1999), *Strukturwandel der europaeischen Integration – Die Europaeische Union und die Veraenderung von Staatlichkeit* (Muenster: Westfaelisches Dampfboot).

Zimmer, R. (2003), 'Europaeische Solidaritaet, Beispiele Positiver Arbeit Europaeischer Betriebsraete', *Arbeitsrecht im Betrieb*, **10**, 620–625.

Zschiedrich, H. (2001), 'Direktinvestitionen als Hoffnungstraeger im EU – BeitrittsProzess Mittel-/ Osteuropaeischer Wirtschaften' *Osteuropa-Wirtschaft*, **46**(3), 205–216.

Name Index

180 *Labour Relations in Central Europe*

Rainnie, Al 77, 82
Rehder, Britta 154, 155
Rondinelli, Dennis 27

Sachs, Jeffrey 16
Schlecht, Otto 16
Schroeder, Wolfgang 26
Schumpeter, Joseph 1
Sisson, Keith 15, 27
Smith, Chris 26, 27, 82
Speidel, Frederic 17
Stark, David 16
Steger, Thomas 161
Stirling, John 68
Streeck, Wolfgang 12, 16, 64, 76
Swain, Adam 77, 82

Thirkell, John 28
Tholen, Jochen 4, 6, 17, 27, 48, 57, 54, 65, 67
Tóth, András 27, 57

Traxler, Franz 15
Tully, Barbara 68

Vallée, Patrick 114
Vatta, Alessia 27, 42
Vickerstaff, Sarah 28
Vincentz, Volkhart 24, 25, 26
Voss, Eckhard 77, 81

Waddington, Jeremy 68
Weber, Max 1
Weinstein, Marc 56
Weiss, Manfred 56, 58
Weitbrecht, Hansjoerg 9
Wood, Stephen 2

Yeaple, Stephen 24

Ziltener, Patrick 13
Zimmer, Reingard 69

Subject Index

International Chemical Workers Trade
    Union 39
International Metal Trade Union Federation
    96
International trade 24, 90, 140
Internationalization 11, 13, 135, 148
Investment processes 35–36, 38–39, 43,
    46–47
Investment strategy 4
IT revolution 2
Italy 58, 68, 94, 118, 161

Jihlava 93–97
Joint Works Council(s) 86, 94, 102, 105,
    115–116, 122–123, 129–130, 138,
    145, 154

Kamp-Lintfort 105
Kassel 84
KIA Motors Company 22
Knowledge 23, 26, 43, 60, 73–74, 85, 92,
    106, 123
Krasnodar 137
Krusovice 145–147
Kvasiny 86

Labour cost(s) 4, 83, 93, 108, 121–122,
    144–145, 153
Labour market 43, 78
Labour relation(s) 5, 14, 27, 63, 69, 143
Latvia 23, 67, 121
Lean production 11
Leba 144
Lithuania 23, 67, 114–115, 119, 121
LMN/ISPAT (Mital Steel) 40
Lodz 103
Lower Saxony 84
Lukoil 41

Maggi 138
Maków Mazowiecki 144
Malta 67
Management concept(s) 1, 5, 47–48, 51,
    53–54, 80, 151
Management culture 48–49, 51, 53, 76, 88,
    111
Mannesmann Rexroth AG 95
Manufacturing industry 6, 23–25, 35, 81,
    152
Marginal inflow 22
Market economy 12, 16, 42, 98, 124, 161

Marketing 25, 114, 144, 147
Matador 108, 110–113
Mediation 5, 53, 63, 71, 75, 95, 103, 123,
    139
Memorandum on Interregional Collective
    Bargaining Policy 38
Mentality 49, 52, 96, 98, 124, 126, 133, 156
Merck & Co 114
Mineral Oil Industry 41
Mirkow 93–94, 96, 98–99
Mladá Boleslav 85
Modernity 1–2, 152
Modernization 1–2, 25–26, 49, 76, 80, 133
Moers 145
Monism 31, 154
Monistic 28, 32, 55, 59, 60, 158
Motorpal 94
Multinational concern 39, 52
Multinational corporation 26, 70–71
Munich 100–101

NAFTA 93
National economy 10, 26, 56
Negotiation 9, 14–15, 36, 38, 68, 71, 77,
    80, 82, 87, 89–90, 99, 104, 108,
    111–112, 114, 117, 151–152, 154,
    161
Nestlé 84, 136–143, 149–150
Netherlands 23, 54, 127, 130
Network 26, 41, 72, 75, 127–128, 140–141,
    145, 158
NGG trade union 39, 145
North America 13, 87, 127, 160
North Rhine-Westphalia 129–130
Nové Zámky 100, 103
NSZZ 29, 86

Oerlinghausen 145
Oetker KG 84, 143–144, 149–150
Olomuoc 138
Onken GmbH 145
OPZZ 29, 39–40, 46–47, 56, 70, 96, 103,
    133, 139–142
Orion 138, 142
Osram 99–107
OZ Chémica 46

Paris 14, 115
Participation 24, 32, 50, 55–56, 63–64, 69,
    78, 102, 113, 130, 134, 155
Partnership 37, 94, 161

Printed in the United States
by Baker & Taylor Publisher Services